THE WITNESS
of Women

THE WITNESS
of Women

Firsthand Experiences and Testimonies from the Restoration

Janiece Johnson and Jennifer Reeder

DESERET
BOOK

Salt Lake City, Utah

The cover painting, *All Assembled Awaiting,* by Paige Crosland Anderson, represents themes the artist encountered while discovering her ancestry: repetition, consistency, veiled connections, endless succession, commitment, diligence, and duty. Her use of patterns and layers refers to the process of uncovering our ancestry and regaining connections to our progenitors.

Back cover photo: Zina D. Young, Bathsheba W. Smith, Emily P. Young, and Eliza R. Snow, credited on the original image as the "Leading Women of Zion." Courtesy of the LDS Church History Library.

Library of Congress Cataloging-in-Publication Data

Names: Johnson, Janiece, author. | Reeder, Jennifer, author.

Title: The witness of women : firsthand experiences and testimonies from the restoration / Janiece Johnson and Jennifer Reeder.

Description: Salt Lake City, Utah : Deseret Book, [2016] | Includes bibliographical references and index.

Identifiers: LCCN 2016036659 | ISBN 9781629722474 (paperbound)

Subjects: LCSH: Women in the Mormon Church. | Women—Religious aspects—The Church of Jesus Christ of Latter-day Saints. | Mormon women.

Classification: LCC BX8643.W66 J64 2016 | DDC 289.3082—dc23

LC record available at https://lccn.loc.gov/2016036659

Printed in the United States of America
Lake Book Manufacturing, Inc., Melrose Park, IL

10 9 8 7 6 5 4 3 2 1

CONTENTS

INTRODUCTION

"My happy soul is witness."[1]

Laura Farnsworth Owen found joy and fellowship in the Restoration, despite enduring much privation in her lifetime. She declared, "I longed for union, and for latter day glory; and my happy soul is witness that it has commenced!" Though her voice is unknown to most Latter-day Saints today, she witnessed to her friends, her family, and her former minister. When she was accused of heresy and delusion by her former church and not allowed to defend herself, she published a tract—*Defence Against the Various Charges That Have Gone Abroad*—making a case for both herself and Mormonism.[2]

Laura felt it was "a duty incumbent upon" her to witness to that which she "verily believed to be the fullness of the gospel."[3] Like other Christian women, female Latter-day Saints studied the Bible, recognized divine patterns, and felt compelled to witness to truth once they had "been an eye and ear witness" themselves.[4] In the Gospel of John, they read that in the early morning darkness, Mary Magdalene was the first to witness Christ's empty tomb. She ran to tell Peter and John. Trusting in Mary's message and following her example, "they ran . . . together" to the empty tomb. After the apostles "went away again," Mary stayed behind at the tomb and became the first to witness the risen Jesus. Following this most poignant reunion, Mary proclaimed the initial witness of the resurrected Christ to his apostles: "she had seen the Lord, and . . . he had spoken these things unto her."[5] Latter-day Saint women observed and followed her example.

Of course, female disciples are not the majority voice in scripture, yet this

1

imbalance further highlights the distinct witness of women. Earlier in John's gospel, many citizens of Samaria "believed on" Jesus due to the witness of the Samaritan woman when she testified to them, "He told me all that ever I did." Her testimony led them to seek out their own.[6] Likewise, as new converts read the Book of Mormon in the nineteenth century, they encountered the first words uttered by a woman in the book. Sariah gained her own witness and testified to her son Nephi, "Now I know of a surety."[7] As Nephi wrote his record thirty years later, her words persisted with him. Though Alma did not know Abish, he chose to include the story of the converted Lamanite woman who "ran forth from house to house" to witness truth to others.[8] (Oh, the running involved with discipleship.) Latter-day Saint women saw themselves in the scripture narrative; they too had an opportunity and a duty to run and witness their experience of truth.

Just after Emma Smith's baptism, Joseph received a revelation for her, the only canonized revelation specifically addressed to a woman. The revelation admonished Emma to "expound scriptures" and "exhort the church."[9] This became a model for Latter-day Saint women. The message was not just for Emma—it was offered "unto all."[10] Women witnessed miraculous events, participated in the expansion of the Restoration from its earliest moments, and told others of their experience. The founding of the Relief Society in 1842 gave women specific roles and responsibilities within the official Church structure. This organization of the Relief Society sharpened their vision of the past as well as their view of eternity. Bathsheba Smith remembered, Joseph Smith "wanted to make us, as the women were in Paul's day, 'A kingdom of priestesses.'"[11]

The editors of the *Times and Seasons* considered Laura Owen's *Defence* "of too much value to be lost" to history, so they published it.[12] Regrettably, many of the voices and much of the vision of these early female Saints are lost to modern members of the Restoration. Yet the story of the Latter-day Saints is not complete without women. Former Relief Society general president Julie B. Beck taught, "We study our history to learn who we are." The more readily we see examples of strong, faithful women, the more opportunities we give all to better "know their identity, value, and importance."[13] Our hope is that *The Witness of Women* will help to create a more inclusive narrative of the early history of the Church as it documents the witness of early Latter-day Saint women in their own voices. These women describe their experience of the Restoration, testifying of the restored gospel and demonstrating how they faithfully applied doctrine and principles. As Latter-day Saints come to understand both their shared identity and individual value, they will better realize their own essential role as the Restoration continues.

This book offers Gospel Doctrine teachers, Young Men and Young Women teachers, religion professors, family history researchers, and Church members in general a resource to incorporate women's experiences and testimonies into their study, teaching, and personal understanding of the Restoration. Our primary goal is to privilege the voices of the women themselves. Often in the chaos of the moment women would not have an opportunity to write of their experience; some of the accounts are later remembered and then written down. In a few instances, if the women haven't left a record of an experience themselves, we include others' descriptions. Inclusion of women in history elevates everyone with a more complete view of the Restoration.

Methodology

This book is not a standard historical narrative; it is a resource offering multiple perspectives organized by subject. Distinct from Latter-day Saint women's biographies, the chapters are arranged topically to make them as accessible as possible for teaching. This organization provides straightforward, uncomplicated access to the powerful testimonies and experiences of early Latter-day Saint women for their sisters and fellow members in Christ today. Though we have arranged the chapters by topic, lives are not ordered topically; themes overlap throughout different chapters in the collection. We recommend referring to the index to find further testimony on a topic beyond its assigned chapter.

We have lightly edited these sources for readability, standardizing spelling and grammar. Each account includes a brief biographical sketch to offer a glimpse into the lives and situations of these women at the time—context that is important to understand each woman and her experience. In most cases, secondary sources have helped us better understand this context.

There is an admitted lack of diversity in these accounts; only a few women are not white, American, or from northwestern Europe. Though there were early members of the Church beyond those categories, often the extant written sources are few. Within this limitation, we have worked to include a variety of ages, levels of education, and visibility in Church leadership; distinct places of origin; and a spectrum from well-known historical figures to lesser-known female members of the Church.

We used archival sources found in various collections of the LDS Church History Library (CHL), Brigham Young University's L. Tom Perry Special Collections in the Harold B. Lee Library, the Utah State Historical Society, private collections, as well as other archives across the United States. We also utilized women's writings from nineteenth-century out-of-print compilation publications such as Edward Tullidge's *Women of Mormondom*, Augusta Joyce Crocheron's *Representative Women of Deseret*, and most significantly the *Woman's Exponent* newspaper. Both Tullidge and Crocheron collected autobiographical writings for their publications. Tullidge carefully inserted women's experiences and their own words into a larger celebratory, hagiographic book, which was often touted in the *Woman's Exponent*.[14] Seven years later, Crocheron gathered biographies and autobiographies of twenty leading Mormon women, some accounts written in the women's own words, some published in the *Exponent*, and others written by friends. Both of these books were compiled during the lifetime of their subjects, and each was approved as an authentic representation of women's lives and experiences.

From 1872 to 1914, the *Woman's Exponent* was the voice of Latter-day Saint women. Initially it was published on a bimonthly basis and later a monthly basis. It was funded, written, and published by women. This is an invaluable source of Church history as women reflect on their personal and collective histories of the Restoration. Brigham Young charged Emmeline B. Wells, second editor of the *Exponent* and leader of the paper's production for nearly forty years, to publish "'the record of [women's] work and a portion of Church history;' he also added 'and I give you a mission to write brief sketches of the lives of the leading women of Zion, and publish them.'"[15] The *Woman's Exponent* is also a significant theological resource, as women would expound

Augusta Joyce Crocheron published this lithograph poster in 1884 to accompany a book of biographies of significant nineteenth-century Latter-day Saint women, Representative Women of Deseret.

scripture and doctrine, exhort others as to its application in their lives, and publish minutes of Relief Society meetings across the Church. Though the *Exponent* at times reprinted the discourses of male leaders, the majority of writings come from the women themselves. Some women in this book served in official capacities for the Relief Society organization of the Church or in their own stakes and wards, and others merely saw an opportunity to serve their sisters and contribute as a part of the body of Christ.

The body of Christ requires that all parts work in union to the same exalted end. Women of the Restoration have consistently participated in and strengthened the body of Christ. As Annie Noble witnessed, "I realize that the foundational knowledge of the principles of the gospel makes us strong, and I rejoice today. . . . I bless the Lord that He has called us in this day to see the light of the gospel. . . . And I feel to rejoice that I have knowledge now which is definite, not only upon this point but on so many other points which have become quite clear to me and to all of us."[16] This clarity was never to be kept to one's self. The witness of women reaches through history to empower and enable us to rejoice in truth today.

~ 1 ~

TRUTH RESTORED

"We knew that the word of the Lord was coming."[1]

The American Revolution resulted in great political and social change, including discussion about religious authority and egalitarian participation. Soon after, the Second Great Awakening challenged conventional, age-old church congregations and created new denominations. One trend was restorationism, an effort to return to New Testament practices. These followers were seeking ways to worship Jesus Christ unimpeded by centuries of corrupted traditions and allowing for a more democratic access to truth.[2]

Joseph Smith organized the Church of Christ, as it was then known, on April 6, 1830. Most of those who would unite with the Mormons were already seeking truth. Many women felt that miraculous events in their lives prepared them to find the Church. For some it was a divine sign or manifestation that led them to recognize Joseph Smith as a prophet. Almost all were well acquainted with the Bible. Some discovered the Church from neighbors and family members, facilitating conversations among believers in a common search for truth. They invested time and effort to carefully study, observe, and investigate different claims of truth. Each woman's experience of seeking for and finding truth reflects careful prayer and personal revelation, followed by a distinct choice to leave the past behind and pursue a new faith.

VISIONS AND DREAMS

"Signs follow those that believe."[3]

Elizabeth Ann Whitney (1800–1882) did not grow up in a religious family, but she remembered her father "was strenuous on all points of honor, honesty, morality, and uprightness." She married Newel K. Whitney. The Whitneys did not belong to any religious denomination before 1830, yet Elizabeth described herself as "naturally religious" with a desire to explore different churches.[4]

We had been praying to know from the Lord how we could obtain the gift of the Holy Ghost. My husband, Newel K. Whitney, and myself, were Campbellites.[5] We had been baptized for the remission of our sins, and believed in the laying on of hands and the gifts of the spirit. But there was no one with authority to confer the Holy Ghost upon us. We were seeking to know how to obtain the spirit and the gifts bestowed upon the ancient saints. . . .

One night—it was midnight—as my husband and I, in our house at Kirtland, were praying to the father to be shown the way, the spirit rested upon us and a cloud overshadowed the house.

It was as though we were out of doors. The house passed away from our vision. We were not conscious of anything but the presence of the spirit and the cloud that was over us.

We were wrapped in the cloud. A solemn awe pervaded us. We saw the cloud and we felt the spirit of the Lord.

Then we heard a voice out of the cloud saying:

Prepare to receive the word of the Lord, for it is coming!

At this we marveled greatly; but from that moment we knew that the word of the Lord was coming to Kirtland.[6]

After this miraculous vision, the Whitneys prayed to find the church of Christ. They heard the gospel preached by Parley P. Pratt and Sidney Rigdon, and they were baptized in November 1830.[7] A short time later, strangers arrived in Kirtland:

Joseph Smith, with his wife, Emma, and a servant girl, came to Kirtland in a sleigh; they drove up in front of my husband's store; Joseph jumped out and went in; he reached his hand across the counter to my husband and called him by name. My husband, not thinking it was anyone in whom he was interested, spoke, saying: "I could not call you by name as you have me." He answered, "I am Joseph the Prophet; you have prayed me here, now what do you want of me?" My husband brought them directly to our own house; we were more than glad to welcome them and share with them all the comforts and blessings we enjoyed. I remarked to my husband that this was the fulfillment of the vision we had seen of a cloud as of glory resting upon our house.[8]

Abigail Calkins Leonard (1795–1880) received a visit from her neighbor, Eleazer Miller, in 1829. With the "light of the gospel," he preached to her of the necessity of a "change of heart."[9] His words sparked a new feeling in Abigail. Here she describes her conversion experience, starting with the night following Miller's visit. Abigail and her husband, Lyman Leonard, were baptized in August 1831.[10]

That night was a sleepless one to me, for all night long I saw before me our Savior nailed to the cross. I had not yet received remission of my sins, and, in consequence thereof, was much distressed. These feelings continued for several days, till one day, while walking alone in the street, I received the light of the spirit.

Not long after this, associated Methodists stopped at our house, and in the morning, while I was preparing breakfast, they were conversing upon the subject of church matters, and the best places for church organization. From the jottings of their conversation, which I caught from time to time, I saw that they cared more for the fleece than the flock. The Bible lay on the table near by, and as I passed I occasionally read a few words until I was impressed with the question: "What is it that separates two Christians?"

For two or three weeks this question was constantly on my mind, and I read the Bible and prayed that this question might be answered to me.

One morning I took my Bible and went to the woods, when I fell upon my knees, and exclaimed: "Now, Lord, I pray for the answer of this question, and I shall never rise till you reveal to me what it is that separates two Christians." Immediately a vision passed before my eyes, and the different sects passed one after another by me, and a voice called to me, saying: "These are built up for gain." Then, beyond, I could see a great light, and a voice from above called out: "I shall raise up a people, whom I shall delight to own and bless." I was then fully satisfied and returned to the house.

Not long after this a meeting was held at our house, during which every one was invited to speak; and when opportunities presented, I arose and said: "Today I come out from all names, sects, and parties, and take upon myself the name of Christ, resolved to wear it to the end of my days."

For several days afterward, many people came from different denominations and endeavored to persuade me to join their respective churches. At length the associated Methodists sent their presiding elder to our house to preach, in the hope that I might be converted. While the elder was discoursing I beheld a vision in which I saw a great multitude of people in the distance, and over their heads hung a thick, dark cloud. Now and then one of the multitude would struggle, and rise up through the gloomy cloud; but the moment his head rose into the light above, the minister would strike him a blow, which would compel him to retire; and I said in my heart, "They will never serve me so."

Not long after this, I heard of the "Book of Mormon," and when a few of us were gathered at a neighbor's we asked that we might have manifestations in proof of the truth and divine origin of this book, although we had not yet seen it. . . . I requested that I might know the truth of this book, by the gift and power of the Holy Ghost, and I immediately felt its presence. Then, when the Book of Mormon came, we were ready to receive it and its truths. The brethren gathered at our house to read it, and such days of rejoicing and thanksgiving I never saw before nor since. We were now ready for baptism.[11]

Seeking Truth in Scripture

"Feast upon the words of Christ." [12]

Eliza R. Snow (1804–1887) came from a family of religious seekers. From her youth, her parents taught her to ponder the teachings of the Bible. They consistently searched for truth, inviting people of diverse religious persuasions into their home. [13]

When studying these interesting [biblical] narratives, my mind, many times, was filled with reflections of the deepest type, and my heart yearned for the gifts and manifestations of which those ancient Apostles testified. Sometimes I wished I had lived when Jesus Christ was on the earth, that I might have witnessed the power of God manifested through the Gospel; or that I could see, and listen to a true Prophet of God, through whom He communicated His will to the children of men. But, alas! that day and those blessings had forever gone by! So said the clergy of my own time, and the clergy professed to know. [14]

In the autumn of 1829, the tidings reached my ears that God had spoken from the heavens; that he had raised up a prophet, and was about to restore the fullness of the gospel with all its gifts and powers. During my brief association with the Campbellite church, I was deeply interested in the study of the ancient prophets, in which I was assisted by the erudite Alexander Campbell himself, and Walter Scott, whose acquaintance I made,—but more particularly by Sidney Rigdon, who was a frequent visitor at my father's house.

But when I heard of the mission of the prophet Joseph I was afraid it was not genuine. It was just what my soul had hungered for, but I thought it was a hoax.

However, I improved the opportunity and attended the first meeting within my reach. . . .

Early in the spring of 1835, my eldest sister, who, with my mother was baptized in 1831, by the prophet, returned home from a visit to the saints in Kirtland, and reported of the faith and humility of those who had received the gospel as taught by Joseph,—the progress of the work, the order of the organization of the priesthood and the frequent manifestations of the power of God.

The spirit bore witness to me of the truth. I felt that I had waited already a little too long to see whether the work was going to "flash in the pan" and go out. But my heart was now fixed; and I was baptized on the 5th of April, 1835. From that day to this I have not doubted the truth of the work.

In December following I went to Kirtland and realized much happiness in the enlarged views and rich intelligence that flowed from the fountain of eternal truth, through the inspiration of the Most High.[15]

Hannah Last Cornaby (1822–1905) and her family were members of the Church of England. One evening, while walking in the garden, Hannah and her father witnessed a sudden flash of light streak across the sky, followed by a whole procession of figures. They immediately returned home and reported the event to Hannah's mother, who believed it was a sign of the last days, according to the book of Revelation. Hannah remembered this moment throughout her life as she developed a desire to recognize the hand of God.[16]

I was early taught by [my parents] to love that Being, who has made the earth so beautiful, and provided so much for His creatures dwelling thereon; thus I was early led to admire and reverence the Creator through His works; and especially from my mother's teaching, learned my duty to Him, as revealed in the Bible. This sacred book was my mother's companion by day and by night; and before able to read, I had committed to memory, under her tuition, many of its holy precepts. . . . My religious desires deepened and my anxiety to understand the plan of human redemption increased. I attended public worship with my parents, who began to be dissatisfied with the religious tenets they had espoused. . . . The foundation of my religious faith had [likewise] been shaken. Accustomed as I was to read my bible, it was impossible not to see many discrepancies between the teachings of the religious sects and those of the Savior; most of all, the lack of promised signs which were to follow believers.

Our minds were not at ease; we were removed from former associations, untrammeled by any religious obligation, and were determined to seek for truth wherever it could be found. With the Bible as our standard, we concluded to take its precepts as our guide.

> Several years later, a Mormon missionary, Elder George Day, came into the Cornabys' bookstore one day and began teaching Hannah and her husband about the restored Church.

I remarked, that I thought we had ministers enough already to preach the gospel; he replied, none of them had authority to preach; but he had been sent with authority as the Savior sent his disciples. I then hastened to call my husband, who received him courteously, and invited him to supper. After supper, he spent the evening with us, telling of the Latter-day work; we listened with great interest until bedtime. We procured lodging for him at a hotel near by, and he breakfasted with us next morning. Before he left, he made an appointment, at our request, to call again that evening and preach to us, we promising to call in our near neighbors to hear him.

All day emotions of hope and fear were battling in our bosoms. Could this wonderful news be true? Was God about to answer our prayers for guidance in this manner? Had we, by receiving this stranger, unexpectedly received the blessing of peace to our troubled spirits? We scarcely dared to hope, yet dared not to doubt. Evening came, and with it Elder Day and the friends we had invited. He preached and we believed, and thought it impossible for any one who heard it to do otherwise.[17]

Susannah Stone Lloyd (1830–1920) was raised in Bristol, England, in a middle-class family of devout Christians. She was the only member of her family to come to Utah, immigrating in 1856 and joining the Willie handcart company.[18]

My father's people belonged to the Church of England, Mother's people to the Wesleyans. I attended the Wesleyan Sunday School. I used to read the scriptures and wish that I had lived in the days of Apostles and Prophets, not knowing then that the Everlasting Gospel had been restored to the earth. When I heard it preached I hailed it with joy. I joined the Church of Jesus Christ of Latter-day Saints about the year 1848 [June 15, 1849]. This caused my heart to rejoice. I have seen that the hand of the Lord has been over me for good from my earliest childhood and I know that His Holy Spirit has been my constant guide and companion. I shall never forget the many manifestations of the Lord's goodness and blessings unto me and mine.[19]

2

JESUS CHRIST

"Follow your Lord and Master." [1]

The vast majority of Latter-day Saint converts in the nineteenth century were already Christian, as were most Americans. However, the religious landscape was in a period of transition as many abandoned the orthodoxy of their ancestors in favor of a wider variety of beliefs and religious experience. They believed in Jesus Christ as Savior, but many questioned the best way to seek salvation.

No two people would seek Christ in the same manner. Some searched for a return to New Testament Christianity. Some looked for a church that would ful-fill biblical prophecy. Some placed prime importance on a church whose beliefs lined up with their own personal experience with the divine. Many saw what they considered the true religion of Jesus Christ within the church that Joseph Smith established. Drusilla Hendricks believed that the Latter-day Saint "elders brought the same light Jesus had in the days of John the Baptist."[2] Some saw Joseph Smith as one who could help bring them to Jesus Christ—spiritually and even literally as they experienced miraculous manifestations.

Those who chose to join with the Latter-day Saints often did so at a cost; how-ever, if it brought them closer to Christ, they would abide the cost. And once they found the Saints, they wanted to be strong themselves and likewise bring their family and friends closer to Christ.

SEEING CHRIST

"When he shall appear we shall be like him, for we shall see him as he is."[3]

> **Nancy Naomi Alexander Tracy** (1816–1902) heard of a "gold bible" shortly after her marriage. Initially she wanted to see a Mormon missionary purely out of curiosity about the sensational stories she had heard. Then she met a Mormon apostle, and her interest quickly transformed into a belief that he was truly a representative of Christ who could teach her "the pure doctrine of our Savior." She believed and was changed by his witness.[4]

That summer we began to hear rumbles about a gold bible that a gold-digger had dug up. Reports came fast and thick. It made quite an excitement. . . . At last there came . . . traveling preachers styling themselves Mormon missionaries. . . . I determined to go and see and hear what those horrid creatures looked like and had to say, for I hardly expected they were human from what I had heard. So I got two other women to go with me and repaired to the place appointed. The house was filled, waiting to see this wonderful man. My astonishment was better felt than described when he appeared: a tall and stately looking man with piercing black eyes filled with the spirit of God. He gave out a hymn and sang, a few joining him. Then he prayed and such a prayer! He was full to the brim. All eyes were upon him and you could have heard a pin drop. It seemed as though his influence put all prejudice under his feet. He took his text from the Bible, but I have forgotten it. However, I well remember his powerful sermon on the first principles of the Gospel as taught by the Savior and his apostles. O how plain and beautiful and easy to understand. I believed with my whole soul and I could see that I had been preserved from uniting with other creeds and was waiting to hear and told the folks that for the first time I had heard the true Gospel preached by David Patten who had been chosen as an Apostle, ordained and set apart to teach the pure doctrine of our Savior. They laughed at me and cried, "Delusion, false prophets," and so on. But the seed had taken root.[5]

Melissa Morgan Dodge (1798–1845) was born blind in New York. On the day of her baptism, her sight was miraculously restored as modern apostles of Christ laid their hands on her head. Choosing to become a Latter-day Saint at times brought difficulty and discouragement; she wrote the following letter to her brother after the Saints were expelled from Missouri. Nevertheless, she was certain she had united with Christ's Church, and her letter would lyrically praise God as she shared her personal experience with God's intercession.[6]

I praise my Maker while I breathe. If I am driven from place to place and serve the Lord for this, I know he has no other Church below. . . . Thanks be to the almighty God, he has preserved us and kept us from the hand of our cruel enemies who were threatening our lives daily. . . . May God grant to give you his Spirit to enable you to see the truth as it is in Christ Jesus that we may meet in the celestial kingdom of God where parting is no more. There we shall sing our maker's praise throughout realms of endless days.[7]

Lucy Mack Smith (1775–1856) grew up in a deeply religious home. With a generally absentee father, her mother ensured that the family was centered on scripture. They believed in prophecies and visions. Lucy readily accepted her son Joseph's message of restoration, believing it to be the fulfillment of familiar biblical prophecies. She read the Book of Mormon and was convinced that Joseph had restored ancient covenants and that those covenants could bring people to Christ. This message of Christ became critical for Lucy to share, and quickly she went about teaching her brothers of Christ. This is an excerpt of a letter written to her brother Solomon Mack and his wife, Ester Hayward.[8]

By searching the prophecies contained in the Old Testament we find it there prophesied that God will set his hand the second time to recover his people the house of Israel. He has now commenced this work. He hath sent forth a revelation in these last days, and this revelation is called the Book of Mormon. It contains the fullness of the gospel to the Gentiles, and is sent forth to show unto the remnant of the house of Israel what great things God hath done for their fathers, that they may know of the covenants of the Lord and that they are not cast off forever, and also of the convincing of both Jew and Gentile that Jesus is the Christ, the Eternal God, and manifests himself unto all nations. It also contains the history of a people which were led out of Jerusalem six hundred years before the coming of Christ in the flesh.[9]

RECEIVING THE GRACE OF CHRIST

"That we may obtain mercy." [10]

Martha Cragun Cox (1852–1932) was born to a Latter-day Saint family. She married polygamously and had eight children, with five surviving to adulthood. She traveled up and down the Wasatch Front in Utah as she worked to provide for her family by teaching. As demonstrated in this dream, her many responsibilities often weighed her down. She turned to "the heavens"—to Christ's grace—to lift her burden.[11]

I had a dream given me that gave me to see the condition into which I was falling. I thought I stood with a chain around my neck. This chain reached to the ground and was heavy with many bundles that were fastened to it, so heavy that I could not raise my head to look upward. Someone said to me, "If you <u>must</u> look at these all the time put them on this rod over your fire place and don't hang them on a chain about your neck or you will never see the sun and stars, and you should look up towards the heavens and not down." I then began to examine the parcels one by one and hang them on the rod. . . . All these while they seemed so heavy while hanging on my neck had no weight at all as I hung them on the rod. . . . That [last] bundle faded out through my fingers as I took it off the chain and lo, the chain was gone and I was free. When I awoke I resolved I would be free.[12]

Bringing the Saints to Christ

"Thy face, Lord, will I seek."[13]

Mary Elizabeth Rollins Lightner (1818–1913) was a girl in Kirtland, Ohio, when she first heard about the Book of Mormon. She and her family joined with the Mormons, and she soon had the opportunity to personally meet Joseph Smith. This meeting with Joseph left her with a powerful impression of Christ and Joseph as his representative.[14]

Joseph got up and began to speak to us. As he began to speak very solemnly and very earnestly all at once his countenance changed and he stood mute. Those who looked at him that day said there was a search light within him, over every part of his body. I never saw anything like it on the earth. I could not take my eyes off of him. He got so white that anyone who saw him would have thought he was transparent. I remember I thought I could almost see the bones through the flesh. I have been through many changes since, but that is photographed in my brain. I shall remember it and see in my mind's eye as long as I remain upon the earth.

He stood some minutes. He looked over the congregation as if to pierce every heart. Said he: "do you know who has been in your midst?" One of the Smiths said "an angel of the Lord." Martin Harris said: "it was our Lord and Savior, Jesus Christ." Joseph put his hands down on Martin and said: "God revealed that to you. Brothers and sisters, the spirit of God has been in your midst. The Savior has been here this night and I want to tell you to remember it. There is a vail over your eyes for you could not endure to look upon Him. You must be fed with milk not with strong meat. I want you to remember this as if it were the last thing that escaped my lips. He has given all of you to me and has sealed you up to everlasting life that where he is there you may be also. And if you are tempted of Satan say "get thee behind me, Satan."

These words are figured upon my brain; and I never took my eyes off his countenance. Then he knelt down and prayed. I have never heard anything like it before or since. I felt that he was talking to the Lord and that power rested down upon us in every fiber of our bodies, and we received a sermon from the lips of the representative of God.[15]

Genevieve Johnson Van Wagenen (1909–2000) was a mother of six, an artist, a seamstress, and a writer who often served in the Relief Society.[16] At a young age, she learned the significance of the testimony of the apostles of Christ. As Joseph Smith taught, "The fundamental principles of our religion is the testimony of the apostles and prophets concerning Jesus Christ . . . all other things are only appendages to these, which pertain to our religion."[17] She recorded her experience when she was Genevieve Johnson.

I shall never forget one sacrament meeting in the Provo First Ward. I was about twelve years old at the time. Apostle Melvin J. Ballard was the speaker. He bore his testimony. It was a truly spiritual experience. His testimony thrilled the audience. He told of seeing the Savior. He wept as he told how the Savior took him in his arms and kissed and hugged him and blessed him. And as Apostle Ballard kissed the Savior's feet he saw the nail prints.

I sat spellbound and enthralled, for I truly felt the Lord's Spirit at the meeting. Apostle Ballard was a wonderful soloist. After speaking, he sang "I Know That My Redeemer Lives." The tears rolled down his cheeks as he sang. They rolled down mine too. I felt very close to the Savior. I knew his testimony was true. I desired to live so that I too could be in my Savior's presence.[18]

Emmeline B. Wells (1828–1921) was a writer, editor, and leader of Latter-day Saint women long before she was Relief Society general president in 1910.[19] The following is an excerpt of an oral history with Ethel C. Newman Lund, who interviewed Wells about her experience with Jesus Christ in the Salt Lake Temple.

Ethel C. Lund (1897–1998) was born in Holladay, Utah. She was a student at LDS High School in Salt Lake City when she was assigned to accompany Wells to speak at the school's devotional. They became acquainted, and Wells told her about the temple. This experience made a significant impression upon Ethel, and she wrote about what Emmeline had told her.[20]

She said that the day before she went to the temple . . . she had a compulsion to press her clothes the night before and see that everything was in order. She said while she always looked nice she wanted it to look special for some reason. She said when she got to the temple that next morning and was dressed, not in her robes but in her white dress, . . . "I saw the Savior." She said, "I'm going to tell you where I saw him and when you go to the temple why always remember that that's a sacred place. I'll tell you right where it is." And she did. They've restored that temple more than once, but they have never changed this place. And she told us specifically how you go, where you go in and where you go to find this place. She said, "When you go up that little ramp into the temple proper and you go turn into this first room, just before you turn to go in the first room the Savior came toward me."

She said he was dressed in a robe and he was in white. She said he was above the floor. She said he wasn't walking. He was just standing above the floor. She said he called her by name, "Emmeline, how beautiful you are in your beautiful dress." Now she didn't elaborate too much. That's all I can remember. But the point was that she said, "When you go to the temple"—this is when you go to do work in the temple or to marry in the temple—"promise me that you will never, never go with soiled clothes or with clothes that are wrinkled because maybe one day you will see the Savior there." It left such an impression on me that I even remembered it the day I was married. When

I went to the temple that morning I followed what she had told me where she saw him. I remember I couldn't step there. I felt like it was holier ground that I should never stop on. In all the years I've been to the temple I've never stepped in that spot where she told me the Savior was. That isn't a figment of my imagination. She told that, but I don't know that it wasn't a figment of her imagination, but I believed her.[21]

Sharing the Message of Christ

"And when ye shall receive these things, I would exhort you that ye would ask God."[22]

> **Rebecca Swain Williams** (1798–1861) believed that she had found Christ's church when she joined with the Mormons. This caused great disappointment for her father, who consistently worked to discourage her from her belief. However, her patriarchal blessing promised her that her father would come to know the truth. In a letter to him, she testified of her faith, quoting scripture of the Restoration, hoping to bring her father to Christ. Though she didn't see that promise come to fruition in mortality, she continued faithful in her belief.[23]

My Father, I hardly know what to say to you. Did you and Mother know the circumstances as we do in relation to this work, I am persuaded you would believe it. My heart mourns for my relation according to the flesh, but all I can do is to commend them to God praying that he would enlighten your minds in the way of truth. . . .

My Dear Father, do you believe that all the Churches are of the Lord? The Lord has said by the mouth of his Servant Joseph that this is the only Church upon the face of the whole earth with which the Lord was well pleased with, speaking unto the Churches collectively and not individually. For I the Lord cannot look upon sin with the least degree of allowance. Nevertheless he that repenteth and doeth the commandments of the Lord shall be forgiven and he that repenteth not from him shall be taken even the light which he hath received. For my Spirit shall not always strive with man saith the Lord of hosts. So then we see all that are pure in heart the Lord will bless.[24]

Phebe Crosby Peck (1800–1849) was a new widow caring for five children in Colesville, New York, when she first heard of the gospel from her sister and brother-in-law, Polly Peck and Joseph Knight. Because of significant persecution in Colesville, Phebe's extended family group left New York. Here Phebe writes to Anna Pratt, the sister of her late husband. Anna had planned to leave New York with the Saints but changed her mind at the last minute to get married. Phebe urgently pled with Anna to choose Christ.[25]

I would exhort you not to reject another call. You have been called to repent of your sins and obey the gospel. You have been convicted from time to time but you could not give up all for Christ. And now I feel to say that if you do not give up all and follow your Lord and Master, you will not be made worthy to partake of the Celestial glories in the kingdom of our God. I hope you will think of these things and ponder them in your Heart for they are of great worth unto the children of men.[26]

Laura Farnsworth Owen (1806–1881) was introduced to the Church when her second husband encouraged her to attend a meeting with missionaries. They were both baptized; however, her husband's belief quickly waned and he joined with apostates. Laura ultimately chose Mormonism over her emotionally abusive husband and followed the Saints as they left Nauvoo. She would not let anything impede her path to Christ. Shortly before her death she left this testament to her posterity, hoping that they, too, would seek out the Christ.[27]

I am now in my 63rd year, have good health, and a glorious future in common with the saints that are striving for the blessings of the gospel of Jesus

Christ as revealed in this the dispensation of the fullness of times. I have a great desire to live to accomplish my work, even all that is my privilege to secure a part in the morning of the first resurrection and I pray my Father in heaven that no device of men or devils shall have power to hinder me from gaining it in the season and time that is my right whatever may be my privations in this life, for I have counted all things but loss and dross. I hunger and thirst to be cleansed from all sin and clothed with the righteousness of Christ, the communion of the Holy Spirit and the fellowship of the true saints of God.[28]

~ 3 ~
THE BOOK OF MORMON
"A marvel and a wonder." [1]

The Book of Mormon played a valuable role in the conversion of early Latter-day Saint women. Women participated in the translation and protection of the gold plates and used the Book of Mormon in their own personal study. Most were very well acquainted with the Bible. The Book of Mormon became a foundation of Latter-day Saint faith, bringing additional "light and intelligence" to add to the biblical message. [2] Testimonies of the Book of Mormon are highly individualized. Each experience is as distinctive as the individual gaining the testimony. Some converts, like Zina Huntington, saw the book and immediately knew it was true. [3] Others read the book for much longer before they believed its divine origins. Eliza R. Snow took years to read and study to gain a testimony of the Book of Mormon. Once these women received a personal confirmation of the Book of Mormon's truth, many felt the need to share the book with others.

BOOK OF MORMON TRANSLATION

"By the gift and power of God."[4]

> **Katharine Smith Salisbury** (1813–1900) was fourteen years old when her older brother, Joseph Smith Jr., began translating the Book of Mormon. Katharine and her family were devoted to helping Joseph, and although none of the immediate family followed the Latter-day Saints to Utah, Katharine maintained her testimony of the Book of Mormon almost sixty years later.[5]

I well remember the trials my brother had, before he obtained the records. After he had the vision, he went frequently to the hill, and upon returning would tell us, "I have seen the records, also the brass plates and the sword of Laban with the breast plate and interpreters." He would ask father why he could not get them? The time had not yet come, but when it did arrive he was commanded to go on the 22d day of September 1827 at 2 o'clock. We had supposed that when he should bring them home, the whole family would be allowed to see them, but he said it was forbidden of the Lord. They could be seen only by those who were chosen to bear their testimony to the world. We had therefore to be content until they were translated and we could have the book to read. Many times when I have read its sacred pages, I have wept like a child, while the Spirit has borne witness with my spirit to its truth. Brothers and Sisters, who have obeyed the gospel and are members of the church of Jesus Christ, you have greater reason to be thankful than all the rest of the world, because the Lord has given you the gospel in its plainness, also revelations for the government of his church, and opened your eyes that you could see the truth, and touched your hearts with a desire to do his will and filled you with peace and love one for another.

After the records were translated and the book printed, we often met together and held prayer meetings. Some of our neighbors would come to these meetings and ask us mockingly, if we expected with our little band to convert the world and make them to believe the golden bible? Thank the Lord, the truth did go forth and the gospel was preached in power and demonstration of the Spirit, to the converting of hundreds and thousands, who are today rejoicing in the liberty wherewith Christ hath made them free, and of the heavenly gifts of the gospel.[6]

Emma Hale Smith (1804–1879) married Joseph Smith on January 18, 1827. The couple first lived in New York and then moved to Pennsylvania to work on the translation of the Book of Mormon. Emma accompanied Joseph when he acquired the plates at the Hill Cumorah and was an eyewitness to the process of translation. She acted as one of his scribes.[7] Her sons Alexander and Joseph Smith III interviewed her in February 1879, shortly before her death, recording her testimony of the Book of Mormon.[8] At that time, Emma was married to Major Lewis C. Bidamon.

I know Mormonism to be the truth; and believe the Church to have been established by divine direction. I have complete faith in it. In writing for your father I frequently wrote day after day, often sitting at the table close by him, he sitting with his face buried in his hat, with the stone in it, and dictating hour after hour with nothing between us.

Q: Had he not a book or manuscript from which he read, or dictated to you?

A: He had neither manuscript nor book to read from.

Q: Could he not have had, and you not know it?

A: If he had had anything of the kind he could not have concealed it from me.

Q: Are you sure that he had the plates at the time you were writing for him?

A: The plates often lay on the table without any attempt at concealment, wrapped in a small linen table cloth, which I had given him to fold them in. I once felt of the plates, as they thus lay on the table, tracing their outline and shape. They seemed to be pliable like thick paper, and would rustle with a metallic sound when the edges were moved by the thumb, as one does sometimes thumb the edges of a book.

Q: Where did father and Oliver Cowdery write?

A: Oliver Cowdery and your father wrote in the room where I was at work.

Q: Could not father have dictated the Book of Mormon to you, Oliver Cowdery and the others who wrote for him, after having first written it, or having first read it out of some book?

A: Joseph Smith could neither write nor dictate a coherent and well-worded letter, let alone dictating a book like the Book of Mormon. And, though I was an active participant in the scenes that transpired, and was present during the translation of the plates, and had cognizance of things as they transpired, it is marvelous to me, "a marvel and a wonder," as much so as to anyone else.

Q: I should suppose that you would have uncovered the plates and examined them?

A: I did not attempt to handle the plates, other than I have told you, nor uncover them to look at them. I was satisfied that it was the work of God, and therefore did not feel it to be necessary to do so.

Major Bidamon: Did Mr. Smith forbid your examining the plates?

A: I do not think he did. I knew that he had them, and was not especially curious about them. I moved them from place to place on the table, as it was necessary in doing my work.

Q: Mother, what is your belief about the authenticity, or origin, of the Book of Mormon?

A: My belief is that the Book of Mormon is of divine authenticity—I have not the slightest doubt of it. I am satisfied that no man could have dictated the writing of the manuscripts unless he was inspired; for, when acting as his scribe, your father would dictate to me hour after hour; and when returning after meals, or after interruptions, he would at once begin where he had left off, without either seeing the manuscript or having any portion of it read to him. This was a usual thing for him to do. It would have been improbable that a learned man could do this; and, for one so ignorant and unlearned as he was, it was simply impossible.[9]

Elizabeth Ann Whitmer Cowdery (1815–1892) became acquainted with Joseph Smith when he moved to the Whitmer home in Fayette, New York, and translated a portion of the Book of Mormon there. She was baptized in April 1830 and later married Joseph's scribe Oliver Cowdery.[10] Elizabeth described Joseph using his seer stone to translate and receive revelation so that the words of the translation could "shine forth in darkness unto light."[11] She wrote this account as an affidavit in 1870.

I cheerfully certify that I was familiar with the manner of Joseph Smith's translating the Book of Mormon. He translated most of it at my Father's house. And I often sat by and saw and heard them translate and write for hours together. Joseph never had a curtain drawn between him and his scribe while he was translating. He would place the director in his hat, and then place his face in his hat, so as to exclude the light, and then [read] to his scribe the words (he said) as they appeared before him.[12]

WITNESSES TO THE BOOK OF MORMON

"The voice of the Lord commanded us that we should bear record of it."[13]

Mary Musselman Whitmer (1778–1856) and her family hosted Joseph Smith and Oliver Cowdery in their Fayette, New York, home as Joseph and Oliver worked to finish the translation. The original manuscript pages were bound together with home-manufactured string, "woolen yarn," which Mary's son, David, remembered as being created from raw wool by Mary herself. Mary was baptized shortly after the organization of the Church in April 1830. Several of her sons are known for later becoming published witnesses to the Book of Mormon, but Mary was also a witness.[14] Her grandson, John C. Whitmer, detailed Mary's experience as she told it to him.

I have heard my grandmother (Mary Musselman Whitmer) say on several occasions that she was shown the plates of the Book of Mormon by an holy angel, whom she always called Brother Nephi. (She undoubtedly refers to Moroni, the angel who had the plates in charge.) It was at the time, she said, when the translation was going on at the house of the elder Peter Whitmer, her husband. Joseph Smith with his wife and Oliver Cowdery, whom David Whitmer a short time previous had brought up from Harmony, Pennsylvania, were all boarding with the Whitmers, and my grandmother in having so many extra persons to care for, besides her own large household, was often

Mary Whitmer made this tattered piece of woolen yarn string, which was used to tie together the Book of Mormon manuscript after Joseph Smith finished the translation in the Whitmer home.

overloaded with work to such an extent that she felt it to be quite a burden. One evening, when (after having done her usual day's work in the house) she went to the barn to milk the cows, she met a stranger carrying something on his back that looked like a knapsack. At first she was a little afraid of him, but when he spoke to her in a kind, friendly tone, and began to explain to her the nature of the work which was going on in her house, she was filled with inexpressible joy and satisfaction. He then untied his knapsack and showed her a bundle of plates, which in size and appearance corresponded with the description subsequently given by the witnesses to the Book of Mormon. This strange person turned the leaves of the book of plates over, leaf after leaf, and also showed her the engravings upon them; after which he told her to be patient and faithful in bearing her burden a little longer, promising that if she would do so, she should be blessed; and her reward would be sure, if she proved faithful to the end. The personage then suddenly vanished with the plates, and where he went, she could not tell. From that moment my grandmother was enabled to perform her household duties with comparative ease, and she felt no more inclination to murmur because her lot was hard. I knew my grandmother to be a good, noble and truthful woman, and I have not the least doubt of her statement in regard to seeing the plates being strictly true. She was a strong believer in the Book of Mormon until the day of her death.[15]

Eliza R. Snow (1804–1887) read the Bible and attended the Baptist church as a young child in Ohio. After studying the New Testament, she began seeking for a prophet of God. In the fall of 1829, she learned about Joseph Smith and the Book of Mormon. She made significant efforts to study the book to discover its truth.[16]

I listened to the testimonials of two of the witnesses of the Book of Mormon. Such impressive testimonies I had never before heard. To hear men testify that they had seen a holy angel—that they had listened to his voice, bearing testimony of the work that was ushering in a new dispensation; that the fullness of the gospel was to be restored and that they were commanded to go forth and declare it, thrilled my inmost soul.[17]

> **Rebecca Swain Williams** (1798–1861) was baptized in 1830 sometime before her husband, Frederick G. Williams. Unhappy with his daughter's decision, Rebecca's father threatened to cut her off.[18] Trying to discourage Rebecca, he wrote her a letter questioning Joseph Smith, the Three Witnesses, and the origins of the Book of Mormon. In response, she witnessed to him.

I have been reading over your letter . . . which I have read over again and again. It gives me pain to hear that your mind is so much disturbed about the Book of Mormon and the *Star*.[19] I feel afraid my Father is in some degree getting into the same Spirit you charge the Editor with, as it regards to the origin of the Book of Mormon. There is no disagreement in the Book between the author and the witnesses. The Book plainly shows for itself, [on pages] 547 and 548: "and unto three shall be shown by the power of God."[20] There is no contradiction. The plates were found in the same manner that the Author says they were in the town of Manchester, Ontario County. I have heard the same story from several of the family and from the three witnesses themselves. I heard them declare in public meeting that they saw an Holy Angel come down from heaven and brought the plates and laid them before their eyes and told them that those was the plates that Joseph Smith was translating the Book of Mormon from. They are men of good character and their word is believed where they are acquainted in anything except when they declare to this unbelieving Generation that they have seen an angel of God and conversed with him.[21]

GAINING A PERSONAL TESTIMONY
OF THE BOOK OF MORMON

"He will manifest the truth of it unto you,
by the power of the Holy Ghost." [22]

Zina Diantha Huntington Young (1821–1901) came from a prominent upstate New York family. Her neighbors experienced a religious controversy in 1831, and her father wanted to understand the truth of the claims of a new "golden Bible." Zina was away at school that winter and came home on a break to learn about the Book of Mormon. She wrote this account in 1893, when she was the Relief Society general president. [23]

One day on my return from school I saw the Book of Mormon, that strange, new book, lying on the window sill of our sitting-room. I went up to the window, picked it up, and the sweet influence of the Holy Spirit accompanied it to such an extent that I pressed it to my bosom in a rapture of delight, murmuring as I did so, "This is the truth, truth, truth!" [24]

Caroline Barnes Crosby (1807–1884) grew up in East Canada. In October 1834, she married Jonathan Crosby, from Massachusetts, who had already joined the Latter-day Saints. Caroline had heard negative rumors about the Church, but she could find no fault with its doctrine. [25]

Shortly after my arrival, we were visited by an elderly gentleman from V[ermon]t, by the name of King, who was an elder of the church of Jesus Christ of Latter-day Saints. He put up at father Crosby's, and stayed some 3 or 4 weeks in the neighborhood, held frequent meetings, had formerly been a Methodist preacher. I was soon convinced of the truth of his doctrine, but considered it best to read the Book of Mormon, and search the scriptures until I was thoroughly convinced that it was the work of the Lord.[26]

Sarah DeArmon Pea Rich (1814–1893) grew up in Glass Prairie, Illinois. Her close extended family held different religious beliefs. Rich's father met two Mormon missionaries and invited them to teach his family.[27] Sarah wrote this account at the age of seventy-one in Salt Lake City.

In the summer of 1835 two Mormon elders came to preach at my father's house by request of my father. . . . The two elders came and held a meeting and preached on the first principles of the gospel, and related to the people about there being a prophet in their church, and told us about the Book of Mormon and about an angel appearing to the prophet and others all of which was new doctrine to the people. So as it was in the afternoon that they held their meeting, my father invited them to stop all night which invitation they accepted. . . .

After supper was over, a number of neighbors gathered in to hear these strange men talk: but I felt anxious to see the Book of Mormon they had told us about and I asked one of the Elders if I could see the book and read some in it that evening. So he gladly handed me the book and I asked the company to excuse me for the evening and I retired to my room and spent the balance of that evening and the most of the night in reading that book. I truly was greatly astonished at its contents that it left an impression upon my mind not to be forgotten for in fact the book appeared to be open before my eyes for weeks, but the next morning those men bid us good by and started on their journey for Ohio. So our family had many things to say about this strange people but still the things they told us left a deep impression on our minds not easy to be forgotten.[28]

Laura Farnsworth Owen (1806–1881) was accused of mental delusion by local ministers when she was baptized; in response, she wrote a defense of the Church demonstrating her extensive knowledge of scripture. In it, she highlighted the simple significance of the Book of Mormon to her.[29]

It has been remarked, that the Book of Mormon has nothing to do with our salvation. First, if God sent an angel from heaven, authorizing them to preach the fullness of the Gospel, and has given them the Holy Spirit to accompany it with power, also a record or history of his covenant people, and of his Gospel, which is so plain that it enables the watchman to see after being enlightened on the subject, that it will have something to do with your salvation.[30]

REVELATION

"I have called upon the Lord for direction."[1]

In the Doctrine and Covenants the Lord speaks, "Wherefore, I the Lord, knowing the calamity which should come upon the inhabitants of the earth, called upon my servant Joseph Smith, Jun., and spake unto him from heaven."[2] Revelation shows us that God "speaketh, not spake."[3] Elder Jeffrey R. Holland declared, "The fundamental fact of the Restoration [is the] spirit of revelation."[4] It can take many forms: personal divine communication, mysteries understood, commandments from God, or collective instruction to the Church. It likewise covers many themes—from the practical to the transcendent. One *Woman's Exponent* author explained, divine revelation is "learning of a better quality."[5] As many Americans searched for new revelation and prophetic authority, Latter-day Saints heard God speaking in their lives.[6] Revelation had the power to combat calamity on an individual level as well as collectively for the Saints as a whole.

TRUTH UNFOLDING

"And to them will I reveal all mysteries."[7]

Eliza R. Snow (1804–1887) often expressed her personal ponderings in verse. Though the subject matter of this poem seems familiar, Eliza wrote "Human Life—What Is It?" in 1829, before she knew Joseph Smith or had likely heard of the angel Moroni; it reflects her search for revelation, referencing one of the angels described by John the Revelator. Though some members of her family joined the Church soon after hearing the gospel message, Eliza studied and prayed for four years. Her answers did not come quickly, but when they came, "her heart [was] fixed." Her belief in the Restoration gave her new subject matter and led her to edit this poem as she copied it into her journal, changing "secret pages" to "long-sealed pages," explicitly referencing the Book of Mormon. Finding and accessing divine revelation changed her view of the world.[8]

But lo! a shining Seraph comes!
Hark! 'tis the voice of sacred Truth;
He smiles, and on his visage blooms,
Eternal youth.
He speaks of things before untold,
Reveals what men nor angels knew,
The secret pages now unfold
To human view.[9]

Phebe Crosby Peck (1800–1849) emigrated from New York to Ohio and went on to Jackson County, Missouri, with her five children because a modern prophet revealed it as Zion. Phebe was among those who heard Joseph and Sidney teach of "the vision" (Doctrine and Covenants 76). Though often engaged in the mundane and the difficult aspects of caring for her children in a new place on her own, Phebe marveled at truth expanded. Several months later she remained transfixed by the revealed plan of salvation and worked to share the plan with her extended family.[10]

For the Lord is revealing the mysteries of the heavenly Kingdom unto his Children. . . . Joseph Smith and Sidney Rigdon made us a visit last spring and we had many joyful meetings while they were here. And we had many mysteries unfolded to our view, which gave me great consolation. We could view the condescension of God in preparing mansions of peace for his children and whoso will not receive the fullness of the gospel and stand as valiant soldiers in the cause of Christ. [They] cannot dwell in the presence of the Father and the Son. But there is a place prepared for all who do not receive, but it is a place of much lesser glory then to dwell in the Celestial kingdom. I shall not attempt to say any farther concerning these things as they are now in print and are going forth to the world.[11] And you perhaps will have an opportunity of reading for yourself and if you do I hope you will read with a careful and a prayerful heart for these things are worthy of notice. And I desire that you may search into them for it is that which lends to our happiness in this world and in the world to come.[12]

Elizabeth Ann Whitney (1800–1882) moved from Connecticut to the "Great West" of Ohio with an adventurous "spinster" aunt at the age of nineteen. In Ohio, she met Newel K. Whitney, a Vermonter seeking his fortune in the West, and they were soon married. Though not affiliated with any religion in their youth, they both sought out religion and joined with the Campbellites. However, after baptism they still desired the gift of the Holy Ghost. When Mormon missionary Parley P. Pratt came to Kirtland, they believed they had found one with the authority they sought. The gift of the Holy Ghost offered Elizabeth Ann this specific connection with the divine through personal revelation.[13]

If there are any principles which have given me strength, and by which I have learned to live more truly a life of usefulness, it seems to me I could wish to impart this joy and strength to others; to tell them what the Gospel has been and is to me, ever since I embraced it and learned to live by its laws. A fresh revelation of the Spirit day by day, an unveiling of mysteries which before were dark, deep, unexplained and incomprehensible; a most implicit faith in a divine power, in infinite truth emanating from God the Father.[14]

SEEKING GUIDANCE

"The Lord thy God shall lead thee by the hand, and give thee answer to thy prayers." [15]

> **Mary Fielding Smith** (1801–1852) first learned of the Mormons in Toronto, Canada. After her baptism she moved to Kirtland, Ohio, where she initially worked as a teacher. She wrote the following letter to her sister Mercy, who was in Canada on a mission. As Mary began the letter, she was uncertain of her future. She had no other support and didn't know how she would take care of herself. Despite her uncertainty, she felt peace with her faith that the answer would come.[16] At the time of writing, Mary was simply Mary Fielding.

I am now in a school which I took for one month; the time expires tomorrow when I expect again to be at liberty or without employment. But I feel my mind pretty much at rest on that subject. I have called upon the Lord for direction and trust he will open my way.

Mary likely worked on this letter for days, using every inch of the paper to share her life with her sister. Before she finished the letter, she had an answer to her dilemma: a position as a governess would enable her to better care for herself.

Since I commenced this letter a kind Sister has proposed my going to stay for a while with her to take charge of 2 or 3 Children who have been in my school. They propose giving something besides my board and I think this will suit me better than a public school if it is but little.[17]

> **Amanda Barnes Smith** (1809–1886) lived at Hawn's Mill, Missouri, in 1838. In late October a Missouri militia attacked the town—before the extermination order was made. Amanda's husband Warren and her son Sardius were amongst the seventeen dead at the blacksmith's shop. She found her

six-year-old son Alma "his hip all shot off and to pieces." In the midst of un-conscionable grief Amanda needed immediate, clear direction to know how she might best help her son. She relied completely on the Lord.[18]

The entire hip joint of my wounded boy had been shot away. Flesh, hip bone, joint and all had been ploughed out from the muzzle of the gun which the ruffian placed to the child's hip through the logs of the shop and deliberately fired.

We laid little Alma on a bed in our tent and I examined the wound. It was a ghastly sight. I knew not what to do. It was night now.

There were none left from that terrible scene, throughout that long, dark night, but about half a dozen bereaved and lamenting women, and the children. . . .

Yet was I there, all that long, dreadful night, with my dead and my wounded, and none but God as our physician and help.

"Oh my Heavenly Father," I cried, "what shall I do? Thou seest my poor wounded boy and knowest my inexperience. Oh, Heavenly Father, direct me what to do!"

And then I was directed as by a voice speaking to me.

The ashes of our fire were still smoldering. We had been burning the bark of the shag-bark hickory. I was directed to take those ashes and make a lye and put a cloth saturated with it right into the wound. It hurt, but little Alma was too near dead to heed it much. Again and again I saturated the cloth and put it into the hole from which the hip joint had been ploughed, and each time mashed flesh and splinters of bone came away with the cloth; and the wound became as white as chicken's flesh.

Having done as directed I again prayed to the Lord and was again instructed as distinctly as though a physician had been standing by speaking to me.

Near by was a slippery elm tree. From this I was told to make a slippery elm poultice and fill the wound with it.

My eldest boy was sent to get the slippery elm from the roots, the poultice was made, and the wound, which took fully a quarter of a yard of linen to cover, so large was it, was properly dressed.

It was then I found vent to my feelings in tears, and resigned myself to the anguish of the hour. . . .

I removed the wounded boy to a house, some distance off, the next day, and dressed his hip; the Lord directing me as before. I was reminded that in my husband's trunk there was a bottle of balsam. This I poured into the wound, greatly soothing Alma's pain.

"Alma, my child," I said, "you believe that the Lord made your hip?"

"Yes, mother."

"Well, the Lord can make something there in the place of your hip, don't you believe he can, Alma?"

"Do you think that the Lord can, mother?" inquired the child, in his simplicity.

"Yes, my son," I replied, "he has showed it all to me in a vision."

Then I laid him comfortably on his face and said: "Now you lay like that, and don't move, and the Lord will make you another hip."

So Alma laid on his face for five weeks, until he was entirely recovered—a flexible gristle having grown in place of the missing joint and socket, which remains to this day a marvel to physicians.

On the day that he walked again I was out of the house fetching a bucket of water, when I heard screams from the children. Running back, in affright, I entered, and there was Alma on the floor, dancing around, and the children screaming in astonishment and joy.

It is now nearly forty years ago, but Alma has never been the least crippled during his life, and he has traveled quite a long period of the time as a missionary of the gospel and a living miracle of the power of God.[19]

Laura Clark Phelps (1807–1842) lived in Far West when her husband, Morris, was arrested at the Siege of Far West with 150 others. Though most were released after a short time, Joseph Smith and others spent months in Liberty Jail. Morris Phelps, Parley P. Pratt, and King Follett ended up in Columbia Jail, where they languished for eight months. Meanwhile, Laura visited them consistently every two weeks, traveling a distance of 139 miles from Far West. As she prepared for yet another visit she decided that she would help the men escape and then dreamed of a way to help them. Her grandson, Will Holmes, detailed her dream.[20]

Here was her plan to free them: She would secret three horses in some brush a short distance from the jail. As an excuse to get the jailer to unlock the prison door, she would suggest to the jailer that he open the door and pass the coffee pot to the prisoners through the open door. . . . Should the jailer unlock the door, it would be the signal to get busy, pull the door wide open, grab the jailer, throw him to the floor and flee for their lives.[21]

When Laura arrived in Columbia she learned that Parley had received a very similar dream twice. His brother Orson soon thereafter arrived "with a firm impression they were about to be delivered," and they moved forward.[22]

The scheme worked but not without difficulties. The second door was unlocked and King Follet pulled the door open and Parley P. Pratt was to follow and grandfather [Morris] Phelps, being an athlete and wrestler, was to throw the jailer down and he would follow. It proved to be an exciting event. . . . it was the fourth of July and nearly hundreds were nearby celebrating.[23]

The plan worked as it had been shown them in their dreams; however, they did not plan the details of where Laura would go after the escape. The jailer exposed her to the mob that had gathered around the jail. Thankfully, a young boy saw what had happened and told his mother. The family rescued Laura from the mob. She gave them a Book of Mormon, sang hymns with them, and left with a promise that if she learned of any great destruction to come upon the state of Missouri she would warn them. Laura did not know that her husband was safe until she met up with him three weeks later.[24]

VOZ DE AMONESTACION

É

INSTRUCCION AL PUEBLO

O SEA INTRODUCCION

A LA FÉ Y DOCTRINAS

DE LA

Iglesia de Jesucristo de los Santos de los últimos dias

Por PARLEY P. PRATT

«Las cosas primeras hé aquí vinieron, y yo anuncio nuevas cosas: ántes que salgan á luz, yo os las haré notorias.» Isaías XLII, 9.

«Alegad vuestra causa, dice Jehová: exhibid vuestros fundamentos, dice el Rey de Jacob.» Isaías XLI, 21.

PRIMERA EDICION ESPAÑOLA

Traducido por los Elders, Trejo, Stewart y Rhodakanáty

Publicado por el Elder Moises Thatcher

MEXICO.—1880

Title page of the Spanish edition of Voz de amonestación (A Voice of Warning), *written by Parley P. Pratt.*

> **Desideria Quintanar de Yañez** (1814–1893) lived her whole life in Nopala, Hildalgo, Mexico. In early 1880, at sixty-six, she dreamed of a pamphlet—*Una voz de amonestación (A Voice of Warning)*—being published by Latter-day Saint missionaries in Mexico City.[25] Mexico City was seventy-five miles to the south, a significant distance for Desideria to travel with her health considerations. Instead her son José made the journey, and he finally found Elder James Z. Stewart while the missionary was correcting printer's proofs of the tract about which Desideria had dreamed. Though the pamphlet was not yet completed, the missionary sent José home with other tracts. After Desideria read the pamphlets, she requested baptism.[26] José María Yañez recorded this experience of his mother's.

He said that before his mother had seen a Mormon that she received a vision, and that in Mexico [were] some men who had a book called "Voice of Warning," so she sent him to Mexico to hunt the book. . . . After hunting for a long time . . . [he arrived] at the Hotel [San Carlos], the Elders knew his mission and told him that he had been sent by his mother. . . . So he accepted the [pamphlets] and went home, and upon arriving his mother was very happy. . . . She knew by inspiration that he had [pamphlets], and shortly after was baptized as well as other members of the family, and his mother who was a descendant of the family of [Cuauhtémoc, an Aztec emperor], was the first woman baptized in this mission.[27]

GAINING A PERSONAL WITNESS

"Thou hast been enlightened by the Spirit of truth."[28]

> **Sarah DeArmon Pea Rich** (1814–1893) and her family were Methodists when they first met Mormon missionaries in 1835. Her father invited the missionaries to stay the night with them, they talked together, and Sarah spent the night reading the Book of Mormon. However, the missionaries quickly left without a plan to return. About six weeks later Sarah had a memorable dream.[29]

Those men would come to our house the next evening just as the sun would be setting, and they would first come in sight at the end of a long lane in front of our house. I also dreamed that I met them on the porch and of the remark that was made both by them and myself.

Because of her dream, she was certain the elders would come. She told her family, but they did not believe her.

"Those two Mormon Elders will be here tonight." "Why," said my father, "have you heard from them?" I said, "No, but I dreamed last night that they would be here, and I feel sure it will be so." Father said I must be crazy for those men were hundreds of miles away. . . . Sure enough, just as the sun was setting they made their appearance just where I dreamed I first saw them. I met them on the porch, and bid them the time of day by saying, "I have been looking for you to come." "Why," said they, "had you heard we were coming?" "No," said I, "but I dreamed last night that you were coming and I felt sure you would be here." "Well," said one of the Elders, "and we had a vision that we were to return here and baptize you and build up a Church in this region." I said, "Well, that is something for the future."

Despite Sarah's initial reluctance, her sister invited the missionaries inside. They taught her family that evening and preached to neighbors in their home over the following days. Quickly Sarah received her own personal witness and acted on that witness.

I was truly convinced that their doctrine was from God, and on the next morning I went forth and was baptized; it was on the 15th of December, and they had to cut the ice and baptize me. I had made it a business of prayer to my Father in Heaven to show me if this was the work of God, and He did. So I was truly convinced that it was the true Gospel, and never have for one moment doubted it since; and it has now been fifty-four years since I embraced Mormonism: and I feel thankful to my Heavenly Father that I ever heard and embraced the truth of His latter day work.[30]

Wilmirth Matilda Greer East (1824–1902) married at the age of fifteen in the Republic of Texas. More than a decade later, she and her husband, Edward, met the Mormons, were baptized, and wanted to gather with the Saints. She wrote in the *Woman's Exponent* of the need to receive revelation herself rather than depend on the testimony or experience of others.[31]

When I first heard a "Mormon" missionary preach, I was twenty-eight years of age; and I believed every word he said. Why? Because I believed the Bible, and he did not preach anything but what could be proved from the sacred book. Now, what was I to do? I had a husband, father and brothers, all intelligent, honorable men. Was it my duty to ask them if the Gospel was true, and whether I must obey it or not? Or had God given me my own agency, to think and act in such matters for myself? My father was a deist, and that was the tradition under which I was brought up. The "Mormon" Elder told the people if they believed and obeyed the requirements of the Gospel, they should know of the doctrine, whether it was of God or of man; and that the signs followed the believers as in ancient times. Well, I thought if God is the same yesterday, today, and forever, I will go to Him on my bended knees and ask him if he has revealed Himself from the Heavens and sent forth messengers to gather His Elect from the four quarters for the earth. I covenanted with the Lord to be a faithful witness to this testimony, provided He gave it to me as I had read of its being given on the day of Pentecost. I would bear testimony to all the world that I received it in answer to my prayer, leaving no room for doubt.[32]

Jane Smith Coleman (1838–1924) was born in Dundee, Scotland, and was baptized with her mother and siblings a few months after the death of her father. Extremely poor, they all labored in factories by day and did "fancywork"—creating lace by hand—at night to save money to gather with the Saints. As they worked to earn money to immigrate, they didn't have extra money for "Easter bonnets and fine clothes and spring suits" as did the other girls at church. Jane's sister Betsey told of how Jane would always "take the back streets as they came home from meeting" hoping to avoid running into other girls from their branch who would tease Jane because of her plain clothes, likely making what follows require even more courage.[33]

When I embraced the gospel, I was in my thirteenth year, and at that early age I received a testimony that was satisfactory to me, that it was true. I well remember being present at a testimony meeting where I felt forcibly constrained to bear testimony to the truth; I tried to argue with myself, that I was too young to get up and say anything—was only a little girl and should not speak. But it was no use, I had to get up and bear testimony that Joseph Smith was a prophet of God, and so forth. I tell you this to encourage you; if you have not got a witness yourself, seek until you do get one. Our Heavenly Father "is the same yesterday, today and forever;" willing at all times to bless and give gifts unto his children. But the steps you have taken will inspire your minds—you will be filled with the light of truth, and you will not be ashamed of the worship of God.[34]

Emma Hale Smith (1804–1879) married her husband, Joseph Smith, before he was a prophet. Though she had more formal education than her husband, his role as prophet also provided an opportunity for her to learn. As he learned through visionary revelatory experiences over the years, she was likewise offered an intimate opportunity to learn with him. Before Joseph left for Carthage, Emma desired a blessing from him, but there was no time. Joseph instructed her to write out a blessing, and he would sign it on his return. The following was taken from this text.[35]

I desire the Spirit of God to know and understand myself, that I might be able to overcome whatever of tradition or nature that would not tend to my exaltation in the eternal worlds. I desire a fruitful, active mind, that I may be able to comprehend the designs of God, when revealed through His servants without doubting.[36]

⁓ 5 ⁓

JOSEPH SMITH

"A prophet of the true and living God."[1]

Many women who knew Joseph Smith personally and interacted with him recorded their convictions of him as a prophet of God. His mother, Lucy Mack Smith, compiled his history entrenched in her own personal conversion and life experiences.[2] Zilpha C. Williams wrote a letter to her family about her first encounter with him.[3] Several wrote from childhood perceptions of the Prophet and his concern and love for people of all ages, races, and backgrounds.[4] Some women saw the Prophet in dreams before they ever met him. They described his physical appearance as well as their feelings as they met him. Some knew he was a prophet the moment they first saw him. For others, spending extended time with him, observing his interactions with others, and hearing him preach and teach provided a spiritual confirmation. Most recognized that something made him different from other people. One thing remains the same across time and age, space and distance: these women gained their own personal witnesses of Joseph Smith as a prophet of God, and they testified in their own words.

First impressions

"After I saw him plain, I was certain he was a prophet because I knew it."[5]

Mary B. Noble (1810–1851) taught school in 1833 in Avon, New York. In the spring of 1834, Joseph Smith came from Kirtland, Ohio, to her father's home.[6]

This was the first time I ever beheld a prophet of the Lord, and I can truly say at the first sight that I had a testimony within my bosom that he was a man chosen of God to bring forth a great work in the last days. His society I prized, his conversation was meat and drink to me. The principles that he brought forth bind the testimony that he bore of the truth of the Book of Mormon [and] made a lasting impression upon my mind. . . .

Brother Joseph and Elder Rigdon held a meeting in Geneva, which was called the Orton neighborhood, in a barn. Elder Rigdon preached, Brother Joseph bore testimony of the truth of the Book of Mormon, and the work that had come forth in these last days. Never did I hear preaching sound so glorious to me as that did. I realized it was the truth of heaven, for I had a testimony of it myself.[7]

Mary Alice Cannon Lambert (1828–1920) was the daughter of George and Ann Quayle Cannon, of Liverpool, England. She was baptized at the age of twelve, and her family arrived in Nauvoo in 1843.[8] She wrote this account in 1905 for the *Young Woman's Journal*.

I first saw Joseph Smith in the spring of 1843. When the boat in which we came up the Mississippi River reached the landing at Nauvoo, several of the leading brethren were there to meet the company of Saints that had come on it. Among those brethren was the Prophet Joseph Smith. I knew him the instant my eyes rested upon him, and at that moment I received my testimony that he was a Prophet of God, for I never had such a feeling for mortal man as thrilled my being when my eyes rested upon Joseph Smith. He was not pointed out to me. I knew him from all the other men, and, child that I was (I was only fourteen) I knew that I saw a Prophet of God.

Many, many times between the time I reached Nauvoo and his martyrdom, I heard him preach. The love the saints had for him was inexpressible. They would willingly have laid down their lives for him. If he was to talk, every task would be laid aside that they might listen to his words. He was not an ordinary man. Saints and sinners alike felt and recognized a power and influence which he carried with him. It was impossible to meet him and not be impressed by the strength of his personality and influence.[9]

Emmeline B. Wells (1828–1921) joined the Church in Massachusetts when she was fourteen years old. The next year she married James Harris, the son of the local branch president, and the following spring, 1844, she moved with James and his family to Nauvoo, where she first encountered Joseph Smith.[10]

As we stepped ashore the crowd advanced, and I could see one person who towered away and above all the others around him; in fact I did not see distinctly any others. His majestic bearing, so entirely different from any one I had ever seen (and I had seen many superior men) was more than a surprise. It was as if I beheld a vision; I seemed to be lifted off my feet, to be as it were walking in the air, and paying no heed whatever to those around me. I made my way through the crowd, then I saw this man whom I had noticed, because of his lofty appearance, shaking hands with all the people, men, women and children. Before I was aware of it he came to me, and when he took my hand, I was simply electrified,—thrilled through and through to the tips of my fingers, and every part of my body, as if some magic elixir had given me new life and vitality. I am sure that for a few minutes I was not conscious of motion. I think I stood still; I did not want to speak, or be spoken to. I was overwhelmed with indefinable emotion. . . .

The one thought that filled my soul was, I have seen the Prophet of God, he has taken me by the hand, and this testimony has never left me in all the "perils by the way." It is as vivid today as ever it was. For many years, I felt it too sacred an experience even to mention. . . .

I heard him preach all his last sermons, and frequently met him and shook hands with him, and always felt in my inmost soul, he is indeed a man unlike all others.

In the Prophet Joseph Smith, I believed I recognized the great spiritual power that brought joy and comfort to the Saints; and withal he had that strong comradeship that made such a bond of brotherliness with those who were his companions in civil and military life, and in which he reached men's souls, and appealed most forcibly to their friendship and loyalty. He possessed too the innate refinement that one finds in the born poet, or in the most highly cultivated intellectual and poetical nature; this extraordinary temperament and force combined is something of a miracle and can scarcely be accounted for except as a "heavenly mystery" of the "higher sort." . . .

The power of God rested upon him to such a degree that on many occasions he seemed transfigured. His expression was mild and almost childlike in repose; and when addressing the people, who loved him it seemed to adoration, the glory of his countenance was beyond description. At other times the great power of his manner, more than of his voice (which was sublimely eloquent to me) seemed to shake the place on which we stood and penetrate the inmost soul of his hearers, and I am sure that then they would have laid down their lives to defend him.[11]

Bathsheba W. Smith (1822–1910) became a member of the Church with most of her family in 1837 in Virginia (now West Virginia) at the age of fifteen. The first time she saw Joseph Smith was in Illinois, after he had been released from Liberty Jail.[12]

The Prophet was a handsome man,—splendid looking, a large man, tall and fair and his hair was light. He had a very nice complexion, his eyes were blue, and his hair a golden brown and very pretty. . . .

My testimony today is, I know Joseph Smith was and is a Prophet, as well as I know anything. I know that he was just what he professed to be. . . . I have seen very many good men, but they had not the gift and blessing Joseph had. He was truly a Prophet of God.[13]

Jane Snyder Richards (1823–1912) lived with her family in Ontario, Canada, when they first heard the gospel message in 1834. Her brother Robert Snyder was the first of the family to join the Church and move to Kirtland. He returned to Canada on a mission and baptized all of his family. They moved to Nauvoo, and Jane married Franklin D. Richards in 1842.[14]

I first saw the Prophet Joseph Smith and shook hands with him, in a dream, about eighteen months before my removal to Nauvoo. Later, at Nauvoo, from the recollections of my dream, I recognized him at first sight, while he was preaching to the people. His was one of the most engaging personalities it has ever been my good fortune to meet. . . . As Seer and Revelator he was fearless and outspoken, yet humble, never considering that he was more than the mouth-piece, through whom God spoke. As the Leader of his people he was ever active and progressive but always modest and considerate of them and their trying circumstances. Socially he was an ideal of affability and always approachable to the humblest of his acquaintances.[15]

> **Margaret Pierce Young** (1823–1907) was born and raised in Pennsylvania by Quaker parents. As a young girl she fell in an icy pond and took cold, developing a fever and heart trouble that made her very ill. Two Mormon missionaries in the area gave her a blessing and saved her life. The following summer, Mormon missionaries returned and the Pierce family chose to be baptized.[16]

In January, 1840, word came that the Prophet Joseph Smith was to visit our Branch on his way from Philadelphia. . . . My Mother served a splendid supper, and then the neighbors gathered to hear the Prophet discourse. I wish that I might describe my feelings at that meeting. Though they are fresh in my memory today, I cannot fall short of expressing myself. So animated with loving kindness, so mild and gentle, yet big and powerful and majestic was the Prophet, that to me he seemed more than a man; I thought almost, that he was an Angel. We were all investigating; none of my people had yet entered the waters of baptism. However, it was a great joy to us to entertain the Prophet Joseph Smith, and hear his wonderful words of wisdom. It was 2 o'clock in the morning before we permitted him to retire. We wanted to listen to him all night.

After he had gone from the room, my mother said, "I don't see how anyone can doubt that he is a Prophet of God. They can see it in his countenance, which is so full of intelligence." "Yes, truly!" my Father replied, "he is a Prophet of God."[17]

> **Mary Isabella Horne** (1818–1905) was born and raised in Kent, England. In 1832, her family immigrated to Canada, where they heard missionaries Orson Pratt and Parley P. Pratt. Mary was baptized in 1836. She wrote this testimony for her descendants before she passed away.[18]

I first met the Prophet Joseph Smith in the fall of 1837, at my home in the town of Scarborough, Canada West. When I first shook hands with him I was thrilled through and through, and I knew that he was a Prophet of God, and that testimony has never left me, but is still strong within me, and has been a monitor to me, so that I can now bear a faithful testimony to the divinity of the mission of the Great Man of God. . . .

I testify that Joseph Smith was the greatest Prophet that ever lived on this earth, the Savior, only, excepted. There was a personal magnetism about him which drew all people who became acquainted with him, to him.

I feel greatly honored when I realize that I have had the privilege of personally entertaining this great man, of ministering to his temporal wants, of shaking hands with him, and listening to his voice. I heard him relate his first vision when the Father and Son appeared to him; also his receiving the Gold Plates from the Angel Moroni. . . . While he was relating the circumstances, the Prophet's countenance lighted up, and so wonderful a power accompanied his words that everybody who heard them felt his influence and power, and none could doubt the truth of his narration. I know that he was true to his trust, and that the principles that he advanced and taught are true.[19]

PERSONAL ACQUAINTANCE

"To mark his 'daily walk and conversation.'" [20]

Mercy Fielding Thompson (1807–1893) was born in England and later immigrated to Canada with her brother and sister, Joseph and Mary Fielding, in 1832. In 1836 the three siblings were baptized after hearing missionary Parley P. Pratt preach. They moved to Kirtland, where Mercy married Robert Thompson, who served as a secretary to Joseph Smith.[21]

We listened with joy and profit to the words of instruction and counsel which fell from the inspired lips of Joseph Smith, each word carrying to our hearts deeper and stronger convictions that we were listening to a mighty Prophet of God. And yet there was not the slightest appearance of ostentation or conscious power on his part; he was as free and sociable as though we had all been his own brothers and sisters, or members of one family. He was as un-assuming as a child. . . .

I have seen the Prophet under a great variety of circumstances, in public, in domestic and social life and in sacred places.

I have seen him as if carried away by the power of God beyond all mortal conception, when speaking to the Saints in their public gatherings; and in less public places I have heard him explaining to the brethren and sisters the glorious principles of the gospel, as no man could, except by prophetic power.

I have seen him in the lyceum[22] and heard him reprove the brethren for giving way to too much excitement and warmth in debate, and have listened to his clear and masterly explanations of deep and difficult questions.

To him all things seemed simple and easy to be understood, and thus he could make them plain to others as no other man could that I ever heard.

In a social gathering of the Saints at the Bowery near the site of the Temple, I saw him rejoicing with the people, perfectly sociable and without reserve, occasionally uttering jokes for their amusement and moving upon the same plane with the humblest and poorest of his friends; to him there were no strangers and by all he was known as the Prophet and a friend of humanity. . . .

I saw him by the bedside of Emma, his wife, in sickness, exhibiting all the solicitude and sympathy possible for the tenderest of hearts and the most af-fectionate of natures to feel. And by the deathbed of my beloved companion, I saw him stand in sorrow, reluctantly submitting to the decree of Providence, while the tears of love and sympathy freely flowed. . . .

I have been present at meetings of the Relief Society and heard him give directions and counsels to the sisters, calculated to inspire them to efforts which would lead to celestial glory and exaltation, and oh! how my heart rejoiced![23]

> **Eliza R. Snow** (1804–1887) grew up in Mantua, Ohio, thirty miles south of Kirtland. Originally Baptist, she and her family followed the Disciples of Christ under the direction of Sidney Rigdon. Her mother and sister joined with the Mormons before Eliza. She studied the Book of Mormon before she met Joseph. Eliza was later sealed to Joseph as a plural wife. She considered him the "choice of my heart and the crown of my life."[24]

In the autumn of [1829 or 1830] I heard of Joseph Smith as a Prophet to whom the Lord was speaking from the heavens; and that a sacred record containing a history of the origin of the aborigines of America, was unearthed. A Prophet of God—the voice of God revealing to man as in former dispensations, was what my soul had hungered for, but could it possibly be true—I considered it a hoax—too good to be true.

In the winter of 1830 and 31, Joseph Smith called at my father's, and as he sat warming himself, I scrutinized his face as closely as I could without attracting his attention, and decided that his was an honest face. My adopted motto, "prove all things and hold fast that which is good,"[25] prompted me to investigation, as incredulous as I was; and the most impressive testimonies I had ever heard were given by two of the witnesses to the Book of Mormon, at the first meeting of the believers in Joseph Smith's mission, which I attended. . . .

In the spring of 1836, I taught a select school for young ladies, and boarded with the Prophet's family. . . . I resided in the family of Joseph Smith, and taught his family school, and had ample opportunity to mark his "daily walk and conversation," as a prophet of God; and the more I became acquainted with him, the more I appreciated him as such. His lips ever flowed with instruction and kindness; and, although very forgiving, indulgent, and affectionate in his temperament, when his Godlike intuition suggested that the welfare of his brethren, or the interests of the kingdom of God demanded it; no fear of censure—no love of approbation could prevent his severe and cutting rebuke.

Though his expansive mind grasped the great plan of salvation and solved the mystic problem of man's destiny—though he had in his possession keys that unlocked the past and the future with its succession of eternities; in his devotions he was humble as a little child.[26]

— 6 —

PRIESTHOOD

"The order of the organization of the priesthood and the frequent manifestations of the power of God." [1]

The priesthood was both essential and central to the Restoration. Women recognized the priesthood as the eternal power and authority of God, used to bless, redeem, and exalt His daughters and sons.[2] They recognized Joseph Smith as one given authority to restore the priesthood as it had been organized in the ancient Church. They studied the Bible and searched for truth in regard to the administration of the Church of God and to the blessings afforded to them as daughters of God.

The restoration of the priesthood through Joseph Smith was indeed a marvelous series of events. Women testified of being both participants in and recipients of the priesthood in the latter days. They observed their fathers, husbands, brothers, and sons ordained to the priesthood and supported them in these administrative positions. They supported priesthood responsibilities of their husbands and local priesthood leaders and exercised priesthood authority in their own callings and in the temple. Women received many blessings through the priesthood.

PRIESTHOOD RESTORATION

"I have conferred upon you the keys and power of the priesthood."[3]

Mary Ann Frost Pratt (1809–1891) was a widow when she joined the Church in Maine in 1835; her first husband had died after only one year of marriage. Having lost dear family members, she was drawn to the promise of life after death. She married Parley P. Pratt, also a widower, in 1837, and accompanied him on missions to England. They lost two children before arriving in Salt Lake City in 1852.[4]

God has said unto us He will restore all things as at the beginning. . . . [The] Melchizedek Priesthood . . . was taken from the earth when those who held it were slain. They held the keys to administer in sacred things. John the Revelator, being banished on the Isle of Patmos, saw what would take place in our day, when the Everlasting Gospel would be preached to every nation, tongue and people, "Saying, give glory to God, for the hour of his judgment has come."[5]

Now it behooves all people to repent of their sins, and receive the Gospel and be saved, for the scripture says, "He that believeth and is baptized shall be saved; he that believeth not shall be damned."[6]

Now, this same John has come and committed this Priesthood to men on the earth, to administer again in sacred ordinances. The angel came with the Everlasting Gospel, having all the gifts and blessings accruing thereunto. I can bear witness to these things; I have heard the gift of tongues, the interpretation given, have seen the sick restored to health by the gift of healing, the evil spirit cast out by prayer and the gift of faith, and I do know for myself that these things are true, for they have been shown to me by the Holy Spirit.

We are told to read the Scriptures, and learn these things for ourselves. I had a testimony before I ever heard a Latter-day Saint preach that the same Gospel that the Apostles taught would be restored to the earth again. I found that I was quite familiar with Bible doctrine, and by the power of the priest-hood I have been enabled to understand more fully. I was no stranger to that which had been taught me in the spirit world before I took this mortal body. Now I expect to obtain an immortal one, if I am faithful to the end.[7]

Eliza R. Snow (1804–1887) studied the Bible as a child, memorizing long passages. As a result, she was sensitive to the priesthood order as outlined in the New Testament. She also grew up with great respect for her father, Oliver Snow, an active community member who served as a justice of the peace in Portage County, Ohio. He was baptized a short time after Eliza.[8] Her understanding of the priesthood in-cluded both the Church institution and the family, as she explained in 1877.

With the restoration of the fullness of the gospel came also the ancient order of patriarchal blessings. Each father, holding the priesthood, stands as a patriarch, at the head of his family, with invested right and power to bless his household, and to predict concerning the future, on the heads of his children, as did Jacob of old.[9]

Supporting Priesthood Offices

"The office of thy calling shall be for a comfort unto . . . thy husband."[10]

Caroline Barnes Crosby (1807–1884) studied the Bible and the Book of Mormon for several months before she was baptized in January 1835. Her husband, Jonathan Crosby, had been baptized the year before. Jonathan was ordained an elder in early 1836 in Kirtland and then a Seventy later that year.[11]

My husband was ordained to the office of an elder, and chosen into the second quorum of seventies. I well recollect the sensations with which my mind was actuated when I learned the fact that my husband had been called and ordained to the Melchizedek priesthood and would undoubtedly be required to travel and preach the gospel to the nations of the earth. I realized in some degree the immense responsibility of the office, and besought the Lord for grace and wisdom to be given him that he might be able to magnify his high and holy calling. The brethren had meetings of some kind almost every evening in the week.[12]

Martha Horne Tingey (1857–1938) was born to Joseph and Mary Isabella Horne in Salt Lake City. As a child, she would often eavesdrop on the conversation of adults in her parents' parlor, many of whom were leaders in the Church and the community. Later she was a counselor in her ward's Primary and Young Women organizations. From 1905 to 1929 she served as general Young Women president.[13] When she wrote this account, she went by Mattie J. Horne.

We the Daughters of Zion . . . heartily coincide with our brothers in those feelings of gratitude to our Heavenly Father and His Holy Priesthood, for our glorious privileges, our surroundings, and our prospects for the future.

We desire in no way to come short of our brothers in the discharge of those duties which are required of us. We wish to share in their trials, tribulations and sacrifices, if by so doing we can help to establish correct principles, and secure to ourselves an exaltation in the kingdom of our God. . . .

We look to our brothers for counsel, protection, and above all, for examples. And would say to them as they have said to us, "Let us work side by side in all the great reforms of the last days." . . .

Brothers, lead out! We are with you, heart and hand in everything that will promote the welfare of Zion.[14]

RECEIVING THE BLESSINGS OF THE PRIESTHOOD

"The power and authority of the higher, or Melchizedek Priesthood, is to hold the keys of all the spiritual blessings of the church."[15]

Cyrena Dustin Merrill (1817–1906) was the only member of her immediate family to join the Church, which she did in March 1837. When she left to join the Saints in Missouri, her parents were grief-stricken at losing their daughter. In April 1838, before departing, Cyrena received her patriarchal blessing from Joseph Smith Sr.[16]

My [patriarchal] blessing has been a great comfort to me in the trials which I have had to pass through and it also assisted to give me the necessary faith, courage, and fortitude to make the sacrifice of leaving home and friends and to start out alone in the world to fight the battle of life among strangers. I went forth trusting in the Lord, in full faith that he would give me grace sufficient to overcome all obstacles and difficulties which might be thrown in my way, and that I might endure to the end.[17]

Vilate Murray Kimball (1806–1867) and her husband, Heber C. Kimball, were baptized in the spring of 1832. Heber was appointed an apostle, and he served a mission to England from 1837 to 1838. Vilate recounted events leading to his second mission to Britain in 1839.[18]

A short time previous to my husband's starting, he was prostrated on his bed from a stitch in his back, which suddenly seized him while chopping and drawing wood for his family, so that he could not stir a limb without exclaiming, from the severity of the pain. Joseph Smith hearing of it came to see him, bringing Oliver Cowdery and Bishop Partridge with him. They prayed for and blessed him, Joseph being mouth, beseeching God to raise him up. He then took him by the right hand and said, "Brother Heber, I take you by the right hand, in the name of Jesus Christ of Nazareth, and by virtue of the holy priesthood vested in me, I command you, in the name of Jesus Christ, to rise, and be thou made whole." He arose from his bed, put on his clothes, and started with them, and went up to the temple, and felt no more of the pain afterwards.[19]

Nancy Naomi Alexander Tracy (1816–1902) remembered the excitement when Mormon missionaries came to her town in New York in the spring of 1833. She and her husband were baptized a year later. Although early Saints were persecuted in the local county, membership increased, and she recorded, "The gifts and blessings of the Gospel were poured out upon those that had embraced it in rich profusion."[20]

A young girl about 20 years of age, Emily Fuller, was staying for a few days at Brother Homer Blakesley's, our presiding Elder's house; she was taken violently ill and kept on getting worse until finally she went into convulsions; she was a good Latter-day Saint but it seemed the evil one was determined to destroy her; Brother Blakesley had gone away to fill an appointment 18 miles from home; there was not an Elder within 14 miles; at last this Elder Thomas Dutcher was sent for to come and administer to this girl; it had now been about twenty-four hours since she was taken ill, everything that could be done for her was done but of no avail; the evil spirit raved in cramping her body. She was in this state when Brother Dutcher came; he immediately repaired to a room alone and prayed mightily for faith and strength in God that he might have power to rebuke the destroyer; and when he came out and went into the room to her bedside he laid his hands upon her head and with the authority of a man clothed upon with the spirit and power of the Priesthood of God commanded her to arise and be made whole from that moment; she obeyed and arose although very weak, she called for water to wash and a comb to arrange her hair and was indeed healed; she became well. This fact I bear testimony of and there is nothing but truth in this statement.[21]

Margarette McIntire Burgess (1824–1913) and her family lived in Nauvoo on the corner of Main Street and Parley Street, a short distance from the Smith family. William P. McIntire, her father, was a bodyguard for Joseph Smith.[22]

The Prophet Joseph was often at my father's house. Some incidents which I recollect of him made deep impressions on my child-mind. One morning when he called at our house, I had a very sore throat. It was much swollen and gave me great pain. He took me up in his lap, and gently anointed my throat with consecrated oil and administered to me, and I was healed. I had no more pain nor soreness.[23]

Women and the Priesthood

"Thou shalt be ordained under his hand to expound scriptures, and to exhort the church."[24]

Mary Isabella Horne (1818–1905) emigrated with her family from England to Canada when she was fourteen years old. She and her husband were baptized in 1836. She joined the Nauvoo Relief Society, where she learned from Joseph Smith about the connection of women to the priesthood. She was the first stake Relief Society president of the Salt Lake Stake.[25]

Through revelation from God the Prophet Joseph Smith organized the first Society of sisters in this last dispensation, saying to the people that the Priesthood was not firmly established on the earth, without an organization of this kind. He gave the sisters much valuable instruction, and predicted a great future for this organization. . . .

We feel much need of the Spirit of God, to enable us in our weakness to discharge our duties in this position. We feel truly thankful that through the blessing of our Heavenly Father, we, His handmaidens are called to be co-laborers with our brethren in building up the kingdom of God upon the earth, in assisting to build Temples, wherein we can receive blessings for time and eternity. In all the ordinances received in the House of the Lord, woman stands beside the man, both for the living and the dead, showing that the man is not without the woman nor the woman without the man in the Lord. Then what manner of women should we be? Faithful in performing all the duties devolving upon us as daughters of God. Sisters, do we appreciate the privileges we enjoy, and the relationship we sustain to God, to each other, and to His kingdom on the earth? We know there are very many faithful sisters, striving with all their might to do all that is required of them. To all such we say, God bless you, sisters! And give you strength to do all your hearts desire to do in righteousness.[26]

Mary Tyndale Baxter Ferguson (1826–1909) came to Utah from Scotland. After her first husband, John Baxter, died in 1869, she married Andrew Ferguson, the missionary who had baptized her. She served in several different positions in Relief Society organizations in Spanish Fork and Goshen, Utah.[27] At the time she recorded this testimony, she was Mary Baxter.

Sisters, do we realize the great and noble calling unto which we are called; do we understand the honor and privileges that are bestowed upon us through the Holy Spirit and everlasting priesthood of God, called with a holy calling to be the daughters and handmaids to labor in the vineyard of our Father, even the Eternal God. To feed the hungry, to clothe the naked, to be eyes to the blind, and strength to the aged and infirm, to wash and anoint in faith believing in the promises of the Lord, living near unto Him at all times, that we may have the influence of His Spirit to guide us in all our actions.[28]

Alice Merrill Horne (1868–1948) was an artist who was born in Salt Lake City. She graduated from the University of Utah and studied art both in Europe and the United States. She was a member of the Utah Legislature and a key force behind the bill that created the Utah Art Institute. She also served on the Relief Society general board.[29]

To all of us there is nothing more beautiful than the organization of this great faith into a Church. Joseph Smith had the broadest comprehension and understanding of woman and when he organized the Relief Society he fully appreciated the necessity and opportunity of women joining with the priesthood, and he said he would make of them high priestesses.[30]

Eliza R. Snow (1804–1887) was appointed secretary of the Nauvoo Relief Society in 1842. She kept careful minutes of the meetings, including the six sermons Joseph Smith gave to the women about their role in connection with the priesthood. These are some of his words as she recorded them.[31]

The Society should move according to the ancient Priesthood, hence there should be a select Society separate from all the evils of the world, choice, virtuous and holy—Said he was going to make of this Society a kingdom of priests as in Enoch's day—as in Paul's day . . . [32]

It is the privilege of those set apart to administer in that authority which is conferred on them—and if the sisters should have faith to heal the sick, let all hold their tongues, and let everything roll on. . . . He said as he had this opportunity, he was going to instruct the Society and point out the way for them to conduct, that they might act according to the will of God—. . . He exhorted the sisters always to concentrate their faith and prayers for, and place confidence, in those whom God has appointed to honor, whom God has placed at the head to lead—that we should arm them with our prayers. . . .

This Society is to get instruction through the order which God has established—through the medium of those appointed to lead—and now I turn the key to you in the name of God and this Society shall rejoice and knowledge and intelligence shall flow down from this time—this is the beginning of better days, to this Society.[33]

~ 7 ~

SHARING THE GOSPEL

"As one that feels for your souls to seek an interest in Christ."[1]

Women embraced the message of the Restoration. They were eager to share the "good news" that had changed their lives. They spoke to their friends, neighbors, and families. They wrote letters. Sarah Layton handed out missionary tracts in nearby villages, as did Ann Rosser, who "took an active part in the gospel, always doing her utmost to announce its 'glad tidings' in England."[2] Sarah Sturtevant Leavitt—one of the few on record who publicly preached in the early nineteenth century—longed, "I wanted very much to get the good will of my neighbors, for I knew that I could have no success in preaching Mormonism unless I did and I was so full of that spirit it was hard to hold my peace."[3] They proclaimed their belief in Joseph Smith, the Book of Mormon, and the authority of the priesthood. Sometimes a chain reaction occurred: Lucy Mack Smith influenced the conversion of her family members, as noted in her letter to her brother Solomon Mack. Lucy's niece, Almira Mack, discovered the Church while visiting her aunt and then brought news and information about the new church to her mother, Temperance Mack. Temperance was baptized, and she and Almira worked for years to share the gospel with other members of their family.[4]

Women were called to serve missions with their husbands in distant lands or in the countries of their own heritage. Mercy Fielding Thompson went with her new husband, Robert B. Thompson, to Canada in 1837.[5] Sisters Caroline Barnes Crosby and Louisa Barnes Pratt traveled with their husbands to Hawaii to preach the gospel.[6] Phoebe Woodruff accompanied her husband, Wilford Woodruff, to England.[7] Like the Book of Mormon prophet Lehi, once these women tasted the love of God, they wanted to share it with those they loved.[8]

FAMILY RELATIONSHIPS

"The hearts of the children shall turn to their fathers."[9]

Lucy Mack Smith (1775–1856), mother of the Prophet Joseph Smith, had always sought true religion and taught her children about things both secular and sacred. She believed that religion could unify her family, and Joseph's experiences brought that much-desired harmony. Lucy was an eager supporter of her son.[10] Hoping that Joseph's truth could further unite her extended family, she wrote this letter to her brother, Solomon Mack, testifying of the Book of Mormon and the restored gospel.

This is the situation which the world is now in, and you can judge for yourselves if we did not need something more than the wisdom of men for to show us the right way. God seeing our situation had compassion upon us and has sent us this revelation that the stumbling block might be removed, that whosoever would might enter. He has now established his church upon the earth as it was in the days of the Apostles. . . . the work is spreading very fast. I must now close my letter by entreating you as one that feels for your souls to seek an interest in Christ and when you have an opportunity to receive this work do not reject it but read it and examine for yourselves. . . . I want you to think seriously of these things for they are the truths of the living God.[11]

Temperance Bond Mack (1771–1850) married Stephen Mack, brother of Lucy Mack Smith. By the time she became acquainted with the Church and was baptized, her husband had already passed away and many of her children were grown. Though Temperance "never wishe[d] herself back to Michigan," to her daughter Harriet she yearned that all her relations might join with her. These excerpts are from two of many letters sent from Temperance to Harriet sharing her desires that they all might come to the truth.[12]

Now, my children, mourn not for your mother, but rather mourn for yourselves. For I was witness unto you perhaps for the last time that I firmly believe this to be the Church of Jesus Christ. Yea the Church of the Living God established on the earth in these last days being built upon the foundation of the apostles and prophets. Jesus Christ being the chief cornerstone. And I again invite you to come under the bond of the new and everlasting covenant—yield to the principles of the Gospel of the Son of God that you may share in the glory of the latter-day dispensation.[13]

On another occasion she again expressed this desire:

O how much more pleasing would it be to me to see all those who are flesh of my flesh and bone of my bone to be gathered with me here; for this I shall not cease to pray.[14]

Almira Mack Covey (1805–1886) learned of the restored gospel as she visited her aunt Lucy Mack Smith in New York. Lucy later shared the gospel with Almira's mother, Temperance. Almira and Temperance worked to offer the rest of their family the joy Aunt Lucy had offered them. Like her mother, Almira also wrote to her sister Harriet desiring to share the truth she had found.[15] At the time of her writing, she was married to William Scobey.

Now Harriet, I do not know what else to write about unless it is about Mormonism (as many call it), and perhaps you will think this to be an old story, but if it is with you it is not with me. My faith is as strong as ever in this thing, and I rejoice that the Lord has suffered me to live in this day when this work has come forth to the children of men. For it ever has been my desire since my remembrance to be prepared to enter into the kingdom of heaven, but how to attain to this blessing I did not know until I heard the ways of salvation proclaimed by this people, who are reproached freely called Mormons. And if I hold out faithful unto the end, I shall have reason in eternity to praise the Lord for sparing my life to this day. But I am liable to go astray and I may yet prove unfaithful and be numbered with the foolish virgins and be cast out of the kingdom; but if I am, I alone shall be to blame for I have had great privileges, and the Lord has given me much light and bestowed many spiritual blessing upon me. . . .

Perhaps some may think me deluded and feel to pity me, but will soon know the truth of these things, for great things await this generation; and it is for this reason that I feel so anxious for you and the rest of my friends, for behold the coming of our Savior is nigh at hand, and this generation will not pass away until he will appear in his glory, and we ought to be prepared for that day. Although we may not either of us live to see that day, yet if we wish to be happy we must be prepared for it, that whether in life or death we may abide the day.[16]

Phebe Crosby Peck (1800–1849) left her native New York in early 1831 with the Colesville Saints. After a short but difficult time in Ohio, they were some of the first Saints to arrive in Jackson County, Missouri, just after Joseph designated it as Zion.[17] Phebe wrote, "I did not know when I left that I should be called to come thus far."[18] She didn't recognize how far-reaching the consequences of her conversion would be. In Missouri, she wrote a letter to Anna Peck Pratt, her late husband's sister, who had decided to remain in New York and elope rather than leave with the Saints.

I shall now attempt to write you the sentiments of my heart in the fear of my God. I can realize that I am separated a great distance from you, but yet my mind will often tra[v]el back to the place of your abode. But Anna, it is not because I wish myself back, but it is because of the feelings I have for you and the rest of my relatives in that part of the world. Yes, we are separated by rolling bellows of water but the Lord's protecting hand has been over us through all our travels and has brought us safely to this land where I shall spend the remainder of my days and if I ever see you again it will be upon this land and I will assure you it would be a joyful meeting to us all.

I well remember the last time I saw you when I took my leave of you the sensations of my heart at that time I think will never be forgotten by me. Although I did not know when I left that I should be called to come thus far and I presume it has bee[n] that which has caused you to almost wonder, but did you know as I know—concerning our leaving Ohio—you would not but you do not. Neither can I tell you but this much I can say, that did you know of the things of God and could you receive the blessings that I have from the hand of the Lord, you would not think it a hardship to come here.[19]

Anna Kirstine Mauritzen Smoot (1833–1894) was born in Norway, where she was baptized. She traveled to Utah in 1855 at the age of twenty-one and became the fourth and final wife of Abraham O. Smoot. Anna served as the stake Primary president in Provo, Utah. Her son, Reed Smoot, visited her birthplace and childhood home on his mission. In an old Mauritzen family Bible, he found this letter, written to Anna's parents on the day she left home to go to America.[20] Reflecting her Norwegian heritage, she had signed it "Kirstine Mauritz-datter."

A few words from your daughter Kirstine, Dear, my parents: Pray God for courage to accept this great truth contained in this book and now restored, so that rejected knowledge may not be a testimony against you on God's great day to come. I pray God that on that great day we may be able to gather together in joy and happiness, and that we may then be crowned to God's glory, and that he may say to us all: "Come now, my faithful children, you shall be rewarded for your labors." This matter, and my desire that you may know the truth and accept it, have made me shed in secret many burning tears, and they have been increased when I have thought of the ungodliness of mankind. The years are speeding on, the day is approaching when all must listen to the Shepherd and render obedience to his will, or receive punishment. The great King is coming to reign and to rule. Sin and evil will be banished. May God grant that you may be among the worthy ones. My heart grows tender when I think of these things. God give that all mankind may repent. I shall pray to my Heavenly Father that all who read these lines may comprehend the true purpose of his holy book, and may lay down the burden of sin. That which I have written is for all who may read these lines. I pray God to lead you into eternal life.[21]

DEVELOPING THE DESIRE

"If ye have desires to serve God ye are called to the work."[22]

Elizabeth Anderson Howard (1823–1893) was born in Ireland and raised a Presbyterian. She married William Howard in 1841. William's health suffered, and the doctor sent him to recover by the sea. He rented a room from Daniel M. Bell and his family, who happened to be Latter-day Saints. Elizabeth warned her husband to beware of such people but then on a visit to her husband, she was impressed with their good manners and kindness. She studied the Bible, the Book of Mormon, and the pamphlet *A Voice of Warning*. Her conversion instilled in her a desire to share the good word with others.[23]

The more I investigated the principles taught by the Latter-day Saints, the more I was satisfied that what I had long been looking for had indeed come, and in the month of August 1851, I was baptized by Mr. Bell, and from that time commenced leading a new life, realizing as I did that my sins were forgiven through obedience to the requirements of the gospel. I felt I had a sure foundation on which to build my hopes of gaining eternal life and felt willing to forget every thing of a worldly nature to attain it. I felt assured I had found the truth, and I was desirous my friends and relations should also come to a knowledge of it. For this purpose, I took every opportunity of presenting to them the principles I had embraced by my books and by correspondence, but failed to make any impression upon them. They were so wrapped up in theories and traditions of their forefathers to accept or even investigate the glorious truths, which had been once more revealed to mankind, but this did not influence me from following on in the path I had commenced to travel. I felt the assurance day by day that God, my Heavenly Father, had accepted of my obedience, and I was quite satisfied that all would work together for good and though my friends turned their backs upon me, I had the satisfaction of knowing that indeed I had made God my friend.[24]

Laura Farnsworth Owen (1806–1881) lived a difficult life trying to maintain her sense of self and her faith while caring for her children through the adversity of abandoning and abusive husbands. Local ministers accused her of mental delusion when she was baptized. In response, she wrote a tract defending the Church and sharing the gospel.[25]

When I was born into the kingdom of God, I was not born a Presbyterian, Methodist, or Baptist, but a child of God. I leave them all alike. I longed for union, and for latter day glory; and my happy soul is witness that it has commenced! And this they call delusion.

If this is delusion—happy delusion![26]

Neighborly Efforts

"It becometh every man who hath been warned to warn his neighbor."[27]

Hannah Tapfield King (1807–1886) was introduced to the Church by her seamstress, Miss Bailey, in 1849 at her home in England. Hannah remembered that Miss Bailey "was a simple-minded girl, but her tact and respectful ingenuity in presenting the subject won my attention, and I listened, not thinking or even dreaming that her words were about to revolutionize my life."[28] Thanks to the "warning" of her employee, Hannah was baptized on November 4, 1850, and she recorded her conversion in an autobiography written in 1864, based on her diary.

Oct. 18th [1849] Sorted my letters. Surely we shall meet the lost and loved on earth in the land of spirits. How dark everything is around us! My mind has been a good deal engrossed by what Miss Bailey has told me of the Latter-day work—I asked many questions and she was kind and gentle in telling me in what their principles consist. Certainly there is nothing in them but what I can test by the Bible, and therefore I know they are truth—They take hold of my mind wonderfully, and I seem to gain strength from them—I feel to prove them all I can, for the Bible says, "Prove all things and hold fast to that which is good."[29]

Sarah Sturtevant Leavitt (1798–1878) was raised in New Hampshire as a Presbyterian. She often read the Bible, and subsequently she began seeking a church similar to that described in the New Testament. In the summer of 1837, a traveler loaned the Leavitts a copy of the Book of Mormon and Parley P. Pratt's *A Voice of Warning*. Sarah was converted and almost immediately wanted to share what she had found.[30]

I wanted very much to get the good will of my neighbors, for I knew that I could have no success in preaching Mormonism unless I did and I was so full of that spirit it was hard to hold my peace. Consequently, I mingled in the society of all, was cheerful and sociable as though I was a great friend, but kept on the side of truth and right. I would go into the tavern when they had balls and help set the table and wait on ladies and was very sociable and talkative. By and by, being free with all, I soon got the good will of some of them. If, we had commenced telling them of their faults and that they were all wrong, which was the case, and they must repent or they would be damned, we could not have got along in that place but should have had to leave. . . .

I gave [Mr. Faulk, the man in whose house we lived] the Voice of Warning. He took it home and read it. Then I gave him other books, all explaining the latter-day message, and at last the Book of Mormon. He would ask questions and answer to my questions, but I could not find out what his mind was concerning what he had read. But as it proved afterwards he believed it to be the truth. . . .

I knelt down in the midst of all that Gentile throng and the Lord gave me great liberty of speech. I prayed with the spirit and understanding, also to Him be the glory. The people were astonished and began to think there was some truth in Mormonism notwithstanding the bad reports about them. After this we were treated with respect.[31]

Elizabeth Jones Lewis (1812–1895) was born in Wales and joined the Baptist church at the age of fifteen. As an adult she kept a tavern, where a Latter-day Saint missionary introduced her to the gospel in 1846. She was baptized in 1847, and her home became a haven for missionaries and Latter-day Saints. She left Wales in 1849 for Utah, and with her wealth she provided passage for several Welsh Saints.[32] She married Dan Jones in Utah. Her letters to friends back in Wales shared her religious convictions.

I promised many dear friends, Saints and others, that I would write from here about the things they doubted there concerning the conditions and nature of this country, its inhabitants, and the religion that is professed; many there promised to believe my testimony from here, if I testify that Mormonism appears still to be true. . . . I consider it my duty to fulfill my promises to them. . . .

With respect to the religion, about whose truthfulness I testified so much while there, I testify today more strongly than ever before, that this is the true gospel of Jesus Christ in its power. I constantly receive additional witnesses of this, and also the like that I could not receive there; all this has confirmed its truthfulness beyond doubt in my mind some time ago. And if my friends there could hear my testimony now, it would be stronger than ever before; and my exhortations would be much more earnest for them to receive their baptism from the servants of God. Oh, you, my dear relatives, believe this my testimony; be wise for your own benefit. You, my acquaintances, I beseeched many of you to give obedience to God's plan to save mankind—from this distance may this final inducement strengthen you to finally settle the debate, that it is best for you to obey the ordinances of heaven, than to go to the trouble to strive to live zealously according to the human traditions of the age; which, in contrast, are nothing more than shadows to the substance. Choose the good part, and be saved, is my constant prayer.[33]

MISSIONARY SERVICE

"The field is white already to harvest."[34]

Louisa Barnes Pratt (1802–1880) and her husband, Addison, were introduced to the Latter-day Saints by Louisa's sister and brother-in-law, Caroline Barnes and Jonathan Crosby. The Pratts were baptized in 1838. In 1843, Addison was called to serve a mission to Hawaii. He completed his first mission and reunited with Louisa in the Salt Lake Valley in 1848. She accompanied him on his second mission, to French Polynesia, in 1849.[35]

My husband went on his mission, but I, with my children, was left to journey afterwards with the body of the church to the Rocky Mountains. We reached the valley in the fall of 1848, and had been there but a week when Elder Pratt arrived, coming by the northern route with soldiers from the Mexican war. He had been absent five years and four months. Only one of his children recognized him, which affected him deeply. One year passed away in comparative comfort and pleasure, when again Mr. Pratt was called to go and leave his family, and again I was left to my own resources. However, six months afterwards several elders were called to join Elder Pratt in the Pacific Isles, and myself and family were permitted to accompany them.

Making the journey by ox-team to San Francisco, on the 15th of September, 1850, we embarked for Tahiti. Sailing to the southwest of that island three hundred and sixty miles we made the Island of Tupuai, where

Mr. Pratt had formerly labored, and where we expected to find him, but to our chagrin found that he was a prisoner under the French governor at Tahiti. After counseling upon the matter we decided to land on Tupuai and petition the governor of Tahiti for Mr. Pratt's release, which we did, aided by the native king, who promised to be responsible for Mr. Pratt's conduct. The petition was granted by the governor, and in due course Mr. Pratt joined us at Tupuai. It was a day of great rejoicing among the natives when he arrived, they all being much attached to him, and it was also a great day for our children.

A volume might be written in attempting to describe the beauties of nature on that little speck in the midst of the great ocean; but I must hasten to speak of the people. . . . they are . . . a most loveable and interesting race. Their piety is deep and sincere and their faith unbounded.[36]

8

CONSECRATION
"My whole heart."[1]

When the Lord commanded the earliest Latter-day Saints to gather in Ohio, he promised them that there they would be given his law. He hinted at the content of the law when he promised, "I say unto you, be one; and if ye are not one ye are not mine."[2]

Ultimately the law of consecration was about unity, love, and serving God with one's whole self. Setting apart and dedicating material goods as well as lives and energies to the kingdom of God transformed the mundane into the transcendent. This law would prepare the Saints to receive celestial glory. They became more focused outward in striving to care for their sisters and brothers as they did for themselves—"Every [wo]man seeking the interest of [her] neighbor."[3] In the nineteenth century, the law was implemented by the Saints in different ways with varying degrees of success.[4] However, they were never exempt from the commandment to "remember the poor."[5] These women thought about consecration whether they were living under the specific economic application of the law or not.

Today the Saints are not asked to sit down with the bishop and determine "wants and needs" for the year; however, consecration remains an eternal principle.[6] As President Gordon B. Hinckley taught, "The law of sacrifice and the law of consecration were not done away with and are still in effect."[7] Ideals of agency, accountability, and stewardship remain.[8] Emmeline Wells explained that the temple helped her to understand the significance and necessity of consecrating one's life. She further observed, "Those who acknowledge God in all things and worship Him in sincerity and truth with His wisdom and providence may be able to stand, although it will require not only obedience to divine laws but the consecration of all one's life and talents to His service."[9] As Emmeline, all need to individually decide what consecration means in the quest for celestial glory.

LIVING THE LAW

"Hearken and hear and obey the law."[10]

Emily M. Coburn Austin (1813–1883) was one of the extended Knight family members who were some of the earliest Mormon converts in Colesville, New York. Her sister Sally Coburn married Newel Knight, and they had joined with the Saints. Despite Emily's initial efforts to convince Sally of her error in following "Joe Smith . . . [Sally] was as firm as the everlasting hills." Emily was eventually baptized and would gather to Kirtland. Though Emily's own conversion did not last, she offered us a view of the consecration in Kirtland.[11]

The church had become numerous within a year or two after we arrived, and we were in a new country, . . . Probably it is indispensably requisite to say that all the money belong[ed] to the wealthy members of the church treasury; and one man had the entire charge of all financial affairs. Had it not been thus, there would have been great suffering among the poor and the aged, who were in this way both fed and clothed. Probably this is the origin of the report that they had all things in common; and this is true. The poor were provided for, as well as those who had put their money in the treasury. They were all satisfied and happy to all appearance, and all seemed to enjoy themselves.[12]

Eliza R. Snow (1804–1887) began to live the law of consecration upon her baptism. The talents she offered to the body of the Saints are well known, but this excerpt illuminates that she likewise consecrated her means—the inheritance received from her parents on leaving their home.[13]

I went into the United Order and all I possessed went in. I had money; I sent for the building committee of the Kirtland Temple, asked if they wanted money; they felt very thankful.[14]

Helen Mar Whitney (1828–1896) was the second daughter of **Vilate Murray Kimball** (1806–1867). Helen used the personal writings of her mother and her father, Heber C. Kimball, as she wrote of early Church history in the *Woman's Exponent*. Her writings became a significant source recording early Church history. Here, she described her mother's efforts to care for others when the Saints were in Winter Quarters.[15]

My mother would go from door to door ministering food and consolation to the sick, and pouring out blessings upon them, during which time she scarcely touched food herself. At meal times, she would only take a cup of milk, saying, when urged to eat, that she had no room for it. She seemed to grow stronger in body, and had an abundance of nurse for her babe; in blessing she was blessed, and there were others enjoying a portion of the same spirit, and by their united faith and works, with fasting and prayer, the sick were healed and made to rejoice more abundantly in the mercy of their Lord, that they were numbered among those who were to come up through much tribulation and be made white in the blood of the Lamb.[16]

H. L. was a pseudonymous *Woman's Exponent* contributor, clearly sensing more significance in her words than in self-acknowledgment. Many Latter-day Saint women contributed to the *Woman's Exponent*. Some used their names, some used initials, and some used pseudonyms.

I have often thought I would like to tell my sisters a little of my experience in the United Order, with which we have been associated for two years, and what the principle teaches us. It teaches us faith and instead of worrying for every little necessity we simply ask our Father in Heaven, for He knows the desires of our hearts, and the way always opens so that we need not suffer; for if we have given all our worldly goods for the upbuilding of His Kingdom, and spend our time and talents for the same; we can have implicit faith that the Lord will care for us.

It teaches us economy, and we try to make things last as long as possible, for every little helps roll on the work; with economy comes industry; unless we are very industrious and careful we cannot keep good things in repair and in order; for we feel the Lord is displeased with us if we are wasteful. It teaches us contentment, yet we sometimes hear complaints; but we feel to do what is required of us, and leave the rest in the hands of the Lord.[17]

Caring for the Poor

"Thou wilt remember the poor."[18]

> **Eliza R. Snow** (1801–1887) kept meticulous notes in her position as the first secretary of the Nauvoo Female Relief Society. At the organizing meeting of the Relief Society, Joseph Smith positioned taking care of the poor as one of the central goals of the organization. The first Relief Society presidency added to this charge. Eliza authored a poem further explaining the purposes of the Relief Society—to care for the poor, whether they were suffering from temporal or spiritual poverty.

17 March 1842 Prest· Smith, & Elders Taylor & Richards return'd and the meeting was address'd by Prest· Smith, to illustrate the object of the Society— that the Society of Sisters might provoke the brethren to good works in looking to the wants of the poor—searching after objects of charity, and in administering to their wants. . . .

Counselor Sarah Cleveland: . . . we design to act in the name of the Lord—to relieve the wants of the distressed, and do all the good we can.—. . . .

Prest· Emma Smith remark'd—we are going to do something <u>extraordinary</u>—when a boat is stuck on the rapids with a multitude of Mormons on board we shall consider <u>that</u> a loud call for <u>relief</u>—we expect extraordinary occasions and pressing calls—

Elder Taylor arose and said—I shall have to concede the point—your arguments are so potent I cannot stand before them—I shall have to give way—

Left to right: Elizabeth Ann Whitney, Emmeline B. Wells, and Eliza R. Snow served in the Relief Society in Utah. Many called them "Mothers in Israel."

Prest J. S. said I also shall have to concede the point, all I shall have to give to the poor, I shall give to this Society—[19]

The Female Relief Society
What Is It?

It is an institution formed to bless
The poor, the widow, and the fatherless;
To clothe the naked and the hungry feed,
And in the holy paths of virtue, lead;
To seek where anguish, grief, and sorrow are,
And light the torch of hope eternal, there;
To prove the strength of consolation's art,
By breathing comfort to the mourning heart.[20]

Jane Elizabeth Manning James (1822–1908) and her family of eight were some of the earliest African-American converts. They first gathered in Nauvoo and then joined the 1847 pioneers. The first years in Utah were demanding, and the Saints had very little. Later Jane expressed, "Oh how I suffered of cold and hunger and keenest of all was to hear my little ones crying for bread, and I had none to give them."[21] In the middle of her own extremity, Jane worked to help a sister in need: **Eliza Partridge Lyman** (1820–1886). These two entries from Eliza's journal concisely illuminate Eliza's need and Jane's sacrifice.

April 13 [1849]: Brother Lyman [Eliza's husband, Amasa] started for California with O. P. Rockwell and others. May the Lord bless and prosper them and return them in safety to their families and friends. Brother Lyman has left us . . . without anything to make bread, it not being in his power to get any.

April 25: Jane James, a colored woman, let me have about two pounds of flour, it being about half she had.[22]

Elizabeth Jones Lewis (1812–1895) was a thirty-four-year-old widow, a mother of six, and the proprietor of successful tavern in Wales when she met the Mormon missionaries. When she decided to go to the United States, she saw a unique opportunity to care for not only herself but for many more of her fellow Saints in Wales also wanting to gather. The Welsh Saints would call her "the Welsh Queen" to celebrate the offering she shared with them. After marrying Captain Dan Jones as a plural wife in 1849, Elizabeth would likewise support her husband's efforts to continue to "bring the [Welsh] Saints home"—to their new American home with the Saints.[23]

Everything was sold including a valuable estate, and I determined to lay it all upon the altar in an endeavor to aid my poorer friends in the church to emigrate also. In 1849, I bade farewell to home, country and friends, and with my six children set out for the far-off Zion. . . . I had paid the passage of forty persons across the ocean and up to Council Bluffs, and from there I provided for and paid the expenses of thirty-two to Salt Lake City.[24]

Donations in Kind
"For the benefit of the church."[25]

Sarah Granger Kimball (1818–1898) dedicated her life to the Lord but did not have her own material assets to offer. Like most nineteenth-century women, Sarah was dependent on her husband for resources. In a clever and progressive move for her time, she asked her husband to monetarily value her work in the home and with their son, enabling her own contribution to the Church. Sarah and her seamstress, Margaret Cook, initiated the women's group that soon resulted in the organization of the Relief Society.[26]

My eldest son was born in Nauvoo . . . when the babe was three days old . . . The walls of the Nauvoo Temple were about three feet above the foundation. The Church was in need of help to assist in raising the Temple walls. I belonged to The Church of Jesus Christ of Latter-day Saints; my husband did not belong to the Church at that time. I wished to help on the Temple, but did not like to ask my husband (who owned considerable property) to help for my sake.

My husband came to my bedside, and as he was admiring our three days old darling, I said, "What is the boy worth?" He replied, "Oh, I don't know; he is worth a great deal." I said, "Is he worth a thousand dollars?" The reply was, "Yes, more than that if he lives and does well." I said, "Half of him is mine, is it not?" "Yes, I suppose so." "Then I have something to help on the Temple." (Pleasantly) "You have?" "Yes, and I am thinking of turning my share right in as tithing." "Well, I'll think about that."

Soon after the above conversation, Mr. Kimball met the Prophet . . . and said, "Sarah has got a little the advantage of me this time. She proposes to turn out the boy as church property." President Smith seemed pleased with the joke, and said. "I accept all such donations, and from this day the boy shall stand recorded, church property." Then turning to Willard Richards, his secretary, he said. "Make a record of this; and you are my witness." Joseph Smith then said, "Major (Mr. Kimball was major in the Nauvoo Legion), you now have the privilege of paying $500 and retaining possession, or receiving $500 and giving possession." Mr. Kimball asked if city property was good currency. President Smith replied that it was. "Then," said Mr. Kimball, "how will that block north of the Temple suit?" President Smith replied, "It is just what we want." The deed was soon made out and transferred in due form.

President Smith said to me, "You have consecrated your first born son. For this you are blessed of the Lord. I bless you in the name of the Lord God of Abraham, of Isaac and of Jacob. And I seal upon you all the blessings that pertain to the faithful."[27]

Time and Talents

"That every [woman] may improve upon [her] talent."[28]

M. A. F. J. is another unknown sister author, who focused on the requirement of developing talents in the quest for discipleship and consecration.

Having a knowledge that God is our Father, and that He holds us accountable for the use we make of the talents He has given us, how necessary it is that we should cultivate and improve those God-given germs and apply them to usefulness in his kingdom. We are living in the day when the Priesthood of God is on earth, and through the great mercy of God man partakes of its blessings; we are not left in darkness and ignorance like those who have not received the fullness of the Gospel. We have many advantages which others do not possess; we have means for acquiring a higher development of mind and of obtaining knowledge which is of the greatest worth.[29]

Alvira Lucy Coolidge Cox (1848–1913) crossed the plains from Nebraska when she was sixteen. She married and moved to Central Utah—Sanpete County. She shared her thoughts with her Relief Society sisters as a young mother with two young children while she was serving as the Relief Society secretary in Manti.[30]

Judging from appearances, one might think that but few, comparatively, really understand and appreciate the blessings which surround us. We not only possess the right of suffrage, a privilege still denied to the great majority of our countrywomen, but we also enjoy a portion of the rights guaranteed by the Constitution, freedom of speech and of the press, notwithstanding the attempts of dishonest officials to deprive us of them. And so far from being what we have been represented by sensationed newspaper writers,—"The poor, oppressed and downtrodden women of Utah," we are quite the reverse; and today are enjoying more freedom than our sisters east or west of us. If our sex is destined to become a power in the land, what should prevent the women of Utah being in the front rank? Certainly not a lack of inclination or ability. Time and opportunity are all that is required to call forth the genius and talents that exist among us. Lest I encroach too far upon your time and space, and weary you or your readers; I will conclude for the present, hoping that you will still continue to be a bold champion for the cause of truth.[31]

Almira Sophronia Jackman Hanks (1856–1931), daughter of Sarah and Levi Jackman, grew up in Spanish Fork, Utah. She was twenty when she wrote this, and she was married a few months later to Joseph Hyrum Hanks. After their marriage, they settled nearby in Salem, Utah.[32]

There are but a few young ladies in this place, consequently our [Retrenchment] Society is composed mostly of small girls, but they attend meetings very faithfully and take great pride in selecting good pieces from the best books and papers, and a good spirit prevails generally; I never enjoy myself better when I attend these meetings. I think it is a great privilege, the young sisters have to improve the talents the Lord has given them in this way. If we could only realize the work we have to perform and the short time we have to do it in, I think we would be more ready and willing to respond to the calls that are made of us from time to time.[33]

Mary Ellen Kimball (1818–1903) was sealed to Heber C. Kimball as a plural wife in the Nauvoo Temple. "A natural teacher," she taught in a variety of schools in the community as well as in Sunday School and Relief Society. She seemed to exemplify the qualities she is here recommending; after her death, she was memorialized as a woman "of a benevolent and sympathetic disposition and charitable in the best sense of the word."[34]

I know you enjoy yourselves better in pursuing a course to develop the abilities God has given you, than in an opposite course. I believe it was for this purpose we were sent to earth, to improve our talents and our times as God assigned. For his designs and purposes are much greater than ours, and will result in the greater good to ourselves, if we learn and follow them. . . . The Prophet Alma in the Book of Mormon speaks of charity accompanied with humility, as one of the greatest gifts of the gospel. In the first place, we should feel our weakness and dependence upon our Heavenly Father and ask his blessing upon all that we do. He says, "Pray three times a day." And again, "Pray in secret." Knowing that our success depends upon his blessing, this is humility. But after this if we neglect to impart of our substance to the poor and needy; and visit not the sick and afflicted, and impart not of our substance to those who are in need, "I say unto you if you do not these things behold your prayer is vain and availeth you nothing; you are as the hypocrites who deny the faith; therefore if ye do not remember to be charitable, ye are as dross which the refiners cast out."[35]

Emmeline B. Wells (1828–1921) often wrote under the pseudonym Blanche Beechwood, as she did in this excerpt. Many of her writings in the *Woman's Exponent* revolved around the theme of consecration and the power of women to do good. She believed that only love might bring "a common consecration to the service of humanity . . . which we hail as the greatest thing in the world."[36]

I believe in women, especially thinking women. Are we human beings, rational and accountable, and yet permit to lie dormant the highest faculty of our nature—thought? Alas we see it every day! But there is a day dawning when we will be better understood, if not appreciated; . . . woman begin to feel and understand that there is something elevating and inspiring, worth living for, worthy of attainment, even though their husbands do not pet them, and spend their whole time and talents, and exhaust the whole English vocabulary in caressing them. . . . Let us not falter by the wayside, but, stimulating, strengthening, encouraging and sympathizing with each other, continue to cultivate and improve our reasoning and reflecting faculties, not only to add to our happiness here, but our eternal felicity hereafter. That it may not be said, of any of us, in that day when all must give an account, that we neglected to improve the talent committed to our care. How to live, how to treat one another, and how to trust in God in matters beyond our mortal comprehension, these are the lessons for us to learn.[37]

ONE'S WHOLE SELF

"Thou shalt love the Lord thy God with all thy heart, with all thy might, mind, and strength."[38]

Elizabeth Ann Whitney (1800–1882) and her husband, Newel, were early residents of Kirtland, Ohio, and members of Sidney Rigdon's congregation when Mormon missionaries arrived. From the time of their baptisms, consecration became a significant theme. The first bishop's storehouse and the School of the Prophets were housed in their store, they invited Joseph and Emma to live in their home, and they consecrated their valuable ashery to the Church.[39]

Just previous to the gospel being preached in Kirtland I had made all needful preparations for a visit to my parents in Connecticut; but after receiving the gospel I abandoned the idea, determining to devote my life, my energies and all that I possessed, towards sustaining and building up the Kingdom of God on the earth. My whole heart was in the great work of the last dispensation, and I took no thought of my own individual comfort and ease. Joseph and Emma were very dear to me, and with my own hands I ministered to them, feeling it a privilege and an honor to do so.[40]

During all these absences and separations from my husband I never felt to murmur or complain in the least . . . yet I was more than satisfied to have him give all, time, talents, and ability into the service of the Kingdom of God; and the change in our circumstances and associations which were consequent upon our embracing the Gospel, never caused me a moment's sorrow. I looked upon it as a real pleasure to give all for the sake of my faith in the religion of Jesus, considering all as naught in comparison with the example of our blessed Savior.[41]

Emmeline B. Wells (1828–1921) had already been editor of the *Woman's Exponent* for a decade when the Edmunds-Tucker Act became a U.S. law in February 1887; among other things, it dissolved the Church corporation, seized Church assets, and disenfranchised the women of Utah (who had received the vote seventeen years earlier). This was an anxious time for the Saints.[42]

The Saints are learning some difficult lessons, that require great patience and the truest humility, and entire devotion to the faith they have espoused; no half-heartedness, but a sublime consecration of one's time and talents in the great and glorious work now being accomplished. After all it seems so little one can do in a lifetime, but when there is a union of effort, more good can be effected.

Sisters, let us not be weary in well-doing, or faint by the wayside, because of trials to be borne, or temptations to be overcome; or allow ourselves to be remiss in any of the duties assigned to us, whether at home or in a public capacity, but press forward to obtain the victory and blessing promised to the faithful. If we seek for wisdom aright to order our daily lives and conversation according to the Gospel plan, it will be given, for the Savior said, "If any lack wisdom let him ask of God, who giveth to all liberally and upbraideth not." It is this wisdom that we all need to carry us safely over and through the dangerous and narrow places that the Saints of God at the present time have to pass, and which, without divine help and assistance, could not be done with safety.[43]

Josephine Meyer Morris (1856–1923) was born in Germany and immigrated to Utah in 1862.[44] She understood hypocrisy as a significant stumbling block to unity and consecration.

We must be saints in very deed. Our whole souls must be in the work, otherwise we can accomplish but very little good. It will not do to say we will accept this and reject that. True saints must embrace every principle pertaining to salvation, advanced by the servants of God, and try to live in accordance with the same. . . . Sisters let us then be united, for in unity there is strength. Let us sustain each other and devote all our time and talents to the building up of the kingdom of the God, so that we may have His spirit at all times.[45]

Susa Young Gates (1856–1933) was the daughter of Lucy Bigelow and Brigham Young. She was very involved in the Relief Society and Young Women organizations, founded the *Young Woman's Journal*, and edited it from 1889 to 1900.[46]

Consecration.

O Builder, let me fill my little niche
With feeble work or strong—
A word of help, a broken crust—choose which—
Or e'en one little song.
Nay, Builder, better—let the midnight toll
No deed of mine today,
If in the doing of it, some weak soul
Would find seeds of decay.
If, Builder, in some hidden tower-stair,
Thou needst a block like me,
On which may climb the toilers upward there,
O, there I fain would be.
Not deeds alone, calm Builder of the sun,
I offer on thy shrine,
But heart of passionate desire to learn
The patience that is Thine.[47]

9

GIFTS OF THE SPIRIT

"I should never lose this gift."[1]

The New Testament reveals the use of spiritual gifts as evidence of God's power and love. According to Mark, "Signs shall follow them that believe," including casting out evil, speaking in tongues, healing, and being healed.[2] Men and women during the Second Great Awakening in early nineteenth-century America likewise sought for the manifestation of spiritual gifts, seeking dreams, visions, healing, and communication according to the order of Christ.[3]

Early Latter-day Saints received and practiced spiritual gifts. Joseph Smith taught, "We believe in the gift of tongues, prophecy, revelation, visions, healing, interpretation of tongues, and so forth."[4] Additionally, Pentecostal events linked the Restoration with the ancient Church. Many looked to the events occurring in Acts 2 after the ascension of Jesus Christ, when the ancient Saints gathered to establish the Church and experienced an outpouring of the Spirit, including hearing a mighty wind and speaking and understanding tongues, to set a level of expectation for establishing the house of the Lord. The dedicatory prayer of the temple in Kirtland made the connection: "Let it be fulfilled upon them, as upon those on the day of Pentecost; let the gift of tongues be poured out upon thy people, even cloven tongues as of fire, and the interpretation thereof. And let thy house be filled, as with a rushing mighty wind, with thy glory."[5]

Women in the restored Church utilized these gifts of the Spirit both to find the Church and to seek God's blessings. Many early Mormon women experienced an outpouring of the Spirit, the gift of tongues, the gift of healing, and the gift of prophecy. In so doing, they blessed each other and their families and they found a united comfort and witness to the Restoration.

PENTECOSTAL EXPERIENCES

"They were all filled with the Holy Ghost." [6]

Mary Fielding Smith (1801–1852) was baptized in Canada in 1834, as were her sister Mercy Fielding (Thompson) and her brother Joseph Fielding. After moving to Kirtland, Ohio, Mercy married and returned to Canada with her new husband to do missionary work. Mary remained in Kirtland and attended meetings in the newly completed temple. Writing as Mary Fielding, she described an experience there in a letter to her sister. [7]

Our Thursday meeting was again better than any former one; the hearts of the people were melted and the Spirit and power of God rested down upon us in a remarkable manner. Many spoke in tongues and others prophesied and interpreted. It has been said by many who have lived in Kirtland a great while, that such a time of love and refreshing has never been known. Some of the Sisters while engaged in conversing in tongues, their countenances beaming with joy; [they] clasped each others' hands and kissed in the most affectionate manner. They were describing in this way the love and felicity of the Celestial World. As the House of the Lord was more than half filled during this time, there were few dry faces. The Brethren as well as the Sisters were all melted down and we wept and praised God together. Some of the prophecies delivered in tongues and interpreted were so great that I cannot begin to describe them. But I do assure you: Brother Hyrum Smith's prediction that from that hour the Lord would begin to bless his people has been verily fulfilled. I believe as do many others that angels were present with us. A bright light shone across the house and rested upon some of the congregation. What I felt that day seemed to outweigh all the affliction and distress of mind I have suffered since I came here. [8]

Presendia L. Kimball (1810–1891) learned about the Book of Mormon from her mother, Zina Huntington. Presendia and her husband, Norman Buell, sold their property and moved to Kirtland, Ohio, where they were baptized in 1836. While in Kirtland, Presendia witnessed Pentecostal outpourings of the Spirit at the temple.[9] At that time, her married name was Presendia Lathrop Buell.

We enjoyed many very great blessings, and often saw the power of God manifested. On one occasion, I saw angels clothed in white, walking upon the Temple. It was during one of our monthly fast meetings, when the saints were in the Temple worshipping, a little girl came to my door, and in wonder called me out, exclaiming, "The meeting is in the top of the meeting house!" I went to the door, and there I saw on the temple, angels clothed in white, covering the roof from end to end. They seemed to be walking to and fro; they appeared and disappeared before I realized that they were not mortal men. Each time in a moment they vanished, and their reappearance was the same. This was in broad daylight in the afternoon. A number of the children in Kirtland saw the same. When the brethren and sisters came home in the evening, they told of the power of God manifested in the Temple that day, and of the prophesying and speaking in tongues. It was also said, in the interpretation of tongues, that the angels were resting down upon the house.

At another fast meeting, I was in the Temple with my sister Zina.[10] The whole congregation was on their knees, praying vocally, for such was the custom, at the close of these meetings when Father Smith [Joseph Smith Sr.] presided, yet there was no confusion. The voices of the congregation mingled softly together. While the congregation was thus praying, we heard from one corner of the room above our heads, a choir of angels, singing most beautifully. They were invisible to us, but myriads of angelic voices seemed to be united in singing some song of Zion, and their sweet harmony filled the Temple of God.

We were also in the Temple at the Pentecost. In the morning, Father Smith prayed for a Pentecost, in opening the meeting. That day the power of God rested mightily upon the Saints. There was poured out upon us abundantly the spirit of revelation, prophecy and tongues. The Holy Ghost filled the house; and along in the afternoon a noise was heard: it was the sound of a mighty rushing wind. But at first the congregation was startled, not knowing what it was. To many it seemed as though the roof was all in flames. Father Smith exclaimed, "Is the house on fire?" "Do you not remember your prayer, this morning, Father Smith?" inquired a brother. Then the patriarch, clasping his hands, exclaimed, "The Spirit of God, like a mighty rushing wind."[11]

THE GIFT OF TONGUES

"It is given to some to speak with tongues; and to another is given the interpretation of tongues."[12]

Zina Diantha Huntington Young (1821–1901) gained a personal testimony of the truthfulness of the Book of Mormon at the young age of ten. Soon after her baptism, she received the gift of tongues, a gift she had to learn how to maintain and develop.[13]

Soon after this, the gift of tongues rested upon me with overwhelming force. I was somewhat alarmed at this strange manifestation, and so checked its utterance. What was my alarm, however, to discover that upon this action upon my part, the gift left me entirely, and I felt I had offended that Holy Spirit by whose influence I had been so richly blessed. One day while mother and I were spinning together, I took courage and told her of the gift . . . and how . . . I had lost it. Mother appreciated my feelings and told me to make it a matter of earnest prayer, that the gift might once more be given me. I walked down to a little spring in one of the meadows, and as I walked I mused on my blessing and how I had turned away the Spirit of God. I knelt down and offered up a prayer to God and told Him if He could forgive my transgression, and give me back the lost gift, I would promise never to check it again, no matter where or when I felt its promptings.[14]

Elizabeth Ann Whitney (1800–1882) grew up in Connecticut in a cultured family, enjoying music and dancing. She had a natural inclination toward singing and was known for her vocal talent. When she received her patriarchal blessing from Joseph Smith Sr. on September 14, 1835, in the Kirtland Temple, Elizabeth Ann was given a very unique gift of the Spirit: singing in tongues.[15]

I received the gift of singing inspirationally, and the first Song of Zion ever given in the pure language was sung by me then, and interpreted by Parley P. Pratt, and written down; of which I have preserved the original copy. It describes the manner in which the ancient patriarchs blessed their families, and gives some account of "Adamondi Ahman." . . . The Prophet Joseph promised me that I should never lose this gift if I would be wise in using it; and his words have been verified.[16]

Elizabeth Ann's friend, Emmeline B. Wells, later wrote about Elizabeth's gift.

The gift of song which Sister Whitney possessed in such a rare degree was often a comfort to the Prophet in those days of trial and gloom. He would sit as it were spell bound and listen to the rich melody of her magnificent voice for the time so absorbed, as to forget his sorrows. . . . She possessed a reverential, prophetic and poetic temperament, and the spirit of the gospel strengthened in her all these exalted attributes.[17]

Lydia Goldthwaite Knight (1812–1884) had a two-year-old child and was pregnant when her alcoholic and abusive husband abandoned the family. Her parents sent her from her home in Massachusetts to Canada to stay with friends, where she heard Joseph Smith speak at a meeting in October 1833. Susa Young Gates related Lydia's experience with the gift of tongues at her baptism on October 27, 1833.[18]

"I would be so glad if someone who has been baptized could receive the gift of tongues as the ancient Saints did and speak to us," said Moses Nickerson.

"If one of you will rise up and open your mouth it shall be filled, and you shall speak in tongues," replied the Prophet.

Everyone then turned as by a common instinct to Lydia and said with one voice, "Sister Lydia, rise up."

And then the great glory of God was manifested to this weak but trusting girl. She was enveloped as with a flame, and unable longer to retain her seat, she rose and her mouth was filled with the praises of God and his glory. The spirit of tongues was upon her, and she was clothed in a shining light, so bright that all present saw it with great distinctness above the light of the fire and the candles.[19]

The Gift of Healing

"To some it is given to have faith to be healed; And to others it is given to have faith to heal."[20]

Rhoda Harriett Foss Richards (1784–1879) suffered from poor health during her childhood. Her cousin, Joseph Young, brother of Brigham Young, visited the Richards family at one point when Rhoda was sick. While the rest of her family was at their church, he remained near Rhoda's bed, where they held their own "church meeting" according to Joseph's new Mormon faith. Rhoda was baptized a year later.[21]

A short time after I was baptized and confirmed I was greatly afflicted with the raging of a cancer, about to break out in my face. I knew too well the symptoms, having had one removed previously. The agony of such an operation, only those who have passed through a like experience can ever imagine. The idea of again passing through a like physical suffering seemed almost more than humanity could endure. One Sabbath, after the close of the morning service, I spoke to the presiding elder, and acquainted him with my situation, requesting that I might be administered to, according to the pattern that God had given, that the cancer might be rebuked and my body healed. The elder called upon the sisters present to unite their faith and prayers in my behalf, and upon the brethren to come forward and lay their hands upon me, and bless me in the name of the Lord Jesus Christ, according to my desire. It was done, and I went home completely healed, and rejoicing in the God of my salvation. Many times have I since been healed by the same power, when, apparently, death had actually seized me as his prey.[22]

Hannah Last Cornaby (1822–1905) and her husband, Samuel, lost a son, Henry, in 1856, and another, Walter, in 1859. After a three-year period of relative peace, health, and tranquility, they lost their year-old daughter, Grace, in 1864. Hannah then experienced her own debilitating illness.[23]

Our Grace faded away like a sweet autumn flower touched by the hand of death. . . . Like David of old, while she was sick we wept and fasted and prayed; but after she was gone, like him, we reasoned, we shall go to her, but she cannot return to us. We resolved not to displease our Father in heaven by pining over this loss, so we set to work to gather up the broken threads of life and to provide for the comfort of the dear ones still left with us.

A week after her death, and while diligently employed, I was suddenly prostrated by sickness, the like of which I had never known. At first we hoped it was only from the heavy strain my system had lately endured, and would soon pass off. We did all that wisdom dictated, all that the love and affection of my family and friends could devise, yet with but short intervals, this debility and weakness lasted nearly six years. . . .

I felt very feeble in body and depressed in mind when Brother William H. Darger, our block teacher, came to administer the sacrament to me. He noticed that I was not as well as usual and asked if I wished to be administered to before he left. My husband anointed my head with consecrated oil, after which they placed their hands upon my head and blessed me. In an instant I felt the healing power in every part of my body. Several persons present at the time also testified to the power that attended the words.

When Brother Darger was leaving, he said, "You will soon be well." I replied that I knew I would. Both my daughters told me they felt that the time for my recovery had come. I did not say much; I was so astonished at this wonderful event that I seemed overpowered by the greatness of the blessing that had come upon me.

Next morning, when alone with my daughter Mary, I told her I was well, and requested her to bring my clothes so I might dress and arise from my bed. She wished me to wait until her father came in, but I wanted no one except her with me. I then got out of bed and, with one hand laid upon her shoulder, walked six times the length of the bed. My darling child was so overjoyed that she exclaimed with uplifted hands, "Oh, Mother, give the glory to God, give all the glory to him, for it is all his work!" and she wept for joy. My husband came in at the time, was astonished, and joined us in thanksgiving to God.[24]

The Gift of Prophecy

"To others it is given to prophesy."[25]

Eliza R. Snow (1804–1887) and **Zina Diantha Huntington Young** (1821–1901) prophesied that a young Heber J. Grant would perform great service in the kingdom. They were blessed to foresee the future of the young man as an apostle. His mother, **Rachel Ivins Grant** (1824–1909), likewise saw great potential in her son and encouraged him to remember that prophecy and behave appropriately.[26] **Lucy Stringham Grant** (1858–1893) was Heber J. Grant's first wife. She too was given the gift of prophecy to aid her family—Heber specifically. In a time of financial desperation, Lucy gave Heber, in his words, "a very remarkable blessing and made many very precious promises to me . . . I have lived to enjoy the blessing promised and to thank the Lord for the gift through which it came. When the blessing was given it was of great comfort to my wife and to me. I can think of nothing that a devoted wife would prize more than to be made instrument in the hands of the Lord in bestowing His blessing upon her husband and the father of her children through the instrumentality of a special gift."[27] All of these women demonstrated the spiritual gift of seeing, a significant manifestation of the gift of prophecy, as they prophesied regarding the life of Heber, the boy who would become the seventh president of the Church. Heber J. Grant would later write about these women.

When I was a little child, in a Relief Society meeting held in the home of the late William C. Staines, corner South Temple and Fifth East streets, my mother was there, "Aunt Em" Wells was there, Eliza R. Snow, Zina D. Young, and many others. After the meeting was over Sister Eliza R. Snow, by the gift of tongues, gave a blessing to each and every one of those good sisters, and Sister Zina D. Young gave the interpretation. After blessing those sisters, she turned to the boy playing on the floor and pronounced a blessing upon my head by the gift of tongues, and Zina D. Young gave the interpretation. I of course did not understand one word that Aunt Eliza was saying. I was astonished because she was talking to me and pointing at me. I could not understand a word, and all I got of the interpretation, as a child, was that some day

Rachel Ivins Grant and Heber J. Grant.

I should be a big man. I thought it meant that I would grow tall. My mother made a record of that blessing. What was it? It was a prophecy, by the gift of tongues, that her boy should live to be an apostle of the Lord Jesus Christ; and oftimes she told me that if I would behave myself, that honor would come to me. I always laughed at her and said: "Every mother believes that her son will become president of the United States, or hold some great office. You ought to get that out of your head, Mother." I did not believe her until that honor came to me.[28]

Hannah Last Cornaby (1822–1905) and her family settled in Spanish Fork, Utah. Her husband, Samuel, went to Salt Lake City for business, leaving Hannah alone with young children and little food. When Hannah learned that Samuel was extremely ill, even near death, she made every effort to join him, but winter roads and lack of transportation and childcare prevented her. She remained in Spanish Fork, worrying about Samuel and attending Church meetings when possible. Her companionship with the Saints bolstered her faith.[29]

Meetings were frequently held in private houses, and were termed Block Meetings, at which the gifts of the gospel were much enjoyed such as speaking in tongues, interpretation, and prophesying. These meetings were a great solace to me. . . .

Heavy snow on New Year's Day nearly prevented Hannah from attending that day's meeting, but a neighbor offered to provide transportation and dinner after the meeting.

Of course I went to the meeting, which was no sooner opened, than the presiding elder, Father John M. Chidester, directed his words to myself; and by the spirit of God, uttered a prophecy in which he told me that my husband was alive, and that the crisis of his sickness was past; that he would live to return home; and that for many years we should enjoy each other's society. I knew by the same spirit, that what he said was true, and my mind became easier.[30]

10

COMMANDMENTS

"I was never happier in my life."[1]

Commandments were certainly not new for most early Latter-day Saints; they came to the restored Church wanting to do what God asked of them. In the Doctrine and Covenants, the Lord teaches, "I give unto you a new commandment, that you may understand my will concerning you; Or, in other words, I give unto you directions how you may act before me, that it may turn to you for your salvation."[2] For some early converts, the Restoration provided new light and knowledge to better understand commandments they already believed to be important. Not all commandments are of the "thou shalt" variety. Believing in a prophet meant being open to the possibility of change. The Restoration would also expand the specific commandments of God and the ways in which the Lord would direct the Saints.

THE FIRST GREAT COMMANDMENT

"Thou shalt love the Lord thy God."[3]

> **Excelette** anonymously expounded scripture about the first great commandment, prioritizing the value of loving God over personal acknowledgment.

Jesus said: 22nd chapter Matthew "Thou shalt love the Lord Thy God with all thy heart and with all thy soul and with all thy mind. This is the first and great commandment; and the second is like unto it. Thou shalt love thy neighbour as thyself. On these two commandments hang all the law and the prophets."

Now we cannot love God with all the affections of the heart, and with all the energies of the mind and the body, without a knowledge of His character and requirements. Hence the necessity of referring to revelation to know His character and his laws. In so doing we find that God is omnipotent, omniscient, unchangeable; a God of justice, judgment, mercy and truth, long suffering, compassionate and impartial, and in every nation he that fears God and works righteousness is accepted of Him.

Believing these revelations of the excellency of God's character, we can but adore and praise the holy name of God our Father; and the inquiry naturally arises, how we shall prove our love to God. Jesus Christ (who is one with the Father) has given us a rule by which we can prove our love to God. St. John 14 chapter 15 verse. "If ye love me, keep my commandments." Again 23rd verse, "If a man love me he will keep my words." 24th verse, "He that loveth me not keepeth not my sayings." Then if we wish to evince our love to God we must keep all His commands as revealed through His Son, and our prophets Joseph Smith, and Brigham Young, not one alone but all their sayings, devoting all our energies mental and physical to His service, with all which he has given us unreservedly. Then we are to show our love to God by imitating the excellency of his character, in all the circumstances of life, showing our love for knowledge by the acquisition of the same; of justice, mercy, truth, long suffering and love, by the exercise of the same in our daily walk and conversation. And like our Father in Heaven [be] no respecter of persons, but one with all those that fear God and work righteousness.[4]

C.R., another anonymous *Woman's Exponent* writer, provided a strong voice and testimony of the spiritual benefits of following divine direction. Gratitude for blessings encourages faithfulness.

As children of a wise Father, who have been privileged to receive light and intelligence from Him, in a greater degree than many others of His creatures, how faithful and diligent should we be in the performance of every duty that is revealed to us from heaven. Laboring earnestly in this Kingdom will enable us to increase in that intelligence which comes from God until we will finally arrive at such a state of perfection that we can do His will here on earth, as it is done in heaven by the angels.[5]

THE WORD OF WISDOM

"A principle with promise."[6]

Ann Marsh Abbott (1797–1849) and her husband, Lewis Abbott, joined the Church together after they learned of Joseph Smith and the Book of Mormon from Ann's brother, Thomas Marsh. Before the revelations were compiled and published, copies of revelations were copied by hand and passed amongst the Saints. Ann Marsh Abbott took the time to write by hand the Word of Wisdom, certainly a sign of its considered importance to her. The surviving manuscript is perhaps the only extant revelation manuscript in a woman's hand.

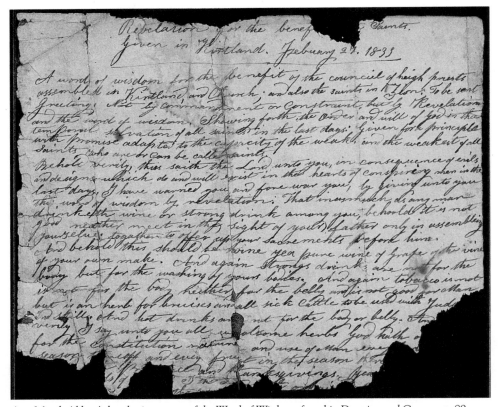

Ann Marsh Abbott's handwritten copy of the Word of Wisdom, found in Doctrine and Covenants 89.

Presendia L. Kimball (1810–1892) was married at sixteen yet remained close to her family of birth, who had converted to the Church. In the summer of 1835, her mother visited her in Lorraine, New York, bringing a handwritten copy of the Word of Wisdom revelation, perhaps much like Ann Marsh Abbott's copy. Like many religiously-minded people of the Second Great Awakening, Presendia considered temperance to show a commitment to God. Presendia immediately believed in the principles taught in the Word of Wisdom—perhaps before deciding to be baptized—and trusted that she would receive the promised blessings if she lived it.[7]

My mother came to visit me and brought the "Word of Wisdom" in writing, it had not yet been printed, and she gave me the first intelligence of the Prophet Joseph Smith and the record taken from the Hill Cumorah. I felt it was true, and I thought I would keep the Word of Wisdom and obtain the blessings promised.[8]

Patty Bartlett Sessions (1795–1892) was methodical and practical in recording the activities of life with apparent precision. Perhaps her work as a midwife required it.[9] Toward the end of her life she shared her simple testimony of following the Word of Wisdom.

I am now eighty-two years of age. I drink no tea nor coffee, nor spirituous liquors; neither do I smoke nor take snuff. To all my posterity and friends I say, do as I have done, and as much better as you can, and the Lord will bless you as he has me.[10]

Tithing

"Prove me now herewith, saith the Lord of hosts."[11]

Mary Fielding Smith (1801–1852), wife of Hyrum Smith, became a widow the same day that she and the rest of the Latter-day Saints lost a prophet. She had six children to care for. Her youngest son, Joseph F. Smith, later remembered the family's struggles once they arrived in the Salt Lake Valley. He also recalled Mary's commitment to pay her tithing and trust in the Lord.[12]

I recollect very vividly a circumstance that occurred in the days of my childhood. My mother was a widow, with a large family to provide for. One spring when we opened our potato pits she had her boys get a load of the best potatoes, and she took them to the tithing office; potatoes were scarce that season. I was a little boy at the time, and drove the team. When we drove up to the steps of the tithing office ready to unload the potatoes, one of the clerks came out and said to my mother: "Widow Smith, it's a shame that you should have to pay tithing." He said a number of other things that I remember well, but they are not necessary for me to repeat here. The first two letters of the name of that tithing clerk was W[illiam] T[hompson], and he chided my mother for paying her tithing, called her anything but wise and prudent; and said there were others able to work that were supported from the tithing office. My mother turned upon him and said: "William, you ought to be ashamed of yourself. Would you deny me a blessing? If I did not pay my tithing I should expect the Lord to withhold His blessings from me; I pay my tithing, not only because it is a law of God but because I expect a blessing by doing it. By keeping this and other laws, I expect to prosper and to be able to provide for my family."[13]

Annie Emma Dexter Noble (1861–1950) was an active member of her local Baptist congregation in Nottingham, England, when she chose to unite with the Latter-day Saints. After her baptism, she continued to attend Baptist services with her husband on Sunday morning and then went to Latter-day Saint cottage meetings in the evenings. As beliefs in her family were divided, sometimes application of commandments was difficult. Here she explains how she received a testimony of tithing. Her husband would later join with the Latter-day Saints, opening the way for further unity in their home.[14]

I had been a member of the Church about six months. I had been taught by the Elders and fully understood the law of tithing and most gladly had paid my dues on some income which was my own. My husband of course was exempt, because he was not a member of the Mormon Church. However, he was a liberal giver in the Baptist Church. One morning as I crossed my kitchen floor to put the breakfast dishes in a cupboard, I suddenly was confronted with the temptation to complain that the Lord expected too much of us when He asked for a tenth. This question of His demands only lasted a moment or two, and feeling deep remorse, I knelt down before the chair which stood by the cupboard and there and then acknowledged my grief and sorrow at such a sin; for my gratitude had known no bounds for the joy and light God had given me in the Gospel. I had felt indeed that I had received from His hands, "The Pearl of Great Price," and for me to begrudge a paltry tenth to Him was indeed despicable.

I bowed my head in shame and begged Him to forgive me, and having heard one of the Elders tell of an answer to his prayer by having a burning in his heart, I too asked the Lord not only to forgive me, but to assure me that never again would I question the principle of tithing, by letting me know by a burning in my heart. At once I felt something like a hot piece of steel boring into my heart. It seemed then that tears literally rained down my face for I was forgiven, and I knew it, and I have never since for a moment doubted, but on the contrary, loved the law of tithing.[15]

THE SABBATH DAY

"Observe the Sabbath day to keep it holy."[16]

Rachel Ivins Grant (1824–1909) lost her parents as a young girl in New Jersey. A close cohort of extended family helped to raise young Rachel and her siblings. Several members of Rachel's kin became converted to the restored gospel, and her older sister Anna Lowrie Ivins's conversion had a great effect on Rachel. Anna and another friend convinced Rachel to go hear the Mormons, though the meeting was on Sunday and Rachel was quite confident that the Mormons were "the false prophets [of which] the Bible speaks." The possibility of breaking the Sabbath to listen to the Mormons caused Rachel serious personal debate. Once she returned home from the meeting she asked God for forgiveness. In the end, she reconsidered the status of her Sabbath-breaking. Her presumed Sabbath-breaking led her to truth.[17]

I attended some more meetings and commenced reading the Book of Mormon, *A Voice of Warning* and other works, and was soon convinced that they were true. A new light seemed to break in on me, the scriptures were plainer to my mind, and the light of the everlasting Gospel began to illume my soul.[18]

FASTING

"This is fasting and prayer, or in other words, rejoicing and prayer." [19]

Zina Diantha Huntington Young (1821–1901) became firmly committed to the Church after she chose baptism. Fasting with the Saints was a commandment that showed her devotion to God as she unified with the Saints. She consistently recorded fast days and accompanying prayers or activities in her journal. She had fasted privately for her sick son Zebulun the week before she wrote this journal entry; this Sunday she fasted again with the body of Saints. [20]

15 [August] 1845 A general fast for the whole Church. Although I am at home with my sick son I feel that the Spirit of God is with the people at the meeting ground to bless the meek. O let me be one of that number for I desire it with all my heart, for I feel to renew my covenant with Thee O God my Heavenly Father, desiring to lay hold on faith and obedience unto salvation, that I may be saved with a fullness of joy among those of the highest Glory. Wilt thou prepare me for this and may I be an honour to those with whom I am concerned. O wilt Thou give me grace in the eyes of the true saints and thy name shall have the honour, worlds with out end, amen and amen. [21]

TEACHING CHILDREN

"Inasmuch as parents have children in Zion." [22]

Phebe Crosby Peck (1800–1849) had recently arrived in Jackson County, Missouri, when the Saints received the revelation found in section 68 of the Doctrine and Covenants. The revelation speaks of the responsibilities of

parents in Zion to teach their children to pray and to prepare them for baptism, with a warning for idle parents who neglect to teach their children and
allow them to grow up in wickedness.[23] Phebe's concerns in this letter appear
to be a direct response to that censure. Rather than allowing her children to
grow up in wickedness, she focused on teaching her children and rejoiced at
the progress they made.[24]

I must tell you the joyful news of the workings of the Lord among the
children. We have had the pleasing view of beholding eleven children from
8 years old to 14 go down into the water in obedience to the commands of
God, among whom was my three oldest. Can we not rejoice in seeing the
rising generation growing up in the knowledge of the Lord? And I think by
giving them good instructions they will grow up and be strong in faith. They
will arise and testify what the Lord has done for them in the presence of a congregation of people. Hezekiah says he enjoys himself well. He will take up his
cross and pray in the family when asked. My children are all contented and I
am very thankful for it.[25]

Emmeline B. Wells (1828–1921) believed there was a great
need to care for and teach children the gospel in the home.
She was the primary example of gospel living for her five
daughters, with limited assistance from their fathers. She
provided for her daughters by teaching school.[26]

Let us teach our little ones the gospel of Jesus as we understand it—tell
them how the Savior loved little children—many of us have been too careless
in regard to our children in times past—let us be wide awake now. The Lord
has abundantly blest us with peace and plenty.[27]

A LIFETIME OF FAITHFULNESS

"Be diligent in keeping my commandments, and you shall be blessed unto eternal life."[28]

Susan Kent Greene (1816–1888) joined with the Latter-day Saints when she was sixteen. She married Evan Molbourne Greene, and they moved west with the Saints. Over time, Susan's testimony of the commandments and particularly the law of the fast grew and strengthened. In Utah, she settled in Smithfield; from there she wrote this letter to the *Woman's Exponent*.[29]

At one of our fast meetings, not long since, when there was a good, large gathering and all seemed to feel well, I had some reflections of which I thought I would like to pen a few for your consideration. The time was entirely occupied with the testimonies borne concerning the truth of the everlasting gospel in these Latter-days. Many brethren testified that they knew that Joseph Smith was a Prophet of God—as great a Prophet as had ever lived since the days of the Savior. And that Brigham Young was his lawful successor, appointed by God, through divine revelation to lead the Church in these last days. As my heart burned within me, almost to the consuming of my flesh, with grateful responses to the truth of those sentiments, I was led to reflect thus. This is a great testimony we have to give. How many of us realize its importance? We believe in all sincerity, that our leaders are inspired men, that they speak to us by the testimony of Jesus, which is the spirit of prophecy; and we believe their teachings to be the word of God unto us, yet—how many of us live by it? Jesus said, man should not live by bread alone, but by every word that proceeded out of the mouth of God. Do our works and our words correspond? . . . My beloved sisters let us strive to live by every word of God, and have faith in Jesus; so shall we receive great blessings, and wisdom through which we may become heirs of Salvation.[30]

Jane Elizabeth Manning James (1822–1908) was baptized at the age of twenty with many members of her family. An African-American woman and daughter of former slaves, Jane and her "little band" walked a thousand miles to join with the Saints. They eagerly anticipated arriving in Nauvoo but were met with "rebuff" from other "Saints" on their arrival. This initial frustration ended when Emma and Joseph invited them into their home; however, it would not be Jane's only frustration as a Latter-day Saint of African descent. Despite hardship, Jane did not regret her decision to join the Church. At the end of her life, she saw commandments as a way to demonstrate her love for God and gratitude for his protection. She considered her offering "feeble," yet her legacy stands in eternity as a powerful example of strength, loyalty, and belief.[31]

I am a widow; my husband Isaac James died in November 1891. I have seen my husband and all my children but two laid away in the silent tomb. But the Lord protects me and takes good care of me in my helpless condition. And I want to say right here that my faith in the gospel of Jesus Christ of Latter-day Saints is as strong today—nay it is if possible stronger—than it was the day I was first baptized. I pay my tithes and offerings, keep the Word of Wisdom. I go to bed early and arise early. I try in my feeble way to set a good example to all.[32]

~ 11 ~

TEMPLES

"Establish . . . a house of God."[1]

In February 1831, the Lord invited his "covenant people" to gather to Independence, Jackson County, Missouri, and declared, "I shall come to my temple."[2] Almost two years later in Kirtland, Ohio, the Lord commanded the Latter-day Saints: "Organize yourselves; prepare every needful thing; and establish a house, even a house of prayer, a house of fasting, a house of faith, a house of learning, a house of glory, a house of order, a house of God."[3] These revelations were the beginning of the building of latter-day temples. After falling behind on the command to build the Kirtland Temple, the Saints never lagged again. They became focused on building temples and would dedicate land for temples in nearly every major Latter-day Saint settlement.

The physical construction of the buildings required great sacrifice. Many women worked fiercely to provide resources for temple construction—first in Kirtland in the 1830s and later in Nauvoo in the 1840s. The Nauvoo Relief Society originated as a sewing society for women to make shirts for temple builders. Women in Utah followed the pattern. Many early Relief Society minute books throughout Utah record the financial and material contributions from women, whether those were rag carpets or altar cloths and veils for the temple interior, money earned from "Sunday eggs" or quilts, or cheese made for construction workers.[4] Just as women contributed to the physical construction of temples, they also participated in the spiritual manifestations of temple dedications, as recorded in letters, diaries, and reminiscences. Such divine demonstrations proved the value of their sacrifice and work and fueled them through additional challenges.

In addition to overseeing the construction and dedication of temples, Joseph Smith received a restoration of sacred ordinances, covenants, and blessings. In Kirtland, only men received the first endowment of washing of feet and early initiatory work. George A. Smith reported "that almost made the women mad, and they said, as they were not admitted into the Temple while this washing was being performed, that some mischief was going on, and some of them were right huffy about it."[5] Joseph received additional revelation in Nauvoo to include women, particularly through the organization of the Relief Society. Thus women participated in the joyous restoration of priesthood ordinances and covenants performed only in the temple. Joseph Smith told Mercy Fielding Thompson that the endowment of blessing would bring her "out of darkness into marvelous light."[6]

SACRIFICE TO BUILD THE TEMPLE

"To do something to help build the temple."[7]

Sarah Granger Kimball (1818–1898) was a teenager in Kirtland and had fond memories of Church activity there.[8] In Utah, years later, she served as a counselor in the retrenchment organization, a women's association initiated by Brigham Young to encourage members to devote more energy to spiritual and mental pursuits rather than fashion and vanity. Sarah spoke at a retrenchment meeting on August 19, 1876, recalling her memories of the Kirtland Temple construction. The minutes were recorded in the *Woman's Exponent*.

Counselor Mrs. Sarah M. Kimball alluded to the time when the Kirtland Temple was being built, when the Saints all considered that what they possessed belonged to the work of the Lord; when the women would churn and cheerfully send their butter to the workmen on the Temple and eat without any on their own tables; then, they were all hopeful and joyous; she had never seen happier days in her life that she knew of.[9]

Eliza R. Snow (1804–1887) had several opportunities to earn money as a young adult in Ohio. She provided secretarial assistance for her father in public office, she won prizes for her needlework, and she published poetry in local newspapers. She left her father's house to teach school in Kirtland and also received an inheritance, which allowed her to contribute a significant amount of money to the construction of the Kirtland Temple, demonstrating her commitment to the Latter-day Saints.[10]

Previous to the completion of the Temple, I proffered a Cash donation to the "Building Committee," which they very much needed. . . . This, like many other trivial events in human life, proved to be one of the little hinges on which events of immense weight occasionally turn.[11]

Eliza R. Snow created this small reticule, or purse pocket, in Ohio, and may have used it to carry her financial donation for the Kirtland Temple. She made it out of green and purple silk and included her initials.

Vilate Murray Kimball (1806–1867) was baptized in 1832 and moved to Kirtland in 1833. Her husband, Heber C. Kimball, gave this account about his wife and her contributions to the construction of the Kirtland Temple. She later joined the Female Relief Society of Nauvoo at its second meeting and was one of the first women to perform ordinances in the Nauvoo Temple.[12]

The brethren were laboring night and day, building the house of the Lord (at Kirtland). Our women were engaged in spinning and knitting, in order to clothe those who were laboring at the building; and the Lord only knows the scenes of poverty, tribulation and distress which we passed through in order to accomplish it. My wife had toiled all summer in lending her aid towards its accomplishment. She took one hundred pounds of wool to spin on shares, which, with the assistance of a girl, she spun in order to finish clothing for those engaged in the building of the temple, and although she had the privilege of keeping half the quantity of wool for herself, as a recompense for her labor, she did not reserve even so much as would make a pair of stockings, but gave it for those who were laboring at the house of the Lord. She spun and wove, and got the cloth dressed and cut, and made up into garments, and gave them to those men who labored on the temple. Almost all the sister[s] in Kirtland labored in knitting, sewing, spinning, for the same purpose.[13]

Polly Johnson Angell (1813–1878) was baptized with her husband, Truman Angell, in 1833. They moved to Kirtland in 1835, where Truman worked on the Kirtland Temple. Polly relates that she and a band of sisters were sewing the veils one day when the Prophet and Sidney Rigdon visited. These veils would hang as curtains dividing the large chapel areas into smaller, more intimate worship spaces.[14]

"Well, sisters," observed Joseph, "you are always on hand. The sisters are always first and foremost in all good works. Mary was the first at the resurrection; and the sisters are now the first to work on the inside of the temple."[15]

Elmeda Stringham Harmon (1829–1923) and her family joined the Church in Jamestown, New York, in about 1832. Because of poor economic activity in New York at the time and the call for Saints to gather, they moved to Kirtland in 1834. Her brothers worked on the temple construction, as did she.[16] Her account sets the story straight that *old* china, rather than best china, was ground to use in the exterior of the temple walls.

The Kirtland temple was finished in the winter time and Briant and Jerry with other boys cut wood to keep the fires to dry the plaster. I, with other little children, gathered bits of glass and broken dishes which were broken up quite fine and mixed with the mortar used in plastering the temple.[17]

The House of the Lord, the first latter-day temple, built in Kirtland, Ohio, dedicated in 1836.

> **Mercy Fielding Thompson** (1807–1893) was serving a mission in Canada with her husband, Robert B. Thompson, when the Kirtland Temple was dedicated. They moved to Nauvoo in 1839, and Mercy developed a fundraising program for the temple there. She received her endowment in Nauvoo in 1844 and worked in the Nauvoo Temple from when it opened in November 1845 until the Saints left Nauvoo. She and her daughter lived in the temple while she performed duties such as recording ordinances, cooking, and laundry for those working in the temple.[18]

At one time after seeking earnestly to know from the Lord if there was anything that I could do for the building up the Kingdom of God a most pleasant sensation came over me with the following words: Try to get the Sisters to subscribe one cent per week for the purpose of buying glass and nails for the temple. I went immediately to Brother Joseph and told him what seemed to be the whispering of the still small voice to me. He told me to go ahead and the Lord will bless you. I then mentioned it to Brother Hyrum who was much pleased and did all in his power to encourage and help by speaking to the Sisters on the subject in private and public, promising them that they should receive their blessings in that temple; all who subscribed the cent per week should have their names recorded in the Book of the Law of the Lord. I assisted by my sister took down and kept a record of all the names and notwithstanding the poverty of the people we had (by the time the committee were ready for the glass and nails) in the treasury about $500 which they gladly received just in time of need.[19]

> At a general retrenchment meeting (an organization encouraging women to focus on spiritual cultivation) in August 1876, Mercy described the value of such a fundraising initiative. The minutes were published in the *Woman's Exponent.*

Sister Mercy Fielding Thompson spoke beautifully concerning the giving of donations for the building of Temples. She considered that the poor saint's dollar, which was given with a grateful hand out of a meagre pittance, would go farther towards purchasing eternal blessings in the kingdom of God, than the dollar of a person whom the Lord has blessed with abundance, so that the small sum given would never be missed.[20]

M. G. H. wrote anonymously about women's contributions to temple building in Utah for the *Woman's Exponent*. She desired to "exhort [the sisters] to live nearer the Lord than we have been doing." She felt that the sisters needed "to become more and more united in our efforts to assist the elders in building up the Kingdom of God," specifically with temple construction.

The scriptures tell us that "the Lord will come suddenly to his temple." Can we imagine that he will come before the Temple is prepared for him? Or can any of us have hopes of being invited to enter into the Temple, and hear the words of life uttered by the Savior and Redeemer of the world, beholding His face and witnessing the glory of His presence, if we are not assisting to make it ready for the reception? We understand that the religion we have embraced is a practical religion, that we must work as well as watch and pray. If any among us cannot, possibly, raise the amount of fifty cents per month in cash, to be given for the building of Temples, it is possible for most of us to do something else, which, in many instances will be quite as well. The men who labor on the Temples must be clothed and fed. Many of us in country places who, in these "hard times," rarely have the spending of a dollar in money, might save a few pounds of butter, a few dozen eggs, knit a pair of good, warm socks or pay in some other similar manner our personal oblations. In some cases, a sister might have a little stocking yarn that she would use for that purpose, if she could get time aside from the incessant care of her young, helpless family. While her neighbor, perhaps, would take the time to knit the socks if she only had or could get the yarn. Let us be neighborly, sisterly, meet and speak often one to another, learn of each others conditions, and under circumstances which I have mentioned, let one donate the material, the other the labor. Here, again, we should find cooperation agreeable and beneficial.[21]

> **Caroline Frances Angell Davis Holbrook** (1825–1908) arrived in Kirtland with her family in 1835. Her brother, Truman Angell, worked on the construction of the temple. Caroline and her mother, Phoebe Angell, aided in building the Kirtland Temple by boarding several workmen.[22] At the time she wrote this, she was Caroline Angell.

The brethren were generally poor but gave freely for the temple for its erection when Mother Smith took her one horse and went around to gather means for glass and nails and also to gather all the broken earthen to put in the outside plaster.[23]

Temple Dedications

"Manifestations of the power of God."[24]

> **Eliza R. Snow** (1804–1887) attended the dedication of the Kirtland Temple on March 27, 1836. She described the event: "The mighty power of God was displayed, and after its dedication enjoyed many refreshing seasons in that holy sanctuary. Many times have I witnessed manifestations of the power of God."[25]

The ceremonies of that dedication may be rehearsed, but no mortal language can describe the heavenly manifestations of that memorable day. Angels appeared to some, while a sense of divine presence was realized by all present, and each heart was filled with joy inexpressible and full of glory.[26]

> **Elvira Stevens Barney** (1832–1909) was born in New York state. She converted with her family in 1844, when they moved to Nauvoo. Shortly after arriving, her father died, followed by her mother a few months later. Elvira stayed with her sister Jane and Jane's family after leaving Nauvoo. She returned to Nauvoo alone to attend multiple sessions of the Nauvoo Temple dedication and wrote about it on the back of a postcard picture of the temple, signing it "Elvira Stevens."[27]

The following written by Sr Elvira Stevens Barney.

-6-

Ruins of the Nauvoo Temple as stood in 1857.

This taken by my Sister Amelia Stevens, whom married Eugene Fronslot; she was an Artist. The Icarian Society then in their colonizing there; she married one of their number; they had near the Temple their residence, and School house, which does not upon this small card show. They were not successful; then moved into Iowa; and broke up their organization.

The Temple appears as I last saw it in 1846. I left there after returning three times across the Mississippi River, the only one from our Company that was westward bound) to witness the Dedication 1st, 2nd, 3rd, days of May 1846. I then only æ 14 y. an Orphan; The Heavenly power was so great I then crossed and re-crossed to be benefited by it; as young as I was; me, Sister Jane and myself were camped across the Mississippi R. on our way in the Company for some western location with wagons, tents, and provisions, and little else; She had married and taken me with her. I am now æ 74, Mar 17th 1906. The only one of 10 in family left. I never saw my Twin Br Barnard after

Postcard from Elvira Barney detailing her experience with the Nauvoo Temple dedication.

Elvira Barney wrote about her experience with the Nauvoo Temple dedication on the back of this 1857 keepsake postcard (detail on page 125).

The heavenly power was so great. I then crossed and recrossed [the Mississippi River] to be benefitted by it, as young as I was.[28]

Nancy Naomi Alexander Tracy (1816–1902) and her husband, Morris, moved to Kirtland in 1835, where Morris contributed financially to the temple.[29] The ritual ordinances performed in Kirtland by Joseph Smith were preparatory ordinances for male members of the priesthood quorums—initiatory work and the washing of the feet. This "endowment," or gift, was preliminary to the later endowment as it was given to both men and women in Nauvoo.

In the spring following, the Temple was finished and dedicated. This continued for two days, and they were two of the happiest days of my life. The fitting hymn that was composed for the occasion was "The Spirit of God Like a Fire is Burning." It was verily true that the heavenly influence rested down upon that house, and the people were glorious and long to be remembered.

Heavenly Beings appeared to many. I attended both days. I felt that it was heaven on earth. . . . Blessings were poured out. Solemn assemblies were called. Endowments were given.[30]

Sylvia Cutler Webb (1832–1916) and her family moved to Kirtland when Sylvia was a young child. The Cutlers followed the Saints to Missouri and Nauvoo, and Sylvia remembered watching her paternal grandfather, Alpheus Cutler, collect tithing donations for the construction of the Nauvoo Temple.[31] Here she describes the momentous dedication of the Kirtland Temple.

One of my earliest recollections was the dedication of the Temple. My father took us up on his lap and told us why we were going and what it meant to dedicate a house to God. And although so very young at that time, I clearly remember the occasion. I can look back through the lapse of years and see as I saw then Joseph the Prophet, standing with his hands raised towards heaven, his face ashy pale, the tears running down his cheeks as he spoke on that memorable day. Almost all seemed to be in tears. The house was so crowded the children were mostly sitting on older people's laps; my sister sat on father's, I on my mother's lap. I can even remember the dresses we wore. My mind was too young at that time to grasp the full significance of it all, but as time passed it dawned more and more upon me, and I am very grateful that I was privileged to be there.[32]

TEMPLE SERVICE

"Step into that temple, your own living heart."[33]

Hannah Tapfield King (1807–1886) came to Utah from England. She frequently published poetry, essays, and biographies in the *Woman's Exponent*. This piece was published in 1874 while the Salt Lake Temple was undergoing construction, nineteen years before its dedication. Hannah was residing in Salt Lake City at the time.

Step into that temple, your own living heart,
Search its innermost cloisters, view every part,
And then worship the God of that scene.
The God who has form'd you—your heart and your brain,
Which are mines of rich wealth all your own—
To work them in wisdom, that you may retain
The gold and the jewels they richly contain,
Adorning hereafter your crown!
Walk slowly, walk softly, walk calmly along,
Seeking wisdom to guide and direct;
That hereafter, when mingling in life's busy throng,
It will plainly be seen to what class you belong,
And may that be to God's own Elect.[34]

> **Hannah Sorensen** (1836–1923) studied at the Royal Hospital in Copenhagen, Denmark, where she graduated in 1861. After her conversion, she experienced trials that she described as being "crushed down in spirit and body," losing hope of future happiness. This discouragement lifted after she attended the temple for the first time.

In the course of time I was impressed to go to the temple, hoping, as I did, that I should receive new hope and courage, through the blessings I could receive there.

Five years ago I went to the temple the first time, . . . I received there my endowment, had many grand blessings pronounced upon my head. . . . It seemed as though Father poured out upon me, after this, a spirit of energy, together with hope, that I might be useful.[35]

> **Esther**—This article was written under a pseudonym. The writer identified herself as born in Salt Lake City and "quite young yet in years." She wrote to defend plural marriage but then went on to talk about the important work done in the temple.

These are powerful testimonies to those who receive them and clearly prove the manner in which we become saviors upon Mt. Zion. Not only are men favored with these great and sacred blessings but women also are saviors of women. There is no inequality even in ministering for the dead. Woman acts in her sphere as man in his. Therefore is man not without the woman, nor the woman without the man in the Lord. The work of performing the ceremonies requires as much labor and falls with as much dignity upon woman as man. Therein is the goodness of our Father to His daughters made manifest. Holy women now minister in the Temple of God.[36]

~ 12 ~

EDUCATION
"The glory of God is intelligence."[1]

A son in a poor family, Joseph Smith had limited learning opportunities outside the home. Along with his own divine tutoring from heaven came instruction to all the Saints about the importance of education in eternity. As the Saints gathered for the first time in Kirtland, Ohio, Joseph received several revelations on education—both spiritual and temporal. These revelations offered the Saints new knowledge as well as a charge to make education central in their lives. Learning the things of God was essential, as was studying the history of the world "out of the best books."[2] They learned that "the glory of God is intelligence," and the Lord petitioned them to "bring up [their] children in light and truth."[3]

As the Saints worked to apply these teachings, Kirtland became home to a broad spectrum of opportunities to learn about things of God and things of the world. Classes were offered for the young and the old, male and female, including both general and specialized classes: a School of the Prophets, a School for the Elders, Hebrew School, geography classes, and more. Though many of these were usually reserved for elders, Sarah M. Kimball attended the School of the Prophets as well as Hebrew School.[4] Eliza R. Snow started a school for girls in Kirtland in 1836 and in Nauvoo in 1842.[5]

While the topic and substance of female education was often debated in the nineteenth century, Latter-day Saint women extended female education beyond the home. In her youth, Maria Morris looked to the example of Mary Magdalene: "When Peter and the other disciples had forsaken the Savior, a woman stood by Him, and followed Him in all His afflictions. She was the last at His tomb, and it was she who embalmed his body, and was the first to discover that He had risen from the dead." As Mary Magdalene taught the apostles what she had learned from the Savior, Maria wanted her sisters to likewise share the education and truths they had received: "We as young ladies have an opportunity of receiving an education in these our meetings, and it devolves upon us all to use the time which is given us in the most profitable way. We can do much good in teaching to others that which we gain here, and we should consider it a duty that we owe to each other, and more especially to God, for the privilege He has blessed us with."[6]

As the Saints moved from place to place they would continue to focus on education, even when in extreme conditions.[7] As Elizabeth Barlow related, "The understanding and knowledge we have of the scriptures makes friends and everything appear in a very different light to me."[8] Learning had the ability to change their entire view of the world and eternity.

Prioritizing Education

"A good education . . . is the greatest legacy."[9]

> **Sarah Eliza Russell** (1840–1913) was a frequent contributor to the *Woman's Exponent* under the pseudonym of "Hope." On the occasion of her death, the *Exponent* republished her last and "most inspired poem," titled "Life Is Worth the Living." It included these lines: "Oh life is worth the living, to know God liveth on high / That the spirit is immortal, and can never never die."[10] She wrote the following under the name "Hope."

How many parents spend all their thoughts, energy and time in striving to gain wealth for their children, when too often it is a greater source of evil than of blessing. A good education, a thorough knowledge of right and wrong, a clear view of the path that leads upward to life and happiness, and the one that leads down to destruction, with the wisdom to learn from other's experience, is the greatest legacy that parents can give to their children.[11]

> **Helen Mar Whitney** (1828–1896) was three years old when her parents, Vilate and Heber C. Kimball, joined the Church. The teachings in the new revelations affected the schooling available to Helen. She wrote about her experience of growing up for the *Woman's Exponent* while Emmeline Wells, her former schoolteacher, was her editor.[12]

The anxiety expressed in my parents' letters concerning their children's going to school, brings up a subject much harped upon by outsiders, who have always declared that "Mormons" were opposed to education. . . . Thousands can testify that wherever our lot has been cast, almost the first building put up has been the school house. In the little town of Far West the Saints had a large and commodious one, far superior to the ones built by the Gentiles in my native town, and in Kirtland, Ohio, where I was taught my earliest lessons. The first thing my parents thought of whenever we stopped was to send us to school.[13]

Lydia Goldthwaite Knight (1812–1884) already knew much sorrow in her life by the time she chose baptism as a Latter-day Saint. She had been deserted by her first husband and lost her first two children. Joseph Smith promised her that the Lord loved her and that he would "overrule all your past sorrows and afflictions." In Kirtland she met a widower, Newel Knight, who likewise knew sorrow, and "her heart ached" for him. They were married and had seven children together before Newel's death in 1847. Lydia was alone again as she wrote this letter asking Brigham Young's advice; she felt the weight of her responsibility to educate her children, even with its central importance.[14]

When I realize the responsibility that rests upon me in regard to rearing up my little ones, I feel [to] ask an interest in your prayers and to so live that I may be guided by the Spirit of truth and wisdom, that every principle that leads to uprightness may be planted in their hearts and grow with their growth.[15]

Emmeline B. Wells (1828–1921) valued education long before she was a Latter-day Saint. However, when she was considering the decision to unite with the Saints, friends offered her educational assistance on the condition that she would not get baptized. Emmeline decided Church membership was more valuable than her friends' enticements. Years later, one of her Latter-day Saint friends, Augusta Crocheron, wrote about how this "Representative Woman of Deseret" continued with her education on her own.[16]

During the year after her coming into the Church she pursued her studies at the same school, yet she had to endure a great deal of ridicule on account of being a Mormon, and her teacher never wearied of persuading and entreating her to give up such foolish ideas, and resume her place among her associates. But though she was as one alone, for there was not another in the school that believed in the peculiar faith she had embraced, and she understood very little herself, still she had an innate conception of the entire consecration necessary for a Latter-day Saint. The next year she taught a country school, receiving her certificate as readily as any of the other young ladies. . . . In Winter Quarters she taught school. . . . Mrs. Wells has been the mother of six children, one son and five daughters, and during their childhood devoted herself almost exclusively to their care and education.[17]

EDUCATION FOR WOMEN

"If 'knowledge is power' why should not woman possess her full quota?"[18]

Lizzie Calkin Smith (1821–1900) had been an immigrant, a pioneer, a widow, a stepmother to seven, and president of both the Primary and the Relief Society in Rockville, Utah, when she wrote this essay encouraging women's education.[19]

It is not uncommon to meet women who have, at some time in life, wished they had been boys; but, happy to say, the noblest minds among us are too sensible of the responsibility laid upon their place in life to crave another which is really no wider or higher. There is much for woman in this saying: "I care not who may deposit the ballots at the polls, if I but bear and rear the voters, may train the voters' wives and mothers." . . . How important, then, that woman should be developed like man; that her education should be comprehensive; that she should be honored and respected; and she should have perfect liberty to follow the vocation which comes to her from God, and of which she alone is judge. I shall always advocate education for woman, and were I to say whether the sons or daughters of the family shall be educated, I would say, "The girls by all means," for if mothers are educated, sons are bound to be.[20]

Eliza R. Snow (1884–1807) was a prime example of gaining both academic and spiritual knowledge during mortality. She saw that women could only reach their full potential when given opportunities for unfettered learning.[21]

In our past, how limited has been the educational advantages of woman! Book-learning was supposed to have very little to do with the requisite acquirements of the ideal housekeeper; the masses really believing that "woman should understand only sufficient geography to know the different apartments in her house, and enough chemistry to keep the kettle boiling." How absurd! If "knowledge is power" why should not woman possess her full quota as well as the sterner sex? She who is entrusted with the sacred responsibility of bearing the souls of men, of ministering to the wants and necessities of her household. Is it not she who must furnish their nutriment, not only to the new-born infant, but 'tis she who must supply the ever-recurring demands of the older and stronger members of the family. Truly the most thorough housekeepers—the best wives and mothers—are those who are best educated.

The true and correct idea of education, is obtaining practical knowledge, knowledge that will enhance our usefulness, and that will give to ourselves the greatest degree of satisfaction. An understanding will enable us to look beyond the surface of all animate and inanimate creation. . . . Then let our wives and daughters study, think and reflect seriously, endeavor to restrain this increasing love of adornment and pleasure, wean our attention from the artifices of dress and vanity to the more solid practical ideas of a true life, of a genuine, true womanhood. Study the beautiful principles of chemistry, physiology and anatomy; that our lives may become more practically and intelligently useful.[22]

ASPIRING WOMEN

An "indomitable spirit."[23]

Elvira Stevens Barney (1832–1909) lost her parents just prior to heading west with the body of the Church. She followed her mother's example and taught school and focused much of her life on educating others. After several years of teaching, at age forty-seven Elvira decided to go to medical school and expand her efforts to serve others. Augusta Crocheron wrote this sketch of Dr. Barney.[24]

Willing to be useful she helped to teach school, studying nights by a chip-fire to keep in advance of her pupils. Many of our public speakers of today, can date their first lessons in elocution and arithmetic to her training. . . . In 1864, went to Wheaton College and returned home after nearly two years absence. From 1859 to 1863 had taught school in ten different places, generally four terms a year. Had during these previous years taken at different times four homeless children in her care until other ways opened for them. In 1873 adopted a boy whom she schooled and provided for for ten years. . . . In 1878 attended the Deseret University. . . . October, 1879, started East to continue her medical studies which she had prosecuted at home for several years, and attended three complete courses; returning home in the spring of 1883, prepared to pursue this her chosen vocation after a long and eventful experience in many fields of usefulness.

Realizing her own early desires for knowledge and the inconvenience of limited privileges, Dr. Barney fitted up her large house to accommodate lady boarders, thus affording them the convenience of home and college under one roof, with the privilege of boarding themselves, and receiving gratuitous medical instructions for one year.[25]

Esther Romania Pratt Penrose (1839–1932) was born into the Church. She attended the Crawfordsville Female Seminary in Ohio after her parents moved the family there from Winter Quarters. She married Parley P. Pratt Jr.

and had seven children, losing two in infancy. Her love of literature was abandoned for medicine when she decided to attend the Woman's Medical College of Philadelphia. She was dedicated to her studies and successfully completed her education. Even after graduation she continued to specialize and further gain skill to better serve others. When she arrived in Utah, she proposed a hospital for women and children. Then, sensing an immediate need, she instituted a school of midwifery.[26] This is a reminiscence written later.

December 1873 I left my children with my mother and went to New York City, with the intention of studying medicine. The first six weeks in New York was spent assisting Mr. Pratt in proofreading his father's autobiography.

After it was ready for the press, I entered a medical college. It was late in the winter, and I merely learned that term how to proceed in my studies. Of course I took a back seat, but all my faculties were on the "qui vive" to learn all I could. I shall not soon forget my extreme confusion on being asked a question during a quiz by a professor who for the moment forgot I was a new student, nor the mischievous smiles of the students, but my revenge was more than complete at the beginning of the next term in witnessing their astonishment because of my advancement. During the summer vacation while they were recreating, sea-bathing and visiting with friends, I daily plodded studiously up the rugged hill of knowledge; reciting as a private student every day to the professor of physiology. . . . I was well prepared to enter the winter term of 1874–75, and made rapid progress in my studies. . . .

The summer vacation of 1875 and 76 I returned to Salt Lake City and once more had the joy of the society of my children and the Saints. . . . In the fall of 1875 I started for Philadelphia to enter the Medical College for Women to finish my medical education. I spent this winter as the one before in attending lectures, clinics, and dissecting. The days all seemed so much alike that it was as one long day. After the spring term a situation in the New England Hospital for Women and Children in Boston was proffered me which I most gladly accepted. The practical experience I gained while there has been of incalculable value to me. I experienced the greatest pleasure in my duties. . . .

With the autumn leaves came the opening of another winter term in college, and I hastened back to Philadelphia to enter upon my last course of lectures. This was a winter full of work, for in addition to my regular studies, I had my thesis to write. At last the winter's days were over and those who successfully passed their examinations stood on the heights of the rugged hill we had been climbing, waving joyfully the flag "Excelsior." On March 15th, 1877 one of the most eventful days of my life arrived—my graduation day. Dressed in black and with throbbing hearts we repaired to Association Hall—the house was crowded full of interested friends and spectators, but alas! Few were mine. A stranger in a strange land, besides being almost a "hiss and a byword" on account of my religion.[27] Nevertheless after we had received our diplomas and a present of the code of Medical Ethics, I received two beautiful bouquets and a book from friends.[28]

An Eternal Responsibility to Learn

"There is no end to intelligence."[29]

> **Mary Jane Crosby** (1816–1889) was born in New York and crossed the plains in 1850.[30] She served as counselor in the East Bountiful Relief Society. Her obituary called her an "active worker."[31] Her editorial in the *Woman's Exponent* offered up her wisdom to her sisters.

Take care of the minutes, and the hours will take care of themselves. We should endeavor to make the best use of our time. . . .

There is no end to intelligence that might be gained by study, by reading, and by reflecting. This world is full of pleasant and beautiful things; learn to prize those priceless gems of intelligence. Character is the eternal temple that each one begins to rear; cultivate highly the raw material furnished by the hearts own fountain; nature in all her laws is just, then cultivate into existence the best attributes that God has sown in the earth of our natures, which gives us independence, and not reject the truthful monitor, the Holy Spirit; and through obedience to every law which God reveals, men become kings and priests, and women queens and priestess[es]. Study self-improvement no matter how old we are we can improve. If we wish to become noble women we must make ourselves such by our own merits. Sisters awake, be up and doing, strive to live the life of saints and the victory will be ours.[32]

Anna Covington (1871–1954) was an Ogden, Utah, native who married and lived there for most of her life. She demonstrated her trust in both spiritual and temporal learning, believing that both were essential to becoming that which God desires.[33]

As minds rule the world, we should read to inform ourselves as to our duty toward God and man, and how best to perform it; to learn from whence we came, wither we are going, and the object of our existence. . . .

We should read to develop the mental powers, such as the memory, imagination, fancy and thinking faculties. We may develop the memory by reading such literature as will be so striking and impressive that we cannot help but remember it. In history we have a broad field for developing this power.

By reading poetry and fiction we may develop the imagination and fancy. The thinking faculties may be developed by reading speeches, pleas, orations and sermons; for by reading these, it will cause us to think, reason and judge for ourselves.

Not only should we read to develop the mental powers, but also the moral powers. By reading we may choose for our companions the works of the good, wise and noble writers of past and present. And these are companions that will not desert us in poverty and in trouble, but they will remain our friends forever and will also aid us in forming our character.[34]

Rachel Amanda Reynolds (1871–1925) was the youngest child in her family. The family immigrated to Utah and settled in South Cottonwood, Salt Lake County, Utah, long before Rachel was born. She was just twenty-one when she shared her insights on earthly education and agency with young women.[35]

If my essay could be as good as my subject, it would be worthy of deepest attention. Life is real, life is earnest; to make life grand is the end of living. God has a great purpose in view in the creation of every human soul. That purpose is its truthful education. Life is God's school, He is its great superintendent, His Son is its primary instructor. The world is his primary school house, or rather our primary school house built by Him. Here we learn the alphabet of things, and learn to read and spell a little from the great book of God. Here we learn our first lesson; here we get ready for that college which God has built for us on Mt. Zion. In this lower school we prepare for the department above. Our position in that department must be determined by our dutifulness and our progress in this. We must be measured by our merit; we must stand in our lot, every [wo]man in [her] order. The deeds done in the body must tell upon the life of the spirit. What we learn for ourselves here shall be ours in the college above. Wisdom gained in life shall not be lost in death, it will leave a brightness, a crown of glory, when death, the last enemy, shall be destroyed.

God did not ask us whether we would come into His primary school or not, neither will He ask us if we will go into the department above. He gave us the one, He will give the other. The use we make of this life is left to us. Our standing we are to choose, to a certain extent. Our characters are to be the workmanship of our own hands. God has given us minds, school, a study room and teachers, all the books of nature, experience, revelation, reason, duty and affection, and now commands us to educate ourselves, promising to be with us and assist us as our kind superintendent in this grand work of life.[36]

Susa Young Gates (1856–1933) was the second daughter born to Lucy Bigelow and Brigham Young. Susa was encouraged to be educated and faithful. Even as a young wife and mother, she spent as much time as possible in "her beloved pursuit" of writing for the Latter-day Saints. Susa inaugurated the *Young Woman's Journal* in 1889 and was the editor for the decade that followed. This particular writing comes from an unpublished manuscript titled "History of Women," found in her voluminous personal papers collection.[37]

Never, for one day, were Mormon women, or men, left without the energizing effects of formal education. A gospel whose scope embraces all eternity, whose shibboleth is "eternal progression," does not contemplate the mental inactivity begotten of fixed creedal formulas. A new angle on an old truth, a fresh facet turned on an understood fact, makes for intellectual elasticity. A Gospel which teaches that "the Bible is the word of God so far as it is translated correctly"[38] permits a true worshipper of divine Truth to answer patiently the geologist with "Why not a million or billion years as an eternal 'day,' so named by Moses or his vision-limited translators?" . . . Education, to the Mormon woman, is not a fad, not a fancy, but a necessity, which accompanies life at birth, marriage, death, and beyond, ever beyond and beyond.[39]

~ 13 ~

Personal Apostasy

"Be not deceived."[1]

As time passed and Church membership grew through avid missionary work and conversion, there were consistently those who fell "out by the way side."[2] Some decided the restored gospel required too much. Some believed that things had changed too much from the time of their baptism. Others had difficulties with Church structure or choices made by Church leadership. There was no single reason for separating oneself from the body of the Church. In the year following the temple dedication, Kirtland became an early center of divergence. Conflicting ideas about governance, economic speculation, and the failure of the Kirtland Safety Society and Anti-Banking Company created chaos in Kirtland.

For Temperance Mack, they were "perilous times."[3] Perhaps ten or fifteen percent of Church membership left during this period; the percentage was greater amongst Church leadership—apostles, Book of Mormon witnesses, and other leaders.[4] This was not a faceless mob of apostates. These were sometimes close friends and family. Disaffiliation and declension became a significant part of the Saints' experience. The new revelations warned the Saints to "be not deceived" and offered them patterns and gifts of the Spirit to help.[5] Those who remained had to personally negotiate the apostasy of others as they considered their own spiritual status and questioned whether they were strong enough to continue to stand faithful.

APOSTASY IN THE CHURCH

"Trials among false brethren."[6]

Caroline Barnes Crosby (1807–1883) and her husband, Jonathan, joined the Saints in Kirtland in 1835, a few months before the temple dedication. Caroline wanted to share her experience with those she loved: "How often while listening to the voice of the prophet have I wished, Oh that my friends, parents, brothers, and sisters, could hear the things that I have heard, and their hearts be made to rejoice in them, as mine did." She enjoyed many "glorious" and "joyful" manifestations of the Spirit in the months surrounding the dedication, and although those spiritual occasions did not last, Caroline remained faithful in the Church.[7]

The Kirtland bank failed, which caused a great deal of distress among the brethren. We had a little garden which was a great help to us, we had no cow, and were obliged to buy milk for the babe. My husband was sued once, by the men who kept the meat market . . . and was obliged to sacrifice twice the amount of the debt in property, to raise the money. Alas thought I, the trials that I had heard the elders preach of were in reality coming upon us. As to poverty we could endure that patiently, but trials among false brethren, who can endure with patience? Many of our most intimate associates were among the apostates.

Warren Parrish was a sort of leader of a party of some 30 or 40 persons, among them was John Boynton and wife, Luke and Lyman Johnson, Harpen Riggs, and others whose names I do not recollect. These were some of our [closest] neighbors and friends. We had taken sweet counsel together, and walked to the house of God as friends. They came out boldly against the prophet, and signed an instrument got up as I understand by Warren Parish and others, renouncing all their alliance with the church. I met Sister Riggs afterwards and asked her if it was true that she had apostatized. She said she was dissatisfied with some things in the church, but that she still believed in the Book of Mormon and thought she always should. I felt very sorrowful, and gloomy, but never had the first idea of leaving the church or forsaking the prophet.[8]

Sally Parker (1799–1852) left her native Maine and moved to Kirtland in the summer of 1837 with her family. She attended meetings at the temple, witnessed the baptism of a 108-year-old man, and marveled at the glorious outpouring of the Spirit. These experiences stood in stark contrast to the concurrent widespread apostasy; those that had "departed from the faith" were the "greatest opposers."[9] The Parkers remained in Kirtland for only a short time due to the chaos there. Sally demonstrated her shock in the disaffection of some leaders in this letter to her brother-in-law John Kempton.[10]

I suppose there are some that are departed from the faith. [They] will hold on to the Book of Mormon, but if they deny that, farewell to all religion. Without doubt you have heard from [former apostles] John Boynton and Warren Parrish. I lived a lone neighbor to Parrish. You remember the piece he put into the paper to send to his parents. He appeared to be a man of God and now he is turned like a dog to his vomit and so forth.[11] He and Boynton they lost their religion and they came out from the Mormons and drew away about thirty and now some have seen their error and gone back but the others have denied the Bible and the Book of Mormon and the whole. Parrish is a lawyer and Boynton is up to all rigs and they are a working against the Mormons. But now they are writing against the heads of the Church. I heard they have sent letters that they were sorry that they deceived the people. I believed that they were praying people. Now they will curse and swear and call upon God to damn anything that does not suit them and they have their debating meetings that there is no religion. Let us begin and hold fast lest at any time we let them slip. The older I grow and the more I see the stronger I feel in my mind. O brother, stand fast in the liberty wherewith Christ has made you free.[12]

Mary Fielding Smith (1801–1852) had gathered with the Saints in Kirtland with her brother and sister, Joseph and Mercy. Soon missions called her siblings away, and Mary was left alone as chaos erupted in Kirtland a few months before her marriage to Hyrum Smith. Mary was a student of the Bible and she understood its stories literally, wondering if the Lord would open the earth to swallow those creating chaos as he had in the book of Numbers. She wrote this letter to her sister.[13]

I have no doubt that you have many trials, but I am inclined to think you have not quite so much to endure as I have. Be this as it may, the Lord knows what our situations are and he will support us and give us grace and strength for the day if we continue to put our trust in him and devote ourselves unreservedly to his service. I do thank my Heavenly Father for the comfort and peace of mind I now enjoy in the midst of all the confusion and perplexity and raging of the devil against the work of God in this place. For although here is a great number of faithful precious souls, yea the Salt of the Earth here. Yet it may truly be called a place where Satan has his seat; he is frequently stirring up some of the people to strife and contention and dissatisfaction with things they do not understand.

I often have of late been led to look back for the circumstances of Korah and his company when they rose up against Moses and Aaron. If you will turn to and read 16th Chapter of Numbers you will there find the [feelings] and conduct of many of the People and even the Elders of Israel in these days exactly described. Whether the Lord will come out in a similar way or not I cannot tell. I sometimes think it may be so, but I pray God to have mercy upon us all and preserve us from the power of the great enemy who knows he has but a short time to work in. . . . We are not yet able to tell where it will end. I have been made to tremble and quake before the Lord and to call upon him with all my heart almost day and night as many others have done of late. I believe the voice of prayer has sounded in the House of the Lord some days from morning till night and it has been by these means that we have hitherto prevailed and it is by this means only that I for one expect to prevail.

I feel more and more convinced that it is through suffering that we are to be made perfected and I have already found it have the effect of driving one nearer to the Lord and so has become a great blessing to me. I have sometimes of late been so filled with the love of God and felt [such a sense] of his favor as has made me rejoice abundantly. Indeed my Heavenly Father has been very gracious unto me both temporally and spiritually.

I fear for Kirtland. O that we as a people may be faithful this is our only hope and all we have to depend upon.[14]

Hepzibah Richards (1795–1838) was the last of her siblings to join with the Latter-day Saints. She followed her family in gathering with the Saints but took her time to be fully convinced of the faith. Though not yet a Latter-day Saint, she suffered with the Saints in Kirtland during this difficult period. She was baptized after leaving Kirtland and arriving in Far West, Missouri, and died shortly thereafter. She described the difficulties in Kirtland to her brother, Willard, and her friends.[15]

At present people are more composed; but the voice to this people, or to the honest in heart is, "Get ye out of this place"[16]—and multitudes are preparing to flee. Some are going almost without any preparation.[17]

I care not how soon I am away from this place. I have been wading in a sea of tribulation ever since I came here. For the last three months we as a people have been tempest tossed; and at times the waves have well nigh overwhelmed us; but we believe there will yet be a way of escape.[18]

Ann Marsh Abbott (1797–1849) first heard the restored gospel from her brother, Thomas Marsh. Her brother was a great influence in leading her and her family to Mormonism. He became one the first apostles in this dispensation, but while in Kirtland, Thomas began to clash with the Prophet Joseph. He would later testify against Joseph and the Saints in Missouri, providing evidence that led to the extermination order. Twenty years later, Thomas would return to fellowship, joining with the Saints in Utah.[19]

We have got to be tried and proved in all things so that we may stand or fall. Many have fallen out by the wayside already: Brother Thomas for one and his family. They live in Missouri, what county or place I cannot tell you.

I have written to them but cannot get an answer. However, I hope he is not lost so but what he can be found again. . . .

I do not hear from my brothers a half so often since we became Mormons as before, but I can tell you this is the greatest blessing the Lord ever bestowed upon me, that I and my family should have the privilege of embracing the true and everlasting gospel as it is in Christ Jesus.[20]

Staying Strong amid Pressure

"Are you such a fool?"[21]

Desdemona Fullmer Smith (1809–1886) was a pragmatic woman who experienced the Spirit in sometimes incredible ways. At one time before her baptism she prayed and "fell to the ground and lay for several hours as dead." A voice told her, "Stop yet a little longer. There is something better for you yet." She waited to join another church until she "heard the Latter-day Saints preach." Once converted, Desdemona would not be swayed. She described her continued commitment amid apostasy in Kirtland.[22]

Oliver Cowdery with others would say to me are you such a fool as still to go to hear Joseph the fallen prophet. I said the Lord convinced me that he was a true prophet. And he has not told me that he is fallen yet.[23]

Jennetta Richards Richards (1817–1845) was considered the first convert baptized in England by Heber C. Kimball. Kimball wrote to missionary Willard Richards the day of Jennetta's baptism, prophetically jesting, "I baptized your wife today." Months passed and Willard and Jennetta heard consistently of each other, but they did not meet until the following March. The first time they met, Willard humorously asked, "Richards is a good name; I never want to change it; do you, Jennetta?" She responded, "No, I do not and I think I never will."[24] The following two letters demonstrate Jennetta's struggles as many friends and family members created imaginative rumors to attempt to separate Jennetta from her conversion, her new church, and her betrothed. Jennetta would eventually decide to separate herself from her friends and family rather than her beliefs. She moved in with Church members until she and Willard were married.[25]

My Dearest Willard,

My Mother says this morning you are gone far in a consumption and that will make them more against you than ever knowing that I have always been very delicate. They think we are two very unfit persons to go together but let them say what they will.[26]

I have had much more to contend with since I came to Kirkham [England] than ever I had before. My brother is uncommonly kind and affectionate and will reason, but Sister has no more reason than a stone. Sister and I were at the Minister's house at Elswich on Monday. I never was so insulted in my life than I was then by no one. Sister and Mr. Edwards were at me as soon as I got there just like two lions.

Jennetta and Willard Richards with their son Heber John, from a daguerreotype. It was likely taken in Nauvoo shortly before Jennetta's death.

After I left you on Saturday Mother told me Mr. Foster said he would take an oath that you told his mother when first you came that you were a widower. And Sister heard so too by someone. She says not through Foster, but Moon saw you told him, that you were now my "Dearest Willard." You know that [I] do not believe that you are, and either Moon or someone must be rolling in untruth or I am deceived. I never asked you the question, but I am satisfied from your own mouth that you are not. I can as soon believe that the gospel you preach is fake as believe that you have a wife and a family in America or that you are a widower.[27]

Laura Farnsworth Owen (1806–1881) and her second husband often found the Church at the center of their arguments. Mr. Owen was baptized, but never truly converted. While the couple lived outside Nauvoo, Mr. Owen became friends with a group of outspoken apostates who frequented the Owen home. Though the Saints did not generally advocate violence, one day Laura had had enough.[28]

One Sabbath morning as we were eating breakfast, an apostate Delap came in and commenced a tirade of abuse against Brother Brigham and all that believed in him. I asked him to stop or leave the house. He said he would say what he pleased and stay as long as he pleased and said Brigham was a dam'd whoremaster and all that believed in him. I told him if he said that again in my house I would put the broomstick over his head. He went over with it again. I took the broomstick and gave him 2 or 3 licks that counted and told him to leave the house. He took it out of my hands. With that I stepped to the fire and took up a long-handled slice (as we called it) and told him to leave or I would split him down with it. He stood his ground. I was as good as my word. I put it into his face with all the power that I had and backed him out of the door, the blood trickling down his cheeks. And as he went, I told him to tell his friends that Sister Owen had given him a decent whipping.

After he was gone, I asked Mr Owen if he was not ashamed to sit still and hear a man abuse me and the Church in such a manner and say nothing. He said he thought I could take my own part very well. I thought it resulted in some good, for I was not troubled any more with that class of beings while I staid there.[29]

Maintaining Faith

"We are determined."[30]

> **Melissa Morgan Dodge** (1798–1845) understood her life through scripture, as did many of the early converts. Born blind, she miraculously received her sight when she was baptized. Melissa had little opportunity for education, yet she clearly knew scripture. She added to her knowledge of the Bible with new Restoration scripture. Through much tribulation the word of God helped her maintain her dogged resolve to "bring forth fruit with patience."[31]

We are still determined [to] maintain the faith which once was delivered to the Saints and not fall away like some have and deny the gospel of Christ. They are those that fell on stony ground—Who when they have h[e]ard the word immediately receive it with gladness and no root in themselves and so endure but for a time afterward. When affliction or persecutions ariseth for the word's sake immediately they are offended.[32] But we are determined by the grace of God, our Lord and Savior Jesus Christ to endure in faith . . . that we may receive the crown that is prepared for his Saints.[33]

> **Temperance Bond Mack** (1771–1850) believed that the Church of Jesus Christ would lead her to Christ, and she left the comforts of home in Michigan to cast her lot with the Saints. Temperance would continue with the Saints even after her sister-in-law, Lucy Mack Smith, stayed behind in Nauvoo. While mixing a few scriptural metaphors, she desired to be the Lord's wheat at the last day, no matter how bitter the mortal experience.[34]

Although the chaff is a scattering off to the four winds, yet there remains some wheat in the granary. We have been sifted, and if we should be [faithful], what remains will be so much the better. And it would be what we are daily looking for.[35] We see the things that many have desired to see and have not seen them, and what if the sup is bitter. The Savior partook of the same and shall we refuse to taste of it?[36] Be assured it is enough for the servant to be as his master.[37]

Emma Hale Smith (1804–1879) married Joseph Smith Jr. in 1827. As his wife, Emma endured all manner of privation. When Joseph left for Carthage, Emma desired a blessing from him, but there was no time. Joseph suggested she "write out the best blessing [she] could think of and he would sign the same on his return."[38] That night, as she possibly sat wondering what was happening in Carthage, she committed her desires to paper. It is revealing that her initial desire was wisdom to discern.[39]

First of all that I would crave as the richest of heaven's blessings would be wisdom from my Heavenly Father bestowed daily, so that whatever I might do or say, I could not look back at the close of the day with regret, nor neglect the performance of any act that would bring a blessing. I desire the Spirit of God to know and understand myself, that I may be able to overcome whatever of tradition or nature that would not tend to my exaltation in the eternal worlds. I desire a fruitful, active mind, that I may be able to comprehend the designs of God, when revealed through his servants without doubting. I desire the spirit of discernment, which is one of the promised blessings of the Holy Ghost.[40]

Almira Mack Covey (1805–1886) knew she was mortal and that she could fall. She had originally chosen truth while visiting her aunt Lucy Mack Smith in New York in 1830. In the years that followed she saw many blessings in her life and the lives of others as they embraced truth. She also saw the experiences of those who fell away. She recognized her blessings and the opportunity to choose her eternal reward herself.[41]

If I hold out faithful unto the end, I shall have reason in eternity to praise the Lord for sparing my life to this day. But I am liable to go astray and I may yet prove unfaithful and be numbered with the foolish virgins and be cast out of the kingdom;[42] but if I am, I alone shall be to blame for I have had great privileges, and the Lord has given me much light and bestowed many spiritual blessing upon me. Therefore it depends upon my faithfulness if I obtain a crown of celestial glory.[43]

～ 14 ～

GATHERING AND BUILDING ZION

*"Upon mount Zion shall be deliverance,
and there shall be holiness."*[1]

Prophets and people throughout time have marveled at the concept of Zion, defined as the household of God: "The Lord shall bless thee out of Zion."[2] As Joseph Smith worked on his new translation of the Bible, the Saints learned that Enoch built the City of Zion, which the Lord defined as both a spiritual state and a place where those who were "of one heart and one mind" dwelt together in righteousness, "and there was no poor among them."[3] The Book of Mormon prophesied that Zion, the New Jerusalem, would be established upon the American continent.[4] In the fall of 1830, Latter-day Saints began to discuss the principle of gathering and building Zion. The geographic location of Zion became more specific over time as the Lord promised he would reveal the place of inheritance; in July of 1831, the Lord designated Independence, Jackson County, Missouri, as the "center place."[5]

Meanwhile, the majority of the Saints gathered to "the Ohio" in 1831, where they formed the headquarters for the Church, increasing in number, receiving vital revelation, building the house of the Lord, and then directing affairs both in "Zion" and in Kirtland. With the Lord's direction, Independence became the new spiritual center of the Church, and the Saints also began to gather to Jackson County. The excitement of gathering and building Zion—the fulfilling of ancient prophecy—was palpable, as recorded by many women.

The Saints' time in Zion did not last. They clashed with Missouri citizens in 1833 and were pushed out. The center place of Zion was thought to be lost. The Lord taught the Saints that Zion was not just about land, but it was also about creating a spiritual state: "I will raise up unto myself a pure people, that will serve me in righteousness."[6] The modern Saints mourned as had ancient Saints for the loss of Zion—"We weep when we remember Zion"—though the Lord promised them that Zion would eventually be redeemed.[7]

Following the initial attempt to build Zion in Jackson County, the Saints continued to gather, first to northern Missouri, then to Nauvoo, and eventually to Utah, perhaps wondering why Zion's redemption did not happen sooner. As Helen Mar Whitney observed in hindsight, "The Church being then in its infancy they understood but very little concerning the plans and purposes of the Almighty. They thought they had sacrificed and suffered enough from the scourgings and oppression of their enemies in Ohio and Missouri and that they would soon be gathered back to their homes from which they had been so cruelly driven. It had not been revealed to them how great and marvelous a work the Saints of God were destined to accomplish."[8]

Gathering meant leaving behind family, friends, and the comforts of home, as well as experiencing poverty in relocation. At each step, women recognized the cost of building Zion but believed that the unity of the Saints in their efforts to build Zion was worth whatever sacrifice. Through experience, they realized that the Lord would bless them, deliver them, and provide a way. Today, stakes and wards work to stretch the boundaries of Zion—the household of God—around the world.

GATHERING WITH THE SAINTS

"The spirit of gathering."[9]

Caroline Barnes Crosby (1807–1883) married a Latter-day Saint, Jonathan Crosby, in November 1834. A few months later she was baptized, and in November 1835 they moved to Kirtland. Though it was difficult to leave friends and family, they felt the "consolations of the holy spirit" in their efforts.[10]

When my husband first broke the subject to his father, he seemed very much distressed, and used all the persuasion he was master of, to induce him to stay, but all in vain; we had set our faces as a flint Zionward and were ready to forsake all to gain that port.

When he saw that we were determined to go, he did what he could to help us away. We bid farewell to the brethren and sisters who wept freely and mourned our departure, but not as those without hope for they intended many of them to join us again at some of the gathering places of the church before many years if it was the Lord's will. . . . [My] husband sold what little stock he had, fixed his buggy in order for travelling with a cover to it, and . . . We bent our course. . . . .

I had the second trial of parting with them. Mother and Catherine wept as before, but I told them it was unnecessary as I thought perhaps I might return in another year as I had then. The zeal and love for the cause in which I was engaged supported me beyond everything, and I only felt to mourn for them because they had not the same consolation that I had.[11]

Emily M. Coburn Austin (1813–after 1900) was baptized in 1830 and joined the Saints in Colesville, New York. She gathered with the Saints in Kirtland the next year and then continued to Missouri. Though she eventually left the Church in Nauvoo, she provided an insightful account of the Saints' attempt to gather to Ohio and build Zion in Missouri.[12]

The winter following I went with several others to Kirtland, Ohio. They were establishing a Mormon church in that thriving little village. The members now numbered about one hundred persons, the greater part of whom were the brightest and best of the community, merchants, lawyers and doctors. All were united in the belief that God had set his hand again—the second time—to recover the house of Israel. . . .

The Mormon elders were sent out into all parts, to build up churches; Kirtland being the placed called by the Saints, one of the stakes of Zion, to prepare to go to the land of promise. Missouri was called the hill of Zion, a land that flows with milk and honey. People were now coming from all parts of the world, and Kirtland was filling with emigrants preparing to go to Missouri. The Colesville church was expected the following summer, and I looked forward to their coming, for I could then enjoy the sweet society of my beloved sister. Preparations were in progress for a final exit to the Hill of Zion; all was hurry and laying plans for the journey. . . .

Now, as time advanced, the little church from Colesville received word from those commissioners who were sent by the church to Missouri to look out lands, and, as preparation had already been made for the journey, we all started for the Ohio river in wagons—twenty-four in number, twelve in each company. . . . We most truly were a band of pilgrims, started out to seek a better country. . . . [13]

It was at this period [1833] we promised ourselves a happy, enjoyable life; a life of peace and plenty; a life devoted to the service of God; a life of benevolence to those who were unfortunate and needy; a life to bind up the broken-hearted and comfort the mourner; a life to teach by example, as well as precept; a life of charity; a life to show to the world that we had been with Christ, and learned of Him.[14]

Bathsheba W. Smith (1822–1910) and her family gathered in stages to northern Missouri, her married sister and family leaving Virginia first. What was exciting for Bathsheba in the fall of 1837 quickly turned to fear as armed men stopped them along their way. One of the men mockingly authorized their continued trip, "As you are Virginians, we will let you go on, but we believe you soon will return for you will quickly become convinced of your folly." Bathsheba and her family relied on "the spirit of the Lord . . . to comfort and sustain us."[15]

The spirit of gathering with the saints in Missouri came upon me, and I became very anxious indeed to go there that fall with my sister Nancy and family, as they had sold out and were getting ready to go. I was told I could not go. This caused me to retire to bed one night feeling very sorrowful. While pondering upon what had been said to me about not going, a voice said to me, "Weep not, you will go this fall." I was satisfied and comforted. . . .

On our journey the young folk of our party had much enjoyment; it seemed so novel and romantic to travel in wagons over hill and dale, through dense forests and over extensive prairies, and occasionally passing through town and cities . . . *and camping in tents at night.*[16]

Augusta Dorius Stevens (1837–1920) was born in Copenhagen, Denmark. When she was thirteen she and her father "embraced the gospel." Copenhagen quickly became a hostile environment for Augusta and her Church family. She left her mother behind to go to Zion in Utah and did not see her again for twenty-two years.[17]

I did not know how many persons had joined the church when I left for Utah. But at that time the spirit of gathering became an important item among the Saints in Copenhagen and there were twenty-eight persons who got ready to emigrate with Elder Erastus Snow when he returned from his first mission to Scandinavia and I was one of this number. . . . My father thought it would be a good thing for one of the family to go to Zion and the rest of the family would come later. So it was arranged for me to go. I thought this was a fine plan and I was happy to think I was the first of the family to go to Zion.[18]

The Cost of Gathering and Building Zion

"Count the cost."[19]

Sarah DeArmon Pea Rich (1814–1893) and her husband, Charles C. Rich, enjoyed the tranquil time in Far West, Caldwell County, Missouri, after the Saints left Jackson County: "We thought we were the happiest couple in all the land." Following political unrest in 1838, Sarah's husband escaped Far West with Hosea Stout, leaving Sarah with Samantha Peck Stout to fend for themselves.[20]

When we parted not knowing whether we should meet again for a long time I felt confident it was the only thing he could do to avoid a maddened mob from taking his life so I felt contented to have him go feeling that the

Lord would spare us to meet again. So him and Hosea Stout made a covenant to stay together until we should meet again and Hosea's wife and I made a covenant that her and I would remain together as true friends until we should meet our husbands again and upon this promise we shook hands with our dear husbands and parted. Her and I then went into my sister-in-law's house and went to bed praying the Lord to protect ourselves and our dear companions until he saw fit to have us meet again.[21]

Elizabeth Haven Barlow (1811–1892) was baptized in 1837 in Massachusetts and moved with her brother to Far West in the spring of 1838. Following the body of Saints to Quincy, Illinois, later that year, Elizabeth worked as a nurse. On February 24, 1839, she wrote a letter to her second cousin, Elizabeth Howe Bullard, who later came to Nauvoo.[22]

To look at our situation at this present time it would seem that Zion is all destroyed, but it is not so, the work of the Lord is on the march. . . .

God moves in a mysterious way his wonders to perform. Many have been sifted out of the church, while others have been rooted and ground in love and are the salt of the earth. . . .

Let all who desire to live with the Saints, count the cost, before they set out on their pilgrimage to Zion. Come prepared to suffer with the Church in all their afflictions, not to flee as many have, in the day of trial when labor was mostly needed. . . .

Ah, Christ says we must forsake all for him. Yes, dear E., let us leave all for Christ.[23]

Presendia L. Kimball (1810–1892) gathered with the Saints in Ohio, Missouri, and Illinois. When her first husband left the Church, Presendia continued faithful and eventually married Heber C. Kimball as a plural wife. She stayed in Nauvoo to work in the temple and then left her home to join the Saints across the river.[24] Even without the assistance and company of her parents, her siblings, and her husband and his varied responsibilities and family members, she remained committed to the cause of Zion.

No tongue can tell my feelings in those days of trial; but I had considered well, and felt I would rather suffer and die with the Saints, than live in Babylon as I had lived before. . . . The excitement and exposure brought on fever and I was very ill. . . . The future that stretched out before me like a great, unknown desert, unrelieved and barren. I had only my Heavenly Father left, and I reached out in faith to the One above to open the heavens for me and aid me in my loneliness. I was in a new, wild country without means.[25]

Eliza R. Snow (1804–1887) followed the Saints from Ohio to Missouri in 1838, where they lost nearly everything to mobs. Even amid physical and emotional discomfort, while fleeing Far West, Eliza recalled that "none but saints can be happy under every circumstance."[26] After leaving Nauvoo in 1846 and arriving in Utah in 1847, she encouraged others to "gather to Zion," but with the admonition to recognize the reality of the frontier situation and that Zion is a spiritual location. In 1856, she wrote this poem to emigrating Saints from Europe.

Think not, when you gather to Zion,
Your troubles and trials are through—
That nothing but comfort and pleasure
Are waiting in Zion for you.
No, no; 'tis design'd as a furnace,
All substance, all textures to try—
To consume all the "wood, hay, and stubble,"
And the gold from the dross purify. . . .
Think not, when you gather to Zion,
The prize and the victory won—

Think not that the warfare is ended,
Or the work of salvation is done.
No, no; for the great Prince of Darkness
A tenfold exertion will make,
When he sees you approaching the fountain
Where the truth you may freely partake.[27]

DIVINE ASSISTANCE IN BUILDING ZION

"I believe the Lord is overruling all things for our good."[28]

Sarah DeArmon Pea Rich (1814–1893) When the Nauvoo temple was completed and dedicated in 1846, Brigham Young assigned Sarah and her husband to assist in giving endowments to as many Saints as possible before they left the city. The effort was long and exhausting, requiring four months of service: "We were to be there at 7 in the morning and remain until the work was done at ten or twelve o'clock at night if necessary."[29] They recognized the divine assistance of God associated with the endowment before crossing the plains, and they were eager to bless others with the same promises.

Many were the blessings we had received in the house of the Lord, which has caused us joy and comfort in the midst of all our sorrows and enabled us to have faith in God, knowing He would guide us and sustain us in the unknown journey that lay before us. For if it had not been for the faith and knowledge that was bestowed upon us in that temple by the influence and help of the Spirit of the Lord, our journey would have been like one taking a leap into the dark. To start out . . . in the winter as it were and in our state of poverty, it would seem like walking into the jaws of death. But we had faith in our Heavenly Father, and we put our trust in Him feeling that we were His chosen people and had embraced His gospel, and instead of sorrow, we felt to rejoice that the day of our deliverance had come.[30]

Mary Fielding Smith (1801–1852) married Hyrum Smith in 1837 and became stepmother to his five children. She bore two children herself, one born while Hyrum was in Liberty Jail. Though she became very sick from exposure and suffered greatly, she continued to seek the divine assistance promised to her. She described her situation in Commerce, Illinois, in this letter to her brother, Joseph Fielding, who was on a mission in England, where their family of origin remained.[31]

The situation is very pleasant; you would be much pleased to see it. How long we may be permitted to enjoy it I know not; but the Lord knows what is best for us. I feel but little concerned about where I am, if I can keep my mind staid upon God; for, you know in this there is perfect peace. I believe the Lord is overruling all things for our good. . . .

I have a hope that our brothers and sisters will also embrace the fullness of the gospel, and come into the new and everlasting covenant; I trust their prejudices will give way to the power of truth. I would gladly have them with us here, even though they might have to endure all kind of tribulation and affliction with us and the rest of the children of God, in these last days, so that they might share in the glories of the celestial kingdom. As to myself, I can truly say, that I would not give up the prospect of the latter-day glory for all that glitters in this world.[32]

A Zion People

"They were of one heart and one mind, . . . and there was no poor among them."[33]

Lucy Mack Smith (1775–1856) joined the Nauvoo Relief Society at the second meeting on March 24, 1842. The minutes record that she wept and told the women "she was advanced in years."[34] A few weeks later, she "spoke very pathetically of her lonely situation."[35] The Saints listened to her counsel and cared for the revered mother of their prophet.

We must cherish one another, watch over one another, comfort one another and gain instruction, that we may all sit down in heaven together.[36]

Ellen Briggs Douglas (1806–1888) arrived in Nauvoo from England in March 1842. Her husband died, and her family experienced illness and extreme poverty.[37] She approached a friend for assistance and soon became a member of the Nauvoo Relief Society, which lived up to its mission to provide for the poor.

After I [had] begun to get well I went down into the city on a visit to where Ann lived, and I stayed two nights. . . . The woman where Ann lived would have me make application to the Female Relief Society for some clothing which I needed for myself and family. I refused to do so, but she said I needed something and that I had been so long sick and if I could not do it myself she would do it for me. . . . We went to one of the sisters, and she asked me what I needed most. I told her that I needed . . . many things. While I was sick my children [wore] out their clothes because I could not [mend] them, so she said she would do the best she could for me. Ann came over in a few days and they brought the wagon and fetched me such a present as I never received before.[38]

Lucy Meserve Smith (1817–1892) worked for Emma Smith in Nauvoo, where she may have become acquainted with Relief Society work. She later served as the first president of the Provo Relief Society. When news came of the impending arrival of the 1856 handcart pioneers gathering to Utah, devastated by early winter snow, hunger, and poverty, Lucy rushed anxiously to assist.[39]

We did all we could, with the aid of the good brethren and sisters, to comfort the needy as they came in with handcarts late in the fall. . . . As our society was short of funds then, we could not do much, but the four bishops could hardly carry the bedding and other clothing we got together the first time we met. We did not cease our exertions [un]til all were made comfortable. . . .

I never took more satisfaction and, I might say, pleasure in any labor I ever performed in my life, such a unanimity of feeling prevailed. I only had to go into a store and make my wants known; if it was cloth, it was measured off without charge. [We] wallowed through the snow until our clothes were wet a foot high to get things together.[40]

15

AFFLICTION
"We have to be tried like gold, seven times tried."[1]

The Book of Mormon prophet Lehi taught that there is opposition in all things.[2] For the early Saints, much of their Missouri experience was a concentrated and collective lesson in opposition and adversity. In 1833, the Saints were expelled from Jackson County, Missouri. Many of them moved to northern counties. By 1838, the bulk of the Latter-day Saints were living in northern Missouri. By the fall, the lives of the Latter-day Saints were in upheaval once more. The governor had signed an order that the Saints "be exterminated or driven from the state."[3] Joseph, Hyrum, and others were imprisoned, and the Saints were preparing to abandon their homes yet again. After leaving Missouri and moving to Illinois, many would express relief that they remained "in the land of the living."[4] Though the specifics of their experience may be distinct, opposition and affliction are components of all of our lives. Despite the difficulties, these Latter-day Saint women found solace in their faith and saw these afflictions as a proving ground that could purify and sanctify.

Providing for a Family Alone

"A feeling I cannot express."[5]

> **Mercy Fielding Thompson** (1807–1893) had a nursing infant, which enabled her to also act as nursemaid for her sister, Mary Fielding Smith, and her newborn, Joseph F. Smith, during the expulsion from Missouri. Though Mercy and her family were in the middle of their own distress, she somehow found the energy to serve her ailing sister.[6]

My husband, with many of the brethren, being threatened and pursued by a mob, fled into the wilderness in November, leaving me with an infant not five months old. Three months of distressing suspense I endured before I could get any intelligence from him, during which time I stayed with my sister, [Mary Fielding Smith,] wife of Hyrum Smith, who, having given birth to a son while his father was in prison, on the 13th of November [Mary] took a severe cold and was unable to attend to her domestic duties for four months. This caused much of the care of her family, which was very large, to fall on me. Mobs were continually threatening to massacre the inhabitants of the city, and at times I feared to lay my babe down lest they should slay me and leave it to suffer worse than immediate death.

About the 1st of February, 1839, by the request of her husband, my sister was placed on a bed in a wagon and taken a journey of forty miles, to visit him in the prison. Her infant son, Joseph F., being then but about eleven weeks old, I had to accompany her, taking my own babe, then near eight months old. The weather was extremely cold, and we suffered much on the journey. This circumstance I always reflect upon with peculiar pleasure, notwithstanding the extreme anxiety I endured from having the care of my sick sister and the two babes. The remembrance of having had the honor of spending a night in prison, in company with the prophet and patriarch, produces a feeling I cannot express.[7]

Mary Fielding Smith (1801–1850) was working as a governess in Kirtland when she met the recent widower and brother of the Prophet Joseph, Hyrum Smith. Eliciting some scorn, they were quickly married and Mary became mother to Hyrum's five children. After only a year and a half of marriage and a move to Missouri, her new husband was in jail in Liberty.[8] As she began this letter to Hyrum, Mary had "mingled feelings of pleasure and grief." It was good to hear from her husband, yet the distance, rumors, and poor communication had caused a number of misunderstandings between the young couple. Despite difficulties, Mary remained committed to her husband. Mary never spoke directly of that traumatic night that she, Mercy, and their babies spent in Liberty Jail. She later revealed to her brother, "I have, to be sure, been called to drink deep of the bitter cup; but you know, my beloved brother, this makes the sweet sweeter."[9]

I must here, my beloved companion, advert to some remarks you make in your last [letter] relative to my having forsaken you, which gave me feelings not to be described. I cannot bear the thought of your having any such suspicion. Surely you had not, if so you are yet unacquainted with the principles of my heart. What? Should I forsake a friend and a bosom friend in the time of adversity and affliction when all the sympathy and affection I am capable of feeling is called for to sooth and comfort as far as possible under such circumstances as you are placed in?

No. Reason, religion, and honor and every feeling of my heart forbids such a thought to enter there. How? I cannot help asking can things have been represented to you so as to indicate any such thing, surely an enemy must have done this, for if you had known the truth, and the endeavors and intentions of my heart towards your family from the time you left me to the present moment, you would I do assure you have had no cause for anxious thoughts, or sleepless nights on their account. It has been my desire and aim to do in your absence both by them and for them as in your presence or even more knowing your great carefulness and concern for our general welfare. . . . if I should again be permitted to enjoy your society I hope to prove to you that I am a never failing friend. I now feel to long to see you. . . . I subscribe myself your most affectionate and faithful friend and companion in tribulation. . . .

We have seen the Epistle[s] to the Church and read them several times. They seem like food to the hungry.[10] We have taken great pleasure in perusing them. I believe all our afflictions will work together for our good altho[ugh] they are not joyous while passing through them. Yours in affection in the fullest sense of the word.[11]

Laura **Clark Phelps** (1807–1841) was trying to make the best out of a difficult situation. With her husband, Morris, in Columbia Jail, she cared for her children alone and prepared to leave Missouri with the Saints, though she was determined not to leave without her husband. She wrote to a friend of her current troubles, the loss of her mother, as well as her resolve to learn and eventually overcome.[12]

I needn't try to express my feelings to you at this time. My heart is full from day to day though I know there is a God that can deliver all his servants. I expect to start in a few days to find Morris if possible. I attended the Court at Richmond April 22. This was a serious time I assure you to leave a companion in the dungeon with half enough to eat. . . . I talked with the lawyers and grand jury; they said that they had no doubt but he was innocent. I have no doubt but Morris would have [been] cleared but they just heard that Brother Joseph and all the others [were] at Liberty.[13] It raised their fury.

I left our home on the 26. I drove my wagon all the way; [it] turned over once with my children under my load but hurt them but little I think. I can safely say I know what trouble is to have my husband torn from the bosom of his family and then having to part with our dear Mother.[14] And had it not been for the power of God I never could have born this [scene]. Her words often roll through my heart, "O Laury, be of good cheer. Remember while you are passing through trouble, I, your Mother, [am] at rest for my work is done. Why can you say stay any longer on earth?"

I can safely say this day I am not sorry I ever joined this Church. . . . I recollect the company that John saw came up through great tribulation.[15] We have to be tried like gold, seven times tried.[16]

The Expulsion from Missouri

"We must flee from the haunts of men." [17]

> **Temperance Bond Mack** (1771–1850), a widow, learned of the Restoration from her youngest daughter, Almira, and her sister-in-law, Lucy Mack Smith, in 1831. She chose baptism and then gathered with the Mormons in Kirtland before moving to Missouri. Here she testifies of her belief to her daughter Harriet as she relayed the trying circumstances that surrounded her and her fellow Saints and her efforts to remain faithful. [18]

Knowing your anxiety for me I will endeavor to inform you of an item of the scenery that has passed around us. Brother Joseph and Hyrum and Sidney Rigdon and a number of others are now in jail and have been in irons. They will have their trial in March if they don't call a special court. They are prisoners of war. They are an offering for the church to save the lives of others. They suffer themselves. The church has agreed to leave here in the spring but where to go they know not.

We don't know but we must flee from the haunts of men to the caves and dens in the rocks like the saints of old, but none of these things move me. Neither do I regret that I have left the eastern states for where the Lord says go. I must obey although my heart is with my children and they are near and dear unto me, yet I am no better than the martyrs. They had to suffer the loss of all things to be an incorruptible crown and so must I, and I do it cheerful knowing I shall reap in due time if I faint not. Fearing as we are under bondage to write you the particulars, yet we are in hopes that the truth will yet reach there and will be published in the papers and you will do well to search them. . . . We are rejoicing that we are found worthy to suffer persecution for the name of Christ. [19]

Amanda Barnes Smith (1809–1886) tragically lost a husband and a son in the Hawn's Mill massacre. She had been miraculously inspired to know how to save another of her sons who had also been a victim of the violent attack. Burying her loved ones certainly must have seemed more than she could endure. And that would not be the end of her suffering; the Missourians continued to harass her and her family. Amanda found divine support, strength, and moments of grace amid the hardship.[20]

One day a mobber came from the mill with the captain's fiat: "The captain says if you women don't stop your d—d praying he will send down a posse to kill every d—d one of you!" And he might as well have done it, as to stop us poor women praying in that hour of our great calamity. Our prayers were hushed in terror. We dared not let our voices be heard in the house in supplication. I could pray in my bed or in silence, but I could not live thus long. This godless silence was more intolerable than had been the night of the massacre.

I could bear it no longer. I pined to hear once more my own voice in petition to my Heavenly Father. I stole down into a cornfield, and crawled into a "stout of corn." It was the temple of the Lord to me at that moment. I prayed aloud and most fervently.

When I emerged from the corn a voice spoke to me. It was a voice as plain as I ever heard one. It was no silent, strong impression of the spirit, but a voice, repeating a verse of the saint's hymn:

That soul who on Jesus hath leaned for repose,

I cannot, I will not desert to its foes;

That soul, though all hell should endeavor to shake,

I'll never, no never, no never forsake![21]

From that moment I had no more fear. I felt that nothing could hurt me. Soon after this the mob sent us word that unless we were all out of the State by a certain day we should be killed.

The day came, and at evening came fifty armed men to execute the sentence. I met them at the door. They demanded of me why I was not gone?

I bade them enter and see their own work. They crowded into my room and I showed them my wounded boy. They came, party after party, until all had seen my excuse. Then they quarreled among themselves and came near fighting.

At last they went away, all but two. These I thought were detailed to kill us. Then the two returned. "Madame," said one, "have you any meat in the house?" "No," was my reply. "Could you dress a fat hog if one was laid at your door?" "I think we could!" was my answer. And then they went and caught a fat hog from a herd which had belonged to a now exiled brother, killed it and dragged it to my door, and departed.

These men, who had come to murder us, left on the threshold of our door a meat offering to atone for their repented intention.[22]

Melissa Morgan Dodge (1798–1845) left few of her own words to document her life. Born in New York, she was blind until apostle David W. Patten healed her eyes at her baptism. Her scrawling hand documented her physical difficulties and the very limited opportunities for schooling she might have received, but this letter written to her brother after the trial of Missouri brims with gratitude and joy.[23]

With thankfulness to the Lord we are yet alive and have this opportunity of letting you know that we are in the land of the living. We have been driven from our home and we are now in Illinois in Adams County, where we rented land. . . .

Although we have been driven by a cruel mob, we can say like Paul, we take the spoiling of our goods joyfully, knowing there is a God in heaven which will bring them to judgment in his own due time.[24] And the day is soon a coming when his Saints shall not be driven and harassed about by a cruel mob. But thanks be to my God. The day is night and the hour is near when he will take vengeance on all the ungodly and give his Children a reward, a crown of righteousness, while the wicked must perish under his wrath. For they have [driven] some from their homes, and some they have killed in a shocking manner. Some they whipped, and some they put in prison.

But all this is to show that the scripture shall be fulfilled and the time draw nigh when the Son of man will come to reign with his Saints. . . . When we were driven from Missouri in February across the prairies, you must realize yourself how you would have felt to have been driven from your home for nothing but for the religion of Jesus Christ in the dead of the winter on the open prairies with your little ones. But thanks be to the Almighty God, he has preserved us and has kept us from the hand of our cruel enemies who were threatening our lives daily.[25]

Ann Marsh Abbott (1797–1849) and her husband, Lewis Abbott, learned of the Book of Mormon from Ann's younger brother, Thomas Marsh, shortly before Thomas became an apostle in the newly organized Church of Christ. However, by the time that Ann wrote the following letter to another brother, Nathan, Thomas had not only left the Church but had had a direct hand in the sufferings of the Church in Missouri. Ann described their Missouri experience and wrote of her steadfast devotion and continued faith amid trials.[26]

I will improve this opportunity and try to write something that you may know we are yet in the land of the living. We are in pretty good health considering what we have had to encounter since we came to this country being driven by mob from time to time which has caused infirmities to come to us, especially my husband [Lewis]. His health is poor, two different times he has had his blood spilt by [a] Missouri mob. However, through the mercy of the Lord he is able to do a good deal of work though he is troubled very much with rheumatism.

Now I can say that through all our trials and afflictions our faith is not lessened but strengthened in Mormonism. And [I] can safely say we have passed through all this for Christ's sake. Neither do we expect that we have passed through all yet. We have got to be tried and proved in all things so that we may stand or fall.[27]

16

ORDINANCES AND COVENANTS

"I have been willing to make covenants."[1]

In July 1830, the Lord told Emma Smith: "Cleave unto the covenants which thou hast made."[2] Emma was baptized into the Church of Christ on June 28, 1830, and this revelation, which came a short time after her baptism, provided a pattern by which Latter-day Saint women made and received covenants and ordinances with the Lord. A key part of the Restoration was the authority by which to seal on earth what could be sealed in heaven—both individuals to Jesus Christ and the Church, and families to each other.[3] Elder David E. Sorensen taught, "Each ordinance is calculated to reveal to us something about Christ and our relationship to God."[4] Therefore, "In the ordinances thereof, the power of godliness is manifest."[5] The ordinances both connect us to God and teach us about becoming like God.

Joseph Smith received, in progression, the Aaronic Priesthood, with the same ordinances and covenants that existed in the ancient Church of Jesus Christ. At a tumultuous time when mortality rates were high and loss was a common occurrence, as well as when different denominations competed for membership, the Restoration of the Church of Christ provided order and ordinances, connecting Saints to God through their covenants in a sacred relationship.[6] The restoration of the Melchizedek Priesthood enabled higher ordinances associated with the temple, including washing and anointing, endowment, and sealing, crowned by the opportunity to perform such necessary ordinances by proxy for the dead. Temperance Mack wrote her daughter describing how she had just been baptized for her deceased father and mother "who had not an opportunity of attending to this ordinance while in the flesh thus releasing them from prison."[7] Eliza R. Snow expressed the joy that this order contained: "Thanks be to God . . . for the holy ordinances of His house and how cheerfully grateful we ought to be that we are the happy participants of these great blessings."[8] The ordinance of the sacrament, or the Lord's Supper, allowed Saints a time to remember and renew all covenants.

Latter-day Saint women celebrated their restored covenants and ordinances, which brought them closer to Christ. Zina D. H. Young recorded confidently in her journal, "O Praise the Lord for all his goodness. . . . He will remember all his covenants to fulfill them in their times."[9] And following years of trials and trouble, Mary Fielding Smith stated, "The more I see of the dealings of our Heavenly Father with us as a people, the more I am constrained to rejoice that I was ever made acquainted with the everlasting covenant. O may the Lord keep me faithful till my change comes!"[10]

BAPTISM

"I wished to be immersed in the water as the Savior was."[11]

Lucy Mack Smith (1775–1856) described the process by which her son, Joseph Smith, received the mandate and instruction to restore the ordinance of baptism. She recounted the baptism of her husband, Joseph Smith Sr., soon after the Church was organized.[12]

In the spring Joseph came up and preached to us after Oliver got through with the Book [of Mormon]. My Husband and Martin Harris were baptized. Joseph stood on the shore when his father came out of the water and as he took him by the hand he cried out "Oh! my God I have lived to see my father baptized into the true church of Jesus Christ," and he covered his face in his father's bosom and wept aloud for joy as did Joseph of old when he beheld his father coming up into the land of Egypt. This took place on the sixth of April 1830, the day on which the church was organized.[13]

Elizabeth Brotherton Pratt (1816–1897) grew up in England, where she pondered over the teachings of Christ and his apostles in the New Testament, particularly the mode of baptism. After several years, a friend gave her a missionary tract about a living prophet. Elizabeth was drawn to the teachings of baptism and the gift of the Holy Ghost. Brigham Young baptized her in September 1840, and Heber C. Kimball confirmed her.[14]

These ordinances were performed by men called to divine authority to preach and administer in "the kingdom, set up in these last days no more to be thrown down nor given to another people." . . .

I received a powerful testimony of the truth which was a great blessing to me in the opposition I had to meet with from my relatives and past friends. Old associates turned their backs on me, but I rejoiced continually because I had received the Gospel of our Savior and had seen the gifts made manifest that were to follow the believer and confirm the word.[15]

Elizabeth Haven Barlow (1811–1892) was about twenty years old and living in Massachusetts when she became a member of the local Congregational church. As she read the Bible, she felt that something was missing. She was baptized and confirmed by Parley P. Pratt in September 1837 and wrote about it under her maiden name, Elizabeth Haven.[16]

I wished to be immersed in the water as the Savior was. I named it to the minister and he said he could immerse me in the water if I wished it, but he said I had better give up the idea as it would make talk for me to be baptized as I was sprinkled when a babe and said that it was not required of us now. So I gave up the idea. . . . But still there was a vacancy in my feelings that never left me until my cousins Brigham Young and Willard Richards came. . . . They stopped with us a day or two and preached the new and everlasting gospel faithfully to us. While there they gave me a Book of Mormon, which I read very attentively. The Spirit of God rested upon me and I felt convinced to say in my heart. "This is the way I long have sought and mourned because I found it not."

I resolved that I would be baptized the first opportunity. . . . I went alone for no one took any interest in the great work of God.[17]

Priscilla Mogridge Staines (1823–1899) was born in England, where she attended the Church of England with her family. She grew dissatisfied with its doctrines and prayed for divine direction. She believed "God had sent the true gospel to me in answer to my prayer" when she discovered The Church of Jesus Christ of Latter-day Saints.[18] Like many other converts in England, Priscilla was baptized in secret to avoid persecution.

Having determined to be baptized, I resolved to at once obey the gospel. . . . On the evening of a bitterly cold day in mid-winter, as before stated, I walked four miles to the house of a local elder for baptism. Arriving at his house, we waited until midnight, in order that the neighbors might not disturb us, and then repaired to a stream of water a quarter of a mile away. Here we found the water, as we anticipated, frozen over, and the elder had to chop a hole in the ice large enough for the purpose of baptism. It was a scene and an occasion I shall never forget. Memory to-day brings back the emotions and sweet awe of that moment. None but God and his angels, and the few witnesses who stood on the bank with us, heard my covenant; but in the solemnity of that midnight hour it seemed as though all nature was listening, and the recording angel writing our words in the book of the Lord. Is it strange that such a scene, occurring in the life of a latter-day saint, should make an everlasting impression, as this did on mine?

Having been thus baptized, I returned to the house in my wet and freezing garments. . . .

The usual confirmation words, pronounced upon my head, "Receive ye the gift of the Holy Ghost," were, indeed, potent. They changed the current of my life. This remarkable and sudden change of mind and the now all-absorbing desire to emigrate with the Saints was my first testimony to the truth and power of the gospel.[19]

> **Eliza Dana Gibbs** (1813–1900) learned about the Church from a hired hand—Elijah Austin, a Latter-day Saint who "enlightened her mind and led her to an understanding." The message resonated with what she had read in the New Testament as a child. Her brother tried to persuade Eliza not to be baptized, telling her that joining with the Mormons would upset her mother. Eliza felt it was "my duty to embrace it, that I should do so and leave Mother in the hands of God."[20]

When the day arrived we had settled upon to obey the gospel we went to meeting, and after meeting to the water, but it was with a heavy heart. I had always implicitly obeyed Mother and it sorely grieved me to cause her pain. Nothing but a sense of duty would have influenced me to have caused her trouble. Both my sister and myself dearly loved our mother and we went forth into the waters of baptism with aching hearts. . . . As soon as I was confirmed the Comforter in very truth rested upon me in so much it would not have disturbed me had the whole world been arrayed against me. My trouble and anxiety in regard to mother and all else were swallowed up in a heavenly peace.[21]

> **Mary Ann Brown Pulsipher** (1799–1886) joined the Methodist church around the age of thirteen. She questioned her preacher about baptism; he told her it was not a necessary ordinance. Yet in her studies of the New Testament, she considered baptism a "duty—a command." When she insisted, he baptized her by pouring water on her head. She recounted, "I was not satisfied." Twenty years later she learned about the Latter-day Saint form of baptism.[22]

It was not long before a Mormon preacher came. We had a great many questions to ask. . . . He said baptism by immersion was the only right way. It was for the remission of sins. I thought that looked right. In a short time some were ready to be baptized. I wanted to be at the first opportunity, but Satan thought he would hinder it. The night before baptism, I was taken lame with rheumatism or something else. I was so sick I could not get around much. As they were fixing to go, Brother Carter said to me, "Sister Pulsipher, if you will do your duty, you shall be healed." I took a cane and hauled to the water and went in. It was a very cold day, but I came out well, left my cane, and went away rejoicing.

I was very ignorant; I had not heard anything about being confirmed, or receiving the Holy Ghost. The next evening I went to meeting and the six that were baptized were there. When he put his hands on my head, he . . . promised great blessings if I would be faithful. The Spirit of the Lord was there. We sang, prayed, and praised God together.[23]

Baptism for the Dead

"Is not this a glorious doctrine?"[24]

> **Jane Harper Neyman** (1792–1880) was baptized in 1838 and moved to Nauvoo in 1840 with her family. Her son, Cyrus, died before they learned about the Church. Their son's early death had been a constant concern for Jane and her husband. When she heard about the doctrine of baptism for the dead in August 1840 from Joseph Smith, she eagerly requested to perform the ordinance for her son that same day. She is considered to be the first person in this dispensation to be baptized for the dead, as noted in this statement.[25] Similarly, Emma Smith and Emmeline B. Wells, among others, were baptized for deceased male family members before the gendered regulation became official.[26] Jane signed the following statement.

Jane Neyman states that Joseph preached Seymour Brunson's funeral sermon and then first introduced the subject of baptism of the dead and said to the people, "I have said the subject of baptism for the dead before you. You may receive or reject it as you choose." She then went and was baptized for her son Cyrus Livingston Neyman by Harvey Olmstead.[27]

Vilate Murray Kimball (1806–1867) was baptized with her husband, Heber C. Kimball, in 1832. He was called as an apostle in 1835. Vilate wrote the following letter to her husband while he was on a mission in England, reporting the new ordinance of work for the dead.[28]

President Smith has opened a new and glorious subject of late which has caused quite a revival in the church. That is, being baptized for the dead. Paul speaks of it in first Corinthians 15th chapter 29th verse. Joseph has received a more full explanation of it by revelation. He says it is the privilege of this church to be baptized for all their kinsfolks that have died before this Gospel came forth, even back to their great Grandfather and Mother if they have been personally acquainted with them. By so doing we act as agents for them, and give them the privilege of coming forth in the first resurrection. He says they will have the Gospel preached to them in Prison. . . . Since this order has been preached here, the waters have been continually troubled. During conference there were sometimes from eight to ten elders in the river at a time baptizing. . . . Those that have no friends on the earth to be baptized for them can [send] ministering spirits to whomsoever they will and make known their request. Thus you see there is a chance for all. Is not this a glorious doctrine? Surely the Gentiles will mock, but we will rejoice in it.[29]

Elizabeth Anderson Howard (1823–1893) joined the LDS Church in 1851 in Ireland with her husband after her neighbors introduced them to the gospel. She recognized that the doctrine resonated with what she found important in the Bible.[30]

I had lived to see the days that by revelation the principle, manners, and customs Jesus taught had been again restored. One principle, among many, I was much impressed with was "Baptism for the Dead." St. Paul touches on it in one of his letters. I was delighted with it. I was satisfied. I knew I had found what my reason, my heart, and my soul had long looked for.[31]

Sally Carlisle Randall (1805–1874) had a fourteen-year-old son, George, who died soon after the family arrived in Nauvoo. She sent the sad report to family members, along with the good news of baptism for the dead, particularly for her mother, who had also lost a child to death.[32]

[George's] father has been baptized for him and what a glorious thing it is that we believe and receive the fulness of the gospel as it is preached now and can be baptized for all of our dead friends and save them as far back as we can get any knowledge of them. I want you should write me the given names of all of our connections that are dead as far back as grandfather's and grandmother's at any rate. I intend to do what I can to save my friends. . . . I expect you will think this is strange doctrine but you will find it to be true. . . . Oh mother, if we are so happy as to have a part in the first resurrection, we shall have our children just as we laid them down in their graves.[33]

ENDOWMENT

"This will bring you out of darkness into marvelous light."[34]

Bathsheba W. Smith (1822–1910) joined the Nauvoo Relief Society at its first meeting. She was struck by Joseph Smith's instructions to the women that "he wanted to make us, as the women were in Paul's day, 'A kingdom of priestesses.' We have the ceremony in our endowments as Joseph taught."[35] Bathsheba was one of the first women in this dispensation to receive the endowment.

I received the ordinance of anointing in a room in Sister Emma Smith's house, in Nauvoo, and the same day, in company with my husband, I received my endowment in the upper room over the Prophet Joseph Smith's store. The endowments were given under the direction of the Prophet Joseph Smith, who afterwards gave us lectures, or instructions, in regard to the endowment ceremonies.[36]

Mary Ellen Kimball (1818–1902) joined the Church in New York in 1842 and moved to Nauvoo in 1844. Later that year she received her endowment, with the ordinance repeated when the temple was completed.[37]

I admired the building from outside: But greater pleasure took possession of my mind when I entered and beheld the beautiful rooms within. I felt a reverential awe knowing this to be the temple of God built by revelation. Sister Vilate Kimball gave me my washing and anointing in this house. I shall never forget how much admiration I felt for her. I knew her to be a saint. No one could fill that position so well without the spirit of our Savior to assist them to do it. I felt to exclaim, "How thankful I am that I can at last throw by my traditions and serve the Lord in deed, with a full purpose of heart."[38]

Hannah Last Cornaby (1822–1905) joined the LDS Church in England in 1852 and arrived in Utah the following year. Her experience with the temple endowment, performed in the Endowment House before the completion of the Salt Lake Temple, was profound.[39]

On the twenty-first of March [1856], we passed through the Endowment House. Those who have enjoyed the privilege, can appreciate the blessing it was to us at this time. Having left all for the gospel's sake, we were repaid a hundred fold. I recollect how happy we felt next morning, as we joined a company going to dig roots. The warm rays of the spring sun seemed to diffuse gladness all around; everybody seemed cheerful; I was as free from care as the birds; and like them, wanted to praise the Creator for all His goodness.[40]

Eternal Marriage

"Sealed under the holy law."[41]

Lydia Goldthwaite Knight (1812–1884) was deserted by her first husband. She moved to Kirtland in 1835 and stayed with Hyrum and Jerusha Smith. There she met Newel Knight, and they fell in love. Below is an account of their wedding in November 1835, written by Susa Young Gates.[42]

The young couple stood up, and the Prophet arose and commenced the ceremony. At its close he pronounced them husband and wife by the authority of the Priesthood which he held. Thus was the first marriage ceremony ever performed by the Prophet Joseph Smith. Here was laid the foundation stone of the grand structure of our marriage ceremony. The revelation of sealing was not given, but after he had united the two he blessed them with fervor. Then turning to the company he exclaimed . . . "The Lord God of Israel has given me authority to unite the people in the holy bonds of matrimony. And from this time forth I shall use that privilege and marry whomsoever I see fit." . . . After Joseph had thus spoken, some of the company asked some questions and he continued to speak and instruct them on the principle of marriage. Much that was entirely new to the Saints was revealed in his conversation, and again Lydia saw that strange, brilliant light shine through his features, like the mellow radiance of an astral lamp, only purer and brighter.[43]

Vilate Murray Kimball (1806–1867) experienced a trial of faith with her husband in Nauvoo. Joseph Smith asked Heber C. Kimball to give him Vilate as a plural wife. Heber agonized over the request, intensely seeking revelation. Upon Heber's obedience, the Prophet joined Heber and Vilate by virtue of his sealing power and authority of the Holy Priesthood, making them husband and wife for eternity. Vilate wrote this letter to her husband, Heber C. Kimball, in his journal on June 8, 1843, just before he left for a mission to the Eastern States.[44]

I write these few lines for you to look upon when you are far distant from me, and when you read them, remember they were penned by one whose warm, affectionate heart is ever the same towards you; yea, it is fixed, firm as a decree which is unalterable. Therefore, let your heart be comforted, and if you never more behold my face in time, let this be my last covenant and testimony unto you: that I am yours in time, and throughout all eternity. This blessing has been sealed upon us, by the Holy Spirit of promise.[45]

SACRAMENT

"Our only access unto God."[46]

Nancy Naomi Alexander Tracy (1816–1902) moved to Kirtland in 1835 with her husband. Her account indicates the comfort and power that came from gathering together to participate in ordinances, including the sacrament.[47]

The elders went from house to house, blessing the Saints and administering the sacrament. Feasts were given. Three families joined together and held one at our house. We baked a lot of bread.[48]

Charity Elizabeth Kinder Savage (1856–1919) was the first president of the Henrieville, Utah, Relief Society and the first Primary president there. Nineteenth-century women often produced the bread, linens, and dishes used for the sacred ordinance of the sacrament. Charity's daughter, Minnie S. Syrett, gave the following account about her mother.[49]

At that time the Bishopric took turns in furnishing the sacrament. When it was father's turn, mother had her own way of preparing it. She cut the crusts off the loaves of bread, then sliced it into half-inch strips. Preparing it this way made it easier for the Priests to break it evenly. She had crystal plates she kept for the sacrament only. She would put the bread on the plates, cover it with a pretty white linen towel that she kept especially for that purpose. Father was always so proud to take it to church.[50]

Eliza R. Snow (1804–1887) wrote several sacrament hymns that continue to be sung today. Each one recognizes Jesus Christ and the sacramental symbols and teaches about the ordinance renewing covenants with God.[51] Eliza told the Gunnison Relief Society in 1878 that each woman "needs the bread of eternal life to keep her up."[52]

> How great the wisdom and the love,
> That fill'd the courts on high,
> And sent the Savior from above
> To suffer, bleed and die! . . .
> In mem'ry of the broken flesh
> We eat the broken bread;
> And witness with the cup, afresh,
> Our faith in Christ, our head.[53]

~ 17 ~
ABRAHAMIC SACRIFICES
"The fellowship of [Christ's] sufferings."[1]

The Lord repeatedly tells the Saints, "I will try you and prove you herewith."[2] Trying, testing, and proving are all part of mortality. However, all adversity is not created equal. Some adversity would push the Saints to their physical, emotional, mental, and spiritual limits. Paul told the Philippians, "I count all things but loss for the excellency of the knowledge of Christ Jesus my Lord: for whom I have suffered the loss of all things." These experiences could enable the Saints to know Christ in their extremity as they joined in "the fellowship of his sufferings."[3] Elder Neal A. Maxwell called this one of the "wintry doctrines" of the gospel.[4] Such knowledge could not be learned in the abstract; it had to be experienced.[5] In the Doctrine and Covenants, the Lord refers to testing and trying the Saints as Abraham.[6] The Lord asked Abraham to give up that which was dearest to him. The manner of testing and trying would be unique for each individual. Abrahamic tests have the ability to not only test loyalty but to transform—the pressure can ultimately create jewels.[7]

One of the Abrahamic tests of the early Saints was the practice of plural marriage. In the revelation on plural marriage, the words of the Lord offer the Saints an example to understand this trial, "I did it . . . to prove you all, as I did Abraham."[8] Plural marriage was certainly a testing and trying doctrine. It was not something easily accepted by a people as Victorian as the early Saints. Eliza R. Snow recorded Joseph Smith describing his own battle "in overcoming the repugnance of his feelings" in regard to plural marriage.[9] Several apostles recorded similar reactions. John Taylor said that all of the Twelve "seemed to put off, as far as we could, what might be termed the evil day."[10] Despite any initial reluctance, they would eventually accept it and live it. Though some women such as Louie Felt quickly "became thoroughly convinced of the truth of the principle of celestial marriage," plural marriage pushed others to extremity.[11] Publicly, Latter-day Saint women would confidently declare their support of the practice of plural marriage.[12] However, the private writings often yield a distinct record, as demonstrated in this chapter.

For many Latter-day Saint women, poetry became a mode of processing tribulation, searching for peace and hope, and finding theological meaning in tragedy. Some would testify that affliction can be transformed. The excavation of one's soul could make room for joy. However, joy was rarely accessible in the middle of extremity. One of the darkest periods of Mary Fielding Smith's life occurred as she was alone, with a newborn, desperately sick, and her new husband in Liberty Jail. A few months later she wrote her brother, "I have, to be sure, been called to drink deep of the bitter cup; but you know, my beloved brother, this makes the sweet sweeter."[13] Though it may take months, years, or a lifetime, the gospel of Jesus Christ carries the eternal possibility of restoration and transformation.

As Abraham

"Do you not want the highest glory?"[14]

> **Drusilla Dorris Hendricks** (1810–1881) was responsible for the care of a paralyzed husband and several young children when the call for Mormon Battalion volunteers came. Though her son William was sixteen, Drusilla felt it would be too difficult to allow him to go. The closer the departure of the Battalion got, the more worried she became. In 1877, Drusilla compiled a life sketch with this account.[15]

One would say to me, Is William going? I answered, "No." . . . But when I was alone the whispering of the Spirit would say to me, "Are you afraid to trust the God of Israel? Has He not been with you in all your trials? Has He not provided for your wants?" Then I would have to acknowledge the hand of God in all His goodness to me. . . .

[The day before the Battalion departed] I spent that day in weeping and when evening came . . . it was a long time before I went to sleep. . . . I thought the number was made up; this is the last thing I thought before I went to sleep and the first thing when I woke up I thought, "Well you have got your boy yet,

Drusilla Hendricks cared for her husband after he was shot in the neck in Missouri; he remained paralyzed for the rest of his life. She also cared for their children and grandchildren.

are you not happy?" . . . I thought how easy something might happen for that was a sickly climate. I got ready to get breakfast and . . . I was asked by the same spirit that had spoken to me before, If I did not want the greatest glory? And I answered with my natural voice, Yes, I did. Then how can you get it without making the greatest sacrifice said the voice. I said it is too late, they are to be marched off this morning. That spirit left me with the heartache.

I got breakfast and called the girls and their father to come to the tent for prayers . . . when Thomas Williams came shouting at the top of his voice, "Turn out, men, turn out, for we do not wish to press you but we lack some men yet in the Battalion." William raised his eyes and looked me in the face. I knew that he would go as well as I know now that he has been.

I could not swallow one bite of breakfast but I waited on the rest thinking I might never have my family all together again. I had no photograph of him, but I took one in my mind and said to myself, "If I never see you again until the morning of the Resurrection, I shall know you are my child."

My husband took his cane and went to where the drum was beating. I went to milk the cows. . . . I thought the cow would be shelter for me and I knelt down and told the Lord if He wanted my child to take him, only spare his life and let him be restored to me and to the bosom of the Church. I felt it was all I could do. Then the voice that talked with me in the morning answered me saying, "It shall be done unto you as it was unto Abraham when he offered Isaac on the altar." I don't know whether I milked or not for I felt the Lord had spoken to me. . . .

I don't think that Abraham felt any worse than we did, I cannot tell the hardships we endured by his going . . . we bore it with the patience of Job.[16]

Forsaking Family for the Gospel

"If I obey the Gospel call,
I find I must forsake you all."[17]

Phoebe K. Pratt (1797–1868) was a Connecticut native who "left her friends and family in the States for the Gospel's sake."[18] She poetically described the pain of this absence, both in her notebook and in a letter to her family.

Its memory oft pains my weeping eyes
But far from thee I now am doomed to dwell
And bid alas my native land farewell
Farewell sweet home my youthful days are o're. . . .

Oh God of orphans wilt thou our way direct
By day o'er see us and by night protect
Each sigh or murmur if thou alone should hear.[19]

Was earthly joys my only theme I would soon return to you again. But if I obey the Gospel call, I find I must forsake you all. I feel an expressible anxiety to see you again. I often think of you and should write oftener, if I could afford time. I am obliged to improve my time to the best advantage to procure.[20]

CHILDREN DYING

"He is gone and I cannot recall him."[21]

Eliza Partridge Lyman (1820–1886) was pregnant when the Saints trekked across Iowa. Her first baby boy, Don Carlos, was born in Winter Quarters on July 14, 1846, leaving Eliza very ill and uncomfortable with the hot sun in the day and cool air in the night.[22] These excerpts are from Eliza Lyman's journal. Winter Quarters was a place of desperate suffering for many Saints.

August 9th Since I last wrote I have been very sick with child bed fever. For many days my life seemed near its end. I am now like a skeleton so much so that those who have not been with me do not know me till told who I am. It is a fearful place to be sick with fever in a wagon with no shade over except the cover and a July sun shining every day. All the comfort I had was the pure cold water from a spring nearby. But the Lord preserved my life for some purpose for which I thank Him. My babe in consequence of my sickness is very poor but as I get better I hope to see him improve. . . .

Oct 25th . . . My hair has nearly all come out, what little is left I have had to cut off. My head is so bare that I am compelled to wear a cap. . . .

Nov 14th Don Carlos weighs 13 lbs, having gained 2 lbs during the last month. He is a great comfort to me. . . .

Dec 12th The baby is dead and I mourn his loss. We have done the best we knew how for him, but nothing has done any good. He continued to fail from the time he was taken sick. My sister Caroline and I sat up every night with him and tried to save him from death for we could not bear to part with him, but we were powerless. The Lord took him and I will try to be reconciled and think that all is for the best. He was my greatest comfort and was nearly always in my arms. But he is gone and I cannot recall him, so I must prepare to meet him in another and I hope a happier world than this. I still have friends who are dear to me, if I had not I should wish to bid this world farewell, for it is full of disappointments and sorrow, but I believe that there is a power that watches over us and does things right. He was buried on the west side of the Missouri on the second ridge back, the eleventh grave on the second row counting from right to left, the first row being farthest from the river. This will be no guide as the place cannot be found in a few years.[23]

Jane Snyder Richards (1823–1912) married Franklin D. Richards in Hancock County, Illinois, in 1842. They would eventually have six children together. She was known as one who consistently was a part of "the great work of helping the distressed." Her friend Annie Wells Cannon wrote, "She knew no place to draw the line when there was a call for help."[24] However, in 1846 at Council Bluffs, Jane had not the strength to help herself. She had lost her baby, Isaac, a few months before. Now Wealthy, her only child, was ailing as well, as was Jane. Franklin was away on a mission to Great Britain.

We seemed to get strength and improve slowly and though it was not until I reached Cutlers Park, [Nebraska] that I had strength even to walk . . . President [Brigham] Young heard of my situation and came back some fifteen miles to counsel me.

He was distressed to find me so ill and to see Wealthy so feeble and he then said if any one had passed through tribulation I had, and if he had known my circumstances he would not have required Mr. Richards to have gone on this mission. Then he gave an order allowing our team to pass on across the [Missouri River] ferry before the rest, some two hundred waiting in turn, and then I was once more with my mother and friends.

Cutlers Park where Brother Brigham was stopping was three hundred miles from Nauvoo and here was my crowning affliction. At last my little daughter after suffering almost incredibly for weeks on the 14th of September [1846] passed from us. There was a time when I had thought she might live and then it seemed as though all I had suffered would seem but a dream. Her life being spared, now [that] she was taken, my own life seemed only a burden. My husband was to be away for two years and the hardships he might suffer made his return seem most uncertain. I only lived because I could not die.[25]

Plural Marriage

"A similar effect to a sudden shock of a small earthquake."[26]

> **Vilate Murray Kimball** (1806–1867) had been married to Heber C. Kimball for twenty years by the time the Saints reached Nauvoo. In mid-1842, Heber returned from a mission with the Twelve to Great Britain. Vilate knew something was amiss. In the excerpt below, her daughter **Helen Mar Whitney** (1828–1896) used Vilate's letters and her own memory to write of her mother's experience.[27]

My mother had noticed a change in [Father's] manner and appearance, and when she enquired the cause, he tried to evade her question. . . . But it so worked upon his mind that his anxious and haggard looks betrayed him daily and hourly, and finally his misery became so unbearable that it was impossible to control his feelings. He became sick in body, but his mental wretchedness was too great to allow of his retiring at night, and instead of going to bed he would walk the floor, and the agony of his mind was so terrible that he would wring his hands and weep, beseeching the Lord with his whole soul to be merciful and reveal to his wife the cause of his great sorrow, for he himself could not break his vow of secrecy. His anguish, and my mother's, were indescribable, and when unable to endure it longer, she retired to her room, where with a broken and contrite heart she poured out her grief to Him who hath said: "If any lack wisdom let him ask of God, who giveth to all men liberally and upbraideth not."[28] "Seek and ye shall find, knock and it shall be opened unto you."[29]

My father's heart was raised at the same time in supplication, and while pleading as one would plead for life, the vision of her mind was opened, and, as darkness fleeth before the morning sun, so did her sorrow and the groveling things of earth vanish away, and before she saw the principle of celestial marriage illustrated in all its beauty and glory, together with the great exaltation and honor it would confer upon her in that immortal and celestial sphere if she would but accept it and stand in her place by her husband's side. She was also shown the woman he had taken to wife, and contemplated with joy the vast and boundless love and union which this order would bring about as well as the increase of kingdoms, power, and glory extending throughout the eternities, worlds without end.

Her soul was satisfied and filled with the Spirit of God. With a countenance beaming with joy she returned to my father, saying, "Heber, what you have kept from me the Lord has shown me." . . .

She covenanted to stand by him and honor the principle, which covenant she faithfully kept, and though her trials were often heavy and grievous to bear, her integrity was unflinching to the end.[30]

Helen Mar Whitney (1828–1896) was just a girl of fourteen when her father, Heber C. Kimball, suggested the possibility of Helen being sealed to Joseph Smith as a plural wife. Helen felt "a similar effect to a sudden shock of a small earthquake."[31] The next morning Joseph taught Helen and her parents the principle of celestial marriage, promising her "If you will take this step, it will ensure your eternal salvation and exaltation and that of your father's household and all of your kindred."[32] Forty years later she would be a fierce and verbose advocate for Mormon

women and polygamy, yet it is difficult to grasp the depth of her initial anguish. In one of her many writings she opined, "No earthly inducement could be held forth to the women who entered this order. It was to be a life-sacrifice for the sake of an everlasting glory and exaltation."[33] In 1881, she wrote an autobiography for her family including this poem. She had not yet forgotten her anguish, but wanted to share her full experience with her posterity. Interestingly, when Helen signed her name to this poem, she inserted "Smith" before "Whitney" as an afterthought.

I thought through this life my time will be my own
The step I now am taking's for eternity alone,
No one need be the wiser, through time I shall be free,
And as the past hath been, the future still will be.
To my guileless heart all free from worldly care
And full of blissful hopes—and youthful visions rare
The world seemed bright the thret'ning clouds were kept
From sight, and all looked fair but pitying angels wept.
They saw my youthful friends grow shy and cold.
And poisonous darts from sland'rous tongues were hurled,
Untutor'd heart in thy gen'rous sacrifice,
Thou dids't not weigh the cost nor know the bitter price;
Thy happy dreams all o'er thou'rt doom'd alas to be
Bar'd out from social scenes by this thy destiny,
And o'er thy sad'nd mem'ries of sweet departed joys
Thy sicken'd heart will brood and imagine future woes,
And like a fetter'd bird with wild and longing heart,
Thou'lt daily pine for freedom and murmur at thy lot;
But could'st thou see the future and view that glorious crown,
Awaiting you in Heaven you would not weep nor mourn.
Pure and exalted was thy father's aim, he saw
A glory in obeying this high celestial law,
For to thousands who've died without the light
I will bring eternal joy and make thy crown more bright.

I'd been taught to revere the Prophet of God
And receive every word as the word of the Lord.
But had this not come through my dear father's mouth,
I should ne'r have received it as God's sacred truth.[34]

Cordelia Morley Cox (1823–1915) was baptized when she was eight years old. Her parents, Lucy Gunn and Isaac Morley, had united with the Latter-day Saints in the first wave of converts in Kirtland in 1831. Just a few weeks before Cordelia's eighth birthday, Joseph Smith revealed that eight was the age of accountability.[35] Twenty years later Cordelia's parents introduced her to plural marriage. Cordelia is another example of family involvement with plural marriage to try to ensure salvation for not only the individual involved but also her family.[36]

In the spring of [18]44, plural marriage was introduced to me by my parents from Joseph Smith, asking their consent and a request to me to be his wife. Imagine if you can my feelings, to be a plural wife, something I never thought I ever could be. I knew nothing of such religion and could not accept it. Neither did I. . . . [After the Martyrdom,] I accepted Joseph Smith's desire and in 1846, January 27, was married to your father [Frederick Walter Cox] in the Nauvoo Temple. While still kneeling upon the altar, my hand clasped in his, now his wife, he gave his consent and I was sealed to Joseph Smith for eternity. I lived with your father and loved him. I was satisfied with the course I had taken. I had three little girls with him. . . .

The Latter-day Saints were preparing to leave and come to Utah. We lived in a settlement where as the Mormons moved away, the Gentiles would buy the improvements until our family was left quite alone with the outside world. Then they began to persecute us. Your father was taken into a Gentile court and tried for breaking laws of the land by living with more than one wife. I had a true companion; her husband was mine also. We were driven from our home in the dead of winter. They told us our religion was false and we had been deceived. I had no one to go to for knowledge or for comfort.

I began to worry and to wonder if I had in these ears been so deceived. I longed for a testimony from my Father in Heaven, to know for myself whether I was right or wrong. I was called a fallen woman. The finger of scorn was pointed at me. I felt that it was more than I could endure and in the humility of my soul, I prayed that I might have a testimony from him who knows the hearts of all. One night I dreamed. I thought I was in the midst of a multitude of people. President Young arose and spoke to the people. He then said there would be a spirit [to] go around to whisper comfort in the ear of everyone. All was silent as death as I sat. Then the spirit came to me and whispered in my ear these words, "Don't ever change your condition or wish it otherwise," for I was better off than thousands and thousands of others. This brought peace to my mind and I have felt satisfied ever since. The Lord has been my guide; in Him I put my trust. I am thankful that I have been true to the covenants I have made with my Father in Heaven. I am thankful for my children that have been given to me. I pray that God will accept us all, and blessed to come forth through a glorious resurrection and receive a crown of eternal life in His kingdom.[37]

Emmeline B. Wells (1828–1921) married James Harris in 1843 after her baptism the previous year. The young couple moved with his family to Nauvoo and had a son, who died shortly after birth. James left the family to seek his fortune, while his parents became disengaged from the Latter-day Saints and left Nauvoo, leaving Emmeline all alone. She taught school for the Whitney family, who took her in. Emmeline wrote this letter to Newel Whitney after he suggested plural marriage. Despite her grief at the possibility, she was sealed to Newel. Years later she would consider it as more of an adoption than a sealing.[38] When Emmeline wrote this passage, she signed it with her name at the time, Emmeline B. Harris.

When the heart is sick and the soul faint and we feel we have no friend on Earth to whom we can go with feelings of perfect confidence and trust the very mind seems ready to burst. Could I go to the Lord and tell him all but I do not know what to say. Since Friday night I have been thinking of some things which makes my heartache. What shall I do or what shall I say? Can I ever be the same happy girl again, at this time feeling as I do? I answer never, no never. When my friends are grieved on my account, what can be worse? Nothing. And yet I must keep up appearances of happiness, because if I do not, I shall be questioned. O I almost despise myself and—if I had one single soul to rest on to whom I could tell my feelings, I should feel relieved. O I could wish life were a dream, a vain delusive dream, but no, O no, it is an awful reality. I have been happy, but I fear I shall never be again. You have represented things to me strangely. I do not know what to think nor what you think of me I am afraid you have lost too much confidence to ever be restored, and yet I could wish for it, pray for it, and I believe live for it. I feel that I could resign the world for peace of mind and live alone in seclusion were it possible. If I only knew what the Lord required of me, I feel almost humble enough to do anything, and I pray that I may be made so.[39]

HOPE

"'Tis faith alone that giveth sight
To see our way thro' darkest night."[40]

Eliza R. Snow (1804–1887) wrote this poem in 1841 looking back at the persecutions of Ohio and Missouri. The poem was first published in the Nauvoo newspaper *Times and Seasons* and was subsequently published as a hymn in the 1856 Liverpool hymnal.[41]

Though outward trials throng your way,
Press on, press on, ye Saints of God!
Ere long, the resurrection day
Will spread its life and truth abroad.
What tho' our rights have been assail'd?
What tho' by foes we've been despoiled?
Jehovah's promise has not fail'd—
Jehovah's purpose is not foil'd.[42]

~ 18 ~

THE DEATH OF JOSEPH AND HYRUM SMITH

"That terrible martyrdom."[1]

When Joseph Smith visited the Nauvoo Relief Society on April 28, 1842, he prophetically told them that "the church would not have his instruction long, and the world would not be troubled with him a great while, . . . God had appointed him elsewhere."[2] Latter-day Saint women were aware of the trouble and danger surrounding Joseph Smith, and they expressed deep concern for him in their efforts to serve him before his death, to care for his family in the aftermath, and to remember him after his martyrdom.

Many women recorded the events leading up to and immediately following the martyrdom, providing a detailed record. Some knew him intimately; others revered him from a distance. The whole community of Saints mourned, both privately and publicly. Even nature itself expressed a depth of grief and despair at the time of the death and burial of Joseph and Hyrum Smith on June 27, 1844. Jane Manning James stated, "I shall never forget that time of agony and sorrow."[3]

In addition to feeling a great sense of loss over the death of their beloved Prophet, many women found hope in the promises of a loving God who would watch over, protect, and lead his Saints through this troubling transition. These women witnessed of their conviction of the Prophet as well as their loyalty to the Church of Jesus Christ.

ANTICIPATING TROUBLE

"I knew he was a servant of God, and [could] only think of the danger he was in."[4]

Mary Ellen Kimball (1818–1902) joined the Church in New York in 1842. A few months before the martyrdom she moved to Nauvoo, where she taught school. She remembered, "The death of the prophet caused us many sorrowful and lonely feelings. But his words were fresh in our memories never to be forgotten."[5]

The last time I saw the Prophet he was on his way to Carthage Jail. He and his brother Hyrum were on horseback, also Brothers John Taylor and Willard Richards. They stopped opposite Sister Clawson's house, at the house of Brother Rosencrans. We were on the porch and could hear every word he said. He asked for a drink of water. Some few remarks passed between them which I do not remember. But one sentence I well remember. After bidding goodbye, he said to Brother Rosencrans, "If I never see you again, or if I never come back, remember that I love you."

This went through me like electricity. I went in the house and threw myself on the bed and wept like a whipped child. And why this grief for a person I had never spoken to in my life, I could not tell. I knew he was a servant of God, and only think of the danger he was in, and how deeply he felt it, for I could see that he looked pale.[6]

Eunice Billings Snow (1830–1914) attended the first Relief Society meetings in Nauvoo with her mother, Diantha Morley Billings. She sang in the Nauvoo choir and attended many of Joseph's sermons.[7] She was fourteen in June 1844.

On the last day which [Joseph Smith] spent in Nauvoo, he passed our house with his brother, Hyrum, both riding. My mother and I were standing in the dooryard, and as he passed, he bowed with uplifted hat to my mother. Hyrum seemed like one in a dream, sad and despondent, taking no notice of anyone. They were on their way to the Carthage jail, and it was the last time I saw the Prophet alive. Shortly after this, my father came home and told my mother that the Prophet and his brother had been murdered, whereupon my mother exclaimed, "How can it be possible? Will the Lord allow anything like that?"[8]

Elizabeth Brotherton Pratt (1816–1897) joined the LDS Church in England in 1840 and arrived in Nauvoo in 1841. She had many opportunities to listen to the words of Joseph Smith and interact with him in Nauvoo.[9]

On the 27th of June 1844 the Prophet and Hyrum his brother were murdered in Carthage Jail. Those who took him as prisoner pledged their word and honor that he would be safe from violence. When word came to Nauvoo of their cruel deaths it was a day of mourning, weeping, and sorrow among all the Saints, for they loved the man of God who had laid down his life for the Gospel's sake. Even the atmosphere and trees seemed to mourn the fate of the murdered dead. I saw them when they were in their coffins and they were just as I saw them in a dream before I knew they were dead. This prepared me for the shock as I could not have believed it, as the Lord had preserved his life so many times.[10]

This engraving of Joseph and Hyrum Smith was created after their deaths from drawings of both men by Sutcliffe Maudsley. The image was reproduced with slight variations and appeared in many different places.

FIRSTHAND WITNESSES

"Mine eyes should witness this awful scene."[11]

> **Eliza Clayton Margetts** (1830–1901) and her family emigrated from England to Nauvoo when Eliza was ten years old. Her older brother was William Clayton, clerk for Joseph Smith. The family moved to Carthage in the fall of 1842, where twelve-year-old Eliza and her older sister Lucy observed the immediate aftermath of the martyrdom.[12] She wrote about her experience during her youth.

In the forenoon of the day on which these atrocious murders were committed some of the neighbors, disguised and with painted faces, came to our house and told mother she had better get out of the way as they were going to kill the Prophet that day. A terrific storm arose that day, and in the afternoon we heard the firing of guns and soon after saw some of the murderers run away howling like fiends. My sister Lucy who was at this time living with the jailer's family, and was at the jail when the shooting commenced, came home and told what had happened. The next day I went with my sister Lucy to the jail, we found the doors and windows open and everything in confusion, as though the people had left in great haste, we went up stairs to the room in which the Prophet and his brother had been shot, everything seemed upset, there were some Church books on the table and portraits of Joseph and Hyrum's families on the mantle piece. Blood in pools on the floor and bespattered on the walls, at sight of which we were overcome with grief and burst into tears. After becoming somewhat collected we gathered up what we supposed belonged to the inmates of the room at the time of the murder, and placed them together on a trunk that was in the room.[13]

> **Zina Diantha Huntington Young** (1821–1901), who lived in Nauvoo and had been privately sealed to Joseph Smith, recorded in her diary the events that transpired between June 24 and July 4, 1844.[14]

June 24, 1844. This night after the brethren left here for Carthage the Heavens gathered blackness, the thunder and lightning was dreadful, the storm arose in the west. . . .

June 28. This afternoon the bodies of the martyrs arrived in town. I went and heard the speeches made by our brethren and friends. They stood where Joseph last stood and addressed the brethren, or he called them sons. Went into his house for the first time and there saw the lifeless speechless bodies of the two martyrs for the testimony which they held. Little did my heart ever think that mine eyes should witness this awful scene.

June 29. The people of the city went to see their beloved Prophet and Patriarch who had laid down their lives for the cause and their Brethren. The night after the brethren were buried we had an awful thunder storm and lightning, so the mob did not come as they intended.

June 30. It is Sunday, a lonely heart-sorrowful day. Also it rains.

July 1. I washed Joseph and Hyrum's clothes. . . .

July 4. Spent the day at Sister Jones's, Carlos Smith's widow [Agnes Coolbright Smith], the girls that reside with her, Louisa Beaman, and Sister Hannah Markham. Very pleasant today, but ah what dreariness and sorrow pervades every bosom.[15]

PRIVATE MOURNING

"My poor heart does ache."[16]

Lucy Mack Smith (1775–1856) described her deep anguish at the death of her two sons when their bodies were returned to Nauvoo.

After the corpses were washed, and dressed in their burial clothes, we were allowed to see them. I had for a long time braced every nerve, roused every energy of my soul, and called upon God to strengthen me; but when I entered the room, and saw my murdered sons extended both at once before my eyes, and heard the sobs and groans of my family, and the cries of "Father! husband!

brothers!" From the lips of their wives, children, brother, and sisters, it was too much; I sank back, crying to the Lord, in the agony of my soul, "My God, my God, why hast thou forsaken this family!" A voice replied, "I have taken them to myself, that they might have rest." Emma was carried back to her room almost in a state of insensibility. Her oldest son approached the corpse, and dropped upon his knees, and laying his cheek against his father's and kissing him, exclaimed, "Oh! my father! my father!" As for myself, I was swallowed up in the depth of my afflictions; and though my soul was filled with horror past imagination, yet I was dumb, until I arose again to contemplate the spectacle before me. Oh! at that moment how my mind flew through every scene of sorrow and distress which we had passed together, in which they had shown the innocence and sympathy which filled their guileless hearts. As I looked upon their peaceful, smiling countenances, I seemed almost to hear them say, "Mother, weep not for us, we have overcome the world by love; we carried to them the gospel, that their souls might be saved; they slew us for our testimony, and thus placed us beyond their power; their ascendancy is for a moment, ours is an eternal triumph."[17]

Martha Ann Smith Harris (1841–1923) was the daughter of Mary Fielding and Hyrum Smith. Very young when her father died, she grew up listening to stories of her father and his death, which likely contributed to her memories. This account, written thirty-seven years after Hyrum's death, describes intimate details of the effect on Martha's family.[18]

I was three years old when my dear father was taken from the bosom of his family and from his friends, when he bid them the last farewell, and he gave them the last farewell kiss.

I remember well the night that he was murdered. I had the measles, I had taken cold and it had settled on my lungs, I could not speak above my breath. I begged of my dear mother to lie down to rest once. She read the Bible a while, then walk again, until the day began to dawn. There was a knock at the door. Mother asked who was there. The answer was, "George Grant." She opened the door and asked. "What is the news?" He gave answer that Joseph and Hyrum were both murdered. My poor mother stepped back calmly exclaiming, "It cannot be." He gave answer, "Yes, it is true."

She fell back against the cupboard and Brother Grant helped her to a chair. The news flew like wildfire through the house. Those cries of agony that went through the soul of everyone were terrible. The anguish and sorrow that was felt can easier be felt than described. It will never be forgotten by those who were called to pass through it.[19]

PUBLIC GRIEF

"Oh the sorrow and sadness of that day!"[20]

> **Caroline Barnes Crosby** (1807–1883) and her family arrived in Nauvoo in June 1842. She remembered the trouble of the Church when Brothers "Joseph and Hyrum were taken prisoners to Carthage, and many of us passed restless days, and sleepless nights."[21]

June 27th 1844 We arose with heavy hearts, full of doubts and fears respecting the safety of our beloved Prophet and Patriarch who were then incarcerated in Carthage jail. . . .

The next morning at an early hour, the news of Joseph and Hyrum's massacre was spread throughout the length and breadth of the city. We would not believe the first report, but finally it was confirmed to us beyond a doubt. And Oh the sorrow and sadness of that day! Many were made sick by the intelligence, others deranged. Many walked the streets mourning and wringing their hands. I lost my strength and appetite, could not attend to any business for several days. PM their bodies were brought home; and arrangements made for their burial. Everybody was invited, or rather had the privilege of seeing them by walking through the house, we went in at one door, passed by their coffins, gave them a short look, and then went out on the opposite side. They were much disfigured. I thought they did not look natural, in the least, could scarcely tell them apart.[22]

Mary Isabella Horne (1818–1905) recognized the prophetic role of Joseph Smith when she first met him and shook his hand in the summer of 1837. The Horne family moved to Nauvoo in 1839, where they often entertained the Smiths.[23]

I took my last look, on earth, of Joseph and Hyrum Smith. May I never experience another day similar to that! I do not wish to recall the scene but for a moment. That terrible martyrdom deeply scarred the hearts and bewildered the senses of all our people. We could scarcely realize the awful event, except in the agony of our feelings; nor comprehend the dark hour, beyond the solemn loneliness which pervaded the city and made the void in our stricken hearts still more terrible to bear. For the moment the sun of our life had set. The majority of the apostles were far from home, and we could do no more than wake the indignation of heaven against the murderers by our lamentations, and weep and pray for divine support in that awful hour.[24]

Vilate Murray Kimball (1806–1867) had gathered with the Saints in Kirtland. Her husband, Heber C. Kimball, was an apostle and was on a mission at the time of the martyrdom. Vilate wrote a letter to Heber on June 30, 1844, describing the events.[25]

Never before, did I take up my pen to address you under so trying circumstances as we are now placed, but as Brother Adams, the bearer of this, can tell you more than I can write I shall not attempt to describe the scene that we have passed through. God forbid that I should ever witness another like unto it. I saw the lifeless corpses of our beloved brethren when they were brought to their almost distracted families. Yea, I witnessed their tears, and groans, which was enough to rent the heart of an adamant. Every brother and sister that witnessed the scene felt deeply to sympathize with them. Yea, every heart is filled with sorrow, and the very streets of Nauvoo seem to mourn. Where it will end the Lord only knows.[26]

Eliza R. Snow (1804–1887) was known as "Zion's Poetess." She published this poem, "The Assassination of Gen'l Joseph Smith and Hyrum Smith," in the *Times and Seasons*, a Nauvoo newspaper, sharing private testimony of the prophetic loss in a public forum, giving voice to Latter-day Saints and to the world at large.

Ye heav'ns attend! Let all the earth give ear!
Let Gods and seraphs, men and angels hear—. . .
We mourn thy Prophet, from whose lips have flow'd
The words of life, thy spirt has bestow'd—. . .
Now Zion mourns—she mourns an earthly head:
The Prophet and the Patriarch are dead! . . .
True to their mission, until death, they stood,
Then seal'd their testimony with their blood.
All hearts with sorrow bleed, and ev'ry eye
Is bath'd in tears—each bosom heaves a sigh—
Heart broken widows' agonizing groans
Are mingled with the helpless orphans' moans!
Ye Saints! be still and know that God is just—
With steadfast purpose in his promise trust.[27]

Nature's Response

"Left the world in total darkness."[28]

Mary Alice Cannon Lambert (1828–1920) had many opportunities to hear Joseph Smith preach after she arrived in Nauvoo in 1843. Here she describes the shock and mourning of those in Nauvoo after the martyrdom.

I well remember the night of the Prophet's death. The spirit of unrest was upon all, man and animal, in the city of Nauvoo. . . . My father was on guard.

LINES

ON THE

ASSASSINATION OF GENERALS JOSEPH SMITH & HYRUM SMITH,

First Presidents of the Church of Latter-Day Saints,

WHO WERE

MASSACRED BY A MOB IN CARTHAGE, HANCOCK COUNTY, ILLINOIS,

ON THE TWENTY-SEVENTH JUNE, 1844.

BY MISS ELIZA R. SNOW.

And when he had opened the fifth seal, I saw under the altar, the souls of them that were slain for the word of God, and for the testimony which they held.

And they cried with a loud voice, saying, How long, O Lord, holy and true, dost thou not judge and avenge our blood on them that dwell on the earth?

And white robes were given unto every one of them; and it was said unto them, that they should rest yet for a little season, until their fellow-servants also, and their brethren, that should be killed as they were, should be fulfilled.—REV. vi. 9, 10, 11.

YE heavens attend! Let all the earth give ear!
Let Gods and seraphs, men and angels hear—
The worlds on high—the universe shall know
What awful scenes are acted here below!
Had nature's self a heart, her heart would bleed;
For never, since the Son of God was slain,
Has blood so noble, flowed from human vein
As that which now on God for vengeance calls
From "freedom's ground"—from Carthage's prison walls.

Oh, Illinois! thy soil has drank the blood
Of Prophets martyr'd for the truth of God.
Once-lov'd America! what can atone
For the pure blood of innocence, thou'st sown?
Were all thy streams in teary torrents shed
To mourn the fate of those illustrious dead:
How vain the tribute, for the noblest worth
That grac'd thy surface, O degraded Earth!

Oh, wretched murderers! fierce for human blood!
You've slain the prophets of the living God,
Who've borne oppression from their early youth,
To plant on earth the principles of truth.

Shades of our patriotic fathers! Can it be,
Beneath your blood-stain'd flag of liberty,
The firm supporters of our country's cause
Are butcher'd, while submissive to her laws?
Yes, blameless men, defam'd by hellish lies,
Have thus been offer'd as a sacrifice
T' appease the ragings of a brutish clan,
That has defied the laws of God and man!

'Twas not for crime or guilt of theirs they fell—
Against the laws they never did rebel.
True to their country, yet her plighted faith
Has prov'd an instrument of cruel death!

Where are thy far-fam'd laws—Columbia? where
Thy boasted freedom?—thy protecting care?
Is this a land of rights? Stern facts shall say,
If legal justice here maintains its sway,
The' official powers of State are sheer pretence
When they're exerted in the Saints' defence.

Great men have fallen, and mighty men have died—
Nations have mourn'd their favourites and their pride;
But TWO, so wise, so virtuous, great and good,
Before, on earth, at once have never stood

Since the creation—men whom God ordain'd
To publish truth where error long had reign'd:
Of whom the world itself unworthy proved:
It KNEW THEM NOT; but men with hatred moved
And with infernal spirits have combin'd
Against the best, the noblest of mankind!

Oh, persecution! shall thy purple hand
Spread utter destruction through the land?
Shall freedom's banner be no more unfurl'd?
Has peace, indeed, been taken from the world?

Thou God of Jacob, in this trying hour
Help us to trust in thy almighty power;
Support thy Saints beneath this awful stroke—
Make bare thine arm to break oppression's yoke.
We mourn thy Prophet, from whose lips have flow'd
The words of life thy Spirit has bestow'd—
A depth of thought no human art could reach,
From time to time, roll'd in sublimest speech
From the celestial fountain through his mind,
To purify and elevate mankind:
The rich intelligence by him brought forth
Is like the sunbeam spreading o'er the earth.

Now Zion mourns—she mourns an earthly head:
The Prophet and the Patriarch are dead!
The blackest deed that men or devils know
Since Calvary's scene, has laid the brothers low!
One in their life, and one in death—they prov'd
How strong their friendship—how they truly lov'd:
True to their mission, until death they stood,
Then seal'd their testimony with their blood.
All hearts with sorrow bleed, and every eye
Is bath'd in tears—each bosom heaves a sigh—
Heart-broken widows' agonizing groans
Are mingled with the helpless orphans' moans!

Ye Saints! be still, and know that God is just—
With steadfast purpose in his promise trust:
Girded with sackcloth, own his mighty hand,
And wait his judgments on this guilty land!
The noble martyrs now have gone to move
The cause of Zion in the courts above.

Nauvoo, July 1st, 1844.

J. HEAP,   PRINTER.

Eliza R. Snow's poem commemorating the death of Joseph and Hyrum Smith was printed in a broadside and widely distributed. It was also published in the Times and Seasons. *Eliza R. Snow, "The Assassination of Gen's Joseph Smith and Hyrum Smith,"* Times and Seasons *5, no. 12 (1 July 1844): 575.*

No one in the house had slept, the dogs were noisy, and even the chickens were awake.

About 3 o'clock the news of the martyrdom was brought to us, and we realized what had kept us awake. And oh, the mourning in the land! The grief felt was beyond expression—men, women and children, we were all stunned by the blow.[29]

Louisa Barnes Pratt (1801–1880) was the sole provider for her family in Nauvoo while her husband, Addison Pratt, was on a mission to the Pacific Islands. She experienced intense agitation with the news of the martyrdom as well as a great sense of trust. "I felt the deepest humility before God. I thought continually of his words, 'Be still and know that I am God.'"[30]

Such consternation was never known, since the rocks were rent and the sun darkened, when Christ the Lamb was slain! I had previously had a presentment that some terrible calamity was at hand, but did not believe the men would be slain! Had the sun and moon both fallen from their orbits, and left the world in total darkness, it would not have betokened a more irretrievable despoliation. I thought the church was ruined forever. I rushed into my garden, when the news was confirmed, and poured out my soul in such bitterness as I had never felt before. . . .

It was a still night, and the moon was at the full. No season was ever more sublime. A night of death, it was, and everything conspired to make it awfully solemn. The noise of war was suddenly heard, the voices of the officers were heard calling the men together and coming in the distance made it fall on the heart like a funeral knell. The women were assembled in groups, weeping and praying. Some wishing terrible punishment on the murderers, others acknowledging the hand of God in the awful event. . . .

From that hour I watched for words of comfort, and drank them in, as I would an antidote to relieve pain.[31]

Moving Forward

"The Lord has begun His work and He will carry it on."[32]

Jane Elizabeth Manning James (1822–1908) felt a distinct affinity to Joseph Smith. When she arrived in Nauvoo, Joseph and Emma Smith had welcomed her into their home and provided support and sustenance when others unfortunately had not.[33]

When he was killed, I would have liked to have died myself, if it had not been for the teachers, I felt so bad.[34] I could have died, just laid down and died; and I was sick abed, and the teachers told me, "You don't want to die because he did. He died for us, and now we all want to live and do all the good we can."[35]

Sally Carlisle Randall (1805–1874) sent detailed letters to her family and friends in the East about life in Nauvoo. This letter was written on July 1, 1844, describing the martyrdom in great detail: "One of the most horrible crimes committed that ever history recorded . . . it seemed that all nature mourned."[36]

There are many that will rejoice and think Mormonism is down now, but they will be mistaken, for the Lord has begun his work and he will carry it on in spite of all mobs and devils.[37]

Postscript

"Unto all."[1]

In the preceding pages, over one hundred different women have testified to the events of the Restoration. No two of these women lived the same experience. The women included here lived in the years between Temperance Bond Mack's birth in 1771 and Genevieve Van Wagenen's death in 2000. They came from and lived in a variety of countries and states. They joined with the Latter-day Saints at different points in their lives and for different reasons. Some would stay with the Church throughout their lives; some would choose to leave. Some of these women were married multiple times; some never married. Some had several children; some adopted children; some never bore children. Some of these women found themselves in the thick of the events of the Restoration; some bore witness from a distance. Despite all of these differences, the Restoration brought these women together.

This is only a small percentage of Latter-day Saint women's voices; there are countless others that likewise believed and testified and could teach us from their own distinct experience. Some of them didn't leave any records, yet many want to speak to us. These women took the scriptural example of women testifying and teaching and lived out their own sacred stories.

As Latter-day Saints, we are a part of this same holy narrative. These women can bring us together. We can further increase our own witnesses and expand our ability to love and serve as we learn of our sisters' experiences. We have the same charge that was given to "elect lady" Emma Smith: to "expound" and "exhort." It is the Lord's voice "unto all."[2]

Notes

INTRODUCTION

1. Laura Owen, "Defence Against the Various Charges that Have Gone Abroad," republished in *Times and Seasons* 2, no. 7 (1 February 1841): 301.

2. Ibid.; see also Laura Owen, "Defence Against the Various Charges that Have Gone Abroad," *Times and Seasons* 2, no. 4 (15 December 1840): 254–56; Laura Owen, "Defence Against the Various Charges that Have Gone Abroad," *Times and Seasons* 2, no. 6 (15 January 1841): 278–80.

3. Laura Owen, "Defence Against the Various Charges that Have Gone Abroad," *Times and Seasons* 2, no. 4 (15 December 1840): 254.

4. Bathsheba W. Smith, in Jill Mulvay Derr, Carol Cornwall Madsen, Kate Holbrook, and Matthew J. Grow, eds., *The First Fifty Years of Relief Society: Key Documents in Latter-day Saint Women's History* (Salt Lake City: The Church Historian's Press, 2016), 314.

5. John 20:4, 10, 18; see also John 20:1–18.

6. John 4:39; see also John 4:39–42.

7. 1 Nephi 5:8.

8. Alma 19:17; see also Alma 19:16–17.

9. Doctrine and Covenants 25:7.

10. Doctrine and Covenants 1:4; 11:27; and 25:16.

11. Clara Clawson, "Pioneer Stake," *Woman's Exponent* 34, no. 2–3 (July and August 1905):14.

12. Laura Owens, "Defence Against the Various Charges that Have Gone Abroad," republished in *Times and Seasons* 2, no. 4 (15 December 1840): 254.

13. Julie B. Beck, "'Daughters in My Kingdom': The History and Work of Relief Society," *Ensign*, November 2010, 114.

14. Edward W. Tullidge, *The Women of Mormondom* (New York: Tullidge and Crandall, 1877). See also Claudia L. Bushman, "Edward W. Tullidge and The Women of Mormondom," *Dialogue: A Journal of Mormon Thought* 33, no. 4 (Winter 2000): 15–27; *The Personal Writings of Eliza R. Snow*, ed. Maureen Ursenbach Beecher (Logan, Utah: Utah State University Press, 2000), 3; "Home Affairs," *Woman's Exponent* 6, no. 6 (15 August 1877): 45; "Home Affairs," *Woman's Exponent* 5, no. 12 (15 November 1876): 92–93.

15. Emmeline B. Wells, "The Jubilee Celebration," *Woman's Exponent* 20, no. 17 (15 March 1892): 132.

16. "Officers' Notes," *Young Woman's Journal* 27, no. 10 (October 1916): 626–27.

Chapter 1—Truth Restored

1. Elizabeth Ann Whitney, in Edward W. Tullidge, *The Women of Mormondom* (New York: Tullidge and Crandall, 1877), 42.
2. Nathan O. Hatch, *The Democratization of American Christianity* (New Haven, CT: Yale University Press, 1989), 3–5, 167–68.
3. Doctrine and Covenants 63:9.
4. Whitney, in Tullidge, *Women of Mormondom*, 32, 34–35; see also Elizabeth Ann Whitney, "A Leaf from an Autobiography," *Woman's Exponent* 7, no. 6 (15 August 1878): 41.
5. Followers of Thomas and Alexander Campbell established a Restoration Movement committed to restoring Christianity as found in the New Testament.
6. Whitney, in Tullidge, *Women of Mormondom*, 41–42.
7. Elizabeth Ann Whitney, "A Leaf from an Autobiography," *Woman's Exponent* 7, no. 7 (1 September 1878): 51.
8. Ibid.
9. Abigail Calkins Leonard, in Tullidge, *Women of Mormondom*, 160–61. Miller was baptized a short time before the Leonards. He later baptized Brigham Young (in 1832). See John G. Turner, *Brigham Young: Pioneer Prophet* (Cambridge, MA: Harvard University Press, 2012), 7.
10. See Tullidge, *Women of Mormondom*, 163.
11. Leonard, in Tullidge, *Women of Mormondom*, 160–63.
12. 2 Nephi 32:3.
13. Eliza R. Snow, "Sketch of My Life," in *The Personal Writings of Eliza R. Snow*, ed. Maureen Ursenbach Beecher (Logan, Utah: Utah State University Press, 2000), 8.
14. Ibid.
15. Eliza R. Snow, in Tullidge, *Women of Mormondom*, 63–64.
16. Hannah Cornaby, *Autobiography and Poems* (Salt Lake City: J. C. Graham, 1881), 9–11.
17. Ibid., 9–25.
18. Susannah Stone Lloyd, "The Sketch of Susanna Stone Lloyd," in Information on Thomas and Susanna Lloyd, ca. 1915, typescript, 3, Church History Library (CHL).
19. Ibid.

Chapter 2—Jesus Christ

1. Phebe Crosby Peck to Anna Pratt, 10 August 1832, photocopy, CHL.
2. Drusilla D. Hendricks, Reminiscences, ca. 1877, typescript, 12, CHL.
3. Moroni 7:48.
4. Nancy Naomi Alexander Tracy, "Reminiscences and Diary," typescript, 4, CHL.
5. Ibid., 4–5.
6. Janiece Johnson, *"Give It All Up and Follow Your Lord": Mormon Female Religiosity, 1831–1843* (Provo, Utah: BYU Studies, 2008), 63–69.
7. Melissa Morgan Dodge to William T. Morgan, June 1839, William T. Morgan Correspondence, 1839–1852, CHL.
8. Johnson, *"Give It All Up and Follow Your Lord,"* 19.
9. Lucy Mack Smith to Solomon Mack; Waterloo, New York; 6 January 1831, CHL.
10. Hebrews 4:16.
11. Martha James Cragun Cox, "Biographical Record of Martha Cox: Written for My Children and My Children's Children, and All Who May Care to Read It," 181–82, CHL.
12. Ibid.; emphasis in original.

13. Psalm 27:8.
14. Mary Elizabeth Rollins Lightner, "Remarks," 14 April 1905, transcript, Brigham Young University, 1–2, CHL.
15. Ibid.
16. "Obituary: Genevieve J. Van Wagenen," Deseret News, 30 September 2000.
17. Joseph Smith, Editorial, *Elders' Journal* 1, no. 3 (July 1838): 44.
18. Genevieve Johnson Van Wagenen, in "History of the Young Women: Our Stories," https://www.lds.org/callings/young-women/leader-resources/history/our-stories.
19. Carol Cornwall Madsen and Cherry B. Silver, "'I Believe in Women, Especially Thinking Women': Emmeline Blanche Woodward Wells (1828–1921)," in *Women of Faith in the Latter Days: Volume Two, 1821–1845*, ed. Richard E. Turley Jr. and Brittany A. Chapman (Salt Lake City: Deseret Book, 2012), 384–86.
20. Ethel C. Lund Oral History, interviewed by Davis Bitton, 1986–1987, typescript, James Moyle Oral History Program, preface, 122, CHL.
21. Ibid., 123–24.
22. Moroni 10:4.
23. Johnson, *"Give Up All and Follow Your Lord,"* 29–32.
24. Rebecca Williams to Isaac Swain, 12 June 1834, CHL.
25. Johnson, *"Give Up All and Follow Your Lord,"* 25–27.
26. Phebe Crosby Peck to Anna Pratt, 10 August 1832, CHL.
27. Laura Farnsworth Owen, Autobiography, CHL.
28. Ibid., 17.

CHAPTER 3—THE BOOK OF MORMON

1. Emma Smith, in Joseph Smith III, "Last Testimony of Sister Emma," *Saints' Herald* 26, no. 19 (1 October 1879): 290.
2. Drusilla Dorris Hendricks, "Historical Sketch of James Hendricks and Drusilla Dorris Hendricks," in *Henry Hendricks Genealogy: A Record of the Ancestry and Descendants of Henry & Sarah (Thompson) Hendricks of Monmouth Co., New Jersey, With Notes on Related Families Including Dorris, Frost, Parsell, Hinton, Schenck, Couwenhoven, Van Pelt and Wyckoff*, ed. Marguerite H. Allen (Salt Lake City: Hendricks Family Organization, 1963), 13.
3. Zina D. H. Young, "How I Gained My Testimony," *Young Woman's Journal* 4, no. 7 (April 1893): 318.
4. "The Testimony of Three Witnesses," Book of Mormon.
5. Kyle R. Walker, "Katharine Smith Salisbury," in *United in Faith: The Joseph Sr. and Lucy Mack Smith Family* (American Fork, Utah: Covenant Communications, 2005), 309–10.
6. Katharine Smith Salisbury to "Dear Sisters," 10 March 1886, in *Saints' Herald* 33, no. 17 (1 May 1886): 260.
7. Mark L. Staker, "'A Comfort unto My Servant, Joseph': Emma Hale Smith (1804–1879)," in *Women of Faith in the Latter Days: Volume One, 1775–1820*, ed. Richard E. Turley Jr. and Brittany A. Chapman (Salt Lake City: Deseret Book, 2011), 343–56.
8. Linda King Newell and Valeen Tippetts Avery, *Mormon Enigma: Emma Hale Smith* (Urbana: University of Illinois Press, 1994), 300–301.
9. Smith, in Joseph Smith III, "Last Testimony of Sister Emma," 289–90.
10. Ronald E. Romig, "Elizabeth Ann Whitmer Cowdery: A Historical Reflection of Her Life," *Mormon Historical Studies* 7, nos. 1, 2 (spring, fall 2006): 1–2.
11. Alma 37:23.

12. Elizabeth Ann Whitmer Cowdery, Affidavit, 15 February 1870, in *Early Mormon Documents*, ed. Dan Vogel (Salt Lake City: Signature Books, 2003), 5:260.

13. "The Testimony of Three Witnesses," Book of Mormon.

14. Andrew Jenson, "Mary Musselman Whitmer," in *Latter-day Saint Biographical Encyclopedia* (Salt Lake City: Deseret News, 1901), 1:283; and Robin Scott Jensen, "A Bit of Old String: Mary Whitmer's Unheralded Contributions," history.lds.org, accessed 18 April 2016.

15. Statement of John C. Whitmer, quoted in Andrew Jenson, "Still Another Witness," *The Historical Record* 7, nos. 8–10 (October 1888): 621. Parenthetical comments in original.

16. Eliza R. Snow, "Sketch of My Life," in *The Personal Writings of Eliza R. Snow*, ed. Maureen Ursenbach Beecher (Logan, Utah: Utah State University Press, 2000), 8–9.

17. Edward W. Tullidge, *The Women of Mormondom* (New York: Tullidge and Crandall, 1877), 63–64.

18. Johnson, *"Give It All Up and Follow Your Lord,"* 29–32.

19. Probably a reference to the nine letters of Ezra Booth that were published in the *Ohio Star* in 1831. In Booth's third letter, he refutes the testimony of the Three Witnesses to the Book of Mormon. Ezra Booth, "Mormonism—No. III," *Ohio Star* (27 October 1831).

20. In the first edition Book of Mormon (1830), these pages are in Ether 2, where Moroni prophesied of the three witnesses. See Ether 5:3 in the current edition.

21. Rebecca Swain Williams to Isaac Swain (1834), CHL.

22. Moroni 10:4.

23. Jennifer Reeder, "'Power for the Accomplishment of Greater Good': Zina Diantha Huntington Young (1821–1901)," in *Women of Faith in the Latter Days: Volume Two, 1821–1845*, ed. Richard E. Turley Jr. and Brittany A. Chapman (Salt Lake City: Deseret Book, 2012), 443, 447–51.

24. Zina D. H. Young, "How I Gained My Testimony," *Young Woman's Journal* 4, no. 7 (April 1893): 318.

25. See Caroline Barnes Crosby, in *No Place to Call Home: The 1807–1857 Life Writings of Caroline Barnes Crosby, Chronicler of Outlying Mormon Communities*, Life Writings of Frontier Women 7, ed. Edward Leo Lyman, Susan Ward Payne, and S. George Ellsworth, (Logan, Utah: Utah State University Press, 2005), 3–4, 17, 31–32.

26. Crosby, in *No Place to Call Home*, ed. Lyman, Payne, and Ellsworth, 32.

27. Sarah P. Rich, Autobiography and Journal, 1885–1890, 1, 13, 23, 25, CHL.

28. Ibid., 25–26.

29. Janiece Johnson, "'My Happy Soul Is Witness': Laura Farnsworth Owen (1806–1881)," in *Women of Faith in the Latter Days: Volume One, 1775–1820*, ed. Richard E. Turley Jr. and Brittany A. Chapman (Salt Lake City: Deseret Book, 2011), 193, 195.

30. Laura Farnsworth Owen, "Mrs. Laura Owen's Defence Against the Various Charges That Have Gone Abroad," Times and Seasons 2, no. 7 (1 February 1841): 301.

CHAPTER 4—REVELATION

1. Mary Fielding to Mercy Thompson, August–September 1837, Mary Fielding Smith Collection, CHL.

2. Doctrine and Covenants 1:17.

3. Ralph Waldo Emerson, in Jeffrey R. Holland, "Prophets, Seers, and Revelators," *Ensign*, November 2004, 8.

4. Jeffrey R. Holland, "Cast Not Away Therefore Your Confidence," BYU Devotional Address, 2 March 1999, 6, speeches.byu.edu, retrieved 14 April 2016.

5. "The Best Learning," *Woman's Exponent* 2, no. 11 (1 November 1873): 86.

6. David Holland, *Sacred Borders: Continuing Revelation and Canonical Restraint in Early America* (Oxford, New York: Oxford University Press, 2011), 127–69.

7. Doctrine and Covenants 76:7.

8. Karen Lynn Davidson and Jill Mulvay Derr, *Eliza: The Life and Faith of Eliza R. Snow* (Salt Lake City: Deseret Book, 2013), 12–15.

9. Eliza R. Snow, "Human Life—What Is It?" Western Courier, 14 February 1829, as cited in *Eliza R. Snow: The Complete Poetry*, ed. Jill Mulvay Derr and Karen Lynn Davidson (Provo, Utah: BYU Press; Salt Lake City: University of Utah Press, 2009), 26.

10. Janiece Johnson, *"Give It All Up and Follow Your Lord": Mormon Female Religiosity, 1831–1843*, (Provo, Utah: BYU Studies, 2008), 25–27.

11. The vision was first published in *The Evening and the Morning Star* in July 1832. See Matthew C. Godfrey, Mark Ashurst-McGee, Grant Underwood, Robert J. Woodford, William G. Hartley, eds., *Documents, Volume 2: July 1831–January 1833*, vol. 2 of Documents series of *The Joseph Smith Papers*, ed. Dean C. Jessee, Ronald K. Esplin, and Richard Lyman Bushman (Salt Lake City: The ChurchHistorian's Press, 2013), 183–206.

12. Phebe Peck to Anna Pratt, 10 August 1832, CHL.

13. Elizabeth Ann Whitney, in Edward Tullidge, *The Women of Mormondom* (New York: Tullidge and Crandall, 1877), 32–35.

14. Elizabeth Ann Whitney, "A Leaf from an Autobiography," *Woman's Exponent* 7, no. 5 (1 August 1878): 33.

15. Doctrine and Covenants 112:10.

16. Johnson, *"Give It All Up and Follow Your Lord,"* 41, 47.

17. Mary Fielding to Mercy Thompson, August–September 1837, Mary Fielding Smith Collection, CHL.

18. Amanda Barnes Smith, Autobiography, 1858, 4, 8, CHL; Tullidge, *Women of Mormondom*, 123.

19. Amanda Barnes Smith, in Tullidge, *Women of Mormondom*, 123–24, 128.

20. Johnson, *"Give It All Up and Follow Your Lord,"* 73, 78.

21. Will R. Holmes (grandson), in Irene H. Budge and Beatrice H. Burgoyne, "Morris Phelps," in Edith Parker Haddock et al., *History of the Bear Lake Pioneers* (Salt Lake City: Daughters of Utah Pioneers, 1968), 601.

22. Parley P. Pratt, *Autobiography of Parley Parker Pratt* (Chicago: Law, King & Law, 1888), 266–67.

23. Will R. Holmes, "Morris Phelps," 601.

24. Johnson, *"Give It All Up and Follow Your Lord,"* 78–79.

25. Parley P. Pratt, *Una voz de amonestación* [A Voice of Warning] (Mexico: El Elder Moises Thatcher, 1880).

26. Clinton D. Christensen, "Solitary Saint in Mexico: Desideria Quintanar de Yañez," in *Women of Faith in the Latter Days: Volume One, 1775–1820*, ed. Richard E. Turley Jr. and Brittany A. Chapman (Salt Lake City: Deseret Book, 2011), 461–72.

27. José María Yañez, as quoted in Alonzo L. Taylor, Journal, 10 July 1903, CHL.

28. Doctrine and Covenants 6:15.

29. Sarah P. Rich, Autobiography and Journal, 1885–1890, 25–26, CHL.

30. Ibid., 26–30.

31. Mary L. Ransom and Sarah Webb, "Biography and Resolutions," *Woman's Exponent* 30, no. 14 (15 May 1902): 111.

32. W. E. [Wilmirth East], "Woman's Agency," *Woman's Exponent* 1, no. 16 (15 January 1873): 125.

33. Sketch of Jane Smith Coleman, https://familysearch.org/photos/documents/7072264,

accessed 14 April 2016; Betsey Smith Goodwin, Memoirs, https://familysearch.org/photos/stories/2170747, accessed 14 April 2016.

34. Jane Smith Coleman, "Words of Encouragement," *Woman's Exponent* 2, no. 16 (15 January 1874): 127.

35. Linda King Newell and Valeen Tippetts Avery, *Mormon Enigma: Emma Hale Smith, 2nd ed.* (Urbana: University of Illinois Press, 1994), 25–26, 31–34, 190.

36. Emma Smith, blessing, 1844, typescript, CHL.

Chapter 5—Joseph Smith

1. Sarah A. Workman, "Joseph Smith, the Prophet," *Young Woman's Journal* 17, no. 12 (December 1906): 542.

2. Lucy Mack Smith, "The History of Lucy Smith Mother of the Prophet," 1845, CHL; also available at josephsmithpapers.org; Lucy Mack Smith, *History of Joseph Smith by His Mother,* ed. Scot Facer Proctor and Maurine Jensen Proctor (Salt Lake City: Bookcraft, 1996); Lucy Mack Smith, *Lucy's Book: A Critical Edition of Lucy Mack Smith's Family Memoir,* ed. Lavina Fielding Anderson (Salt Lake City: Signature Books, 2001).

3. Zilpha C. Williams to Samuel Cilley, 16 July 1845, CHL.

4. See Susan E. J. Martineau, Sarah A. Workman, "Joseph Smith, the Prophet," *Young Woman's Journal* 17, no. 12 (December 1906): 541–42; Jane Manning James, "Joseph Smith, the Prophet," *Young Woman's Journal* 16, no. 12 (December 1905): 551–53.

5. Jane Manning James was in her early twenties when she arrived in Nauvoo and met Joseph Smith. She wrote of his kindness to her and of his handsome physical appearance. Jane Manning James, "Joseph Smith, the Prophet," Young Woman's Journal 16, no. 12 (December 1905): 552–53.

6. Mary A. Noble, "A Journal of Mary A. Noble," in Joseph Bates Noble Reminiscences, 1836–1866, CHL.

7. Ibid.

8. Her Children, *Life Sketch of Mary Alice Cannon Lambert* (Salt Lake City, 1908), 1–5.

9. Mary Alice Cannon Lambert, "Joseph Smith, the Prophet," *Young Woman's Journal* 16, no. 12 (December 1905): 554.

10. Carol Cornwall Madsen and Cherry B. Silver, "'I Believe in Women, Especially Thinking Women': Emmeline Blanche Woodward Wells (1828–1921)," in *Women of Faith in the Latter Days: Volume Two, 1821–1845*, ed. Richard E. Turley Jr. and Brittany A. Chapman (Salt Lake City: Deseret Book, 2012), 384.

11. Emmeline B. Wells, "Joseph Smith, the Prophet," *Young Woman's Journal* 16, no. 12 (December 1905): 555–56.

12. Bathsheba W. Smith, "Joseph Smith, the Prophet," *Young Woman's Journal* 16, no. 12 (December 1905): 549.

13. Ibid., 549–50.

14. Annie Wells Cannon, "Jane Snyder Richards: In Memoriam," *Woman's Exponent* 41, no. 3 (November 1912): 17.

15. Jane Snyder Richards, "Joseph Smith, the Prophet," *Young Woman's Journal* 16, no. 12 (December 1905): 550.

16. Margaret Pierce Whitesides Young, "Journal Excerpts," typescript, (n.d.), 1–2, CHL.

17. Ibid.

18. "A Representative Woman: Mary Isabella Horne," *Woman's Exponent* 10, no. 24 (15 May

1882): 185; "A Representative Woman: Mary Isabella Horne," *Woman's Exponent* 11, no. 1 (1 June 1882): 1.

19. Mary Isabella Horne, "Testimony," 10 June 1905, CHL.

20. Eliza R. Snow, "Sketch of My Life," in *The Personal Writings of Eliza R. Snow*, ed. Maureen Ursenbach Beecher (Logan, Utah: Utah State University Press, 2000), 11.

21. Jennifer Reeder, "'The Blessing of the Lord has Attended Me': Mercy Fielding Thompson," in *Women of Faith in the Latter Days: Volume One, 1775–1820*, ed. Richard E. Turley Jr. and Brittany A. Chapman (Salt Lake City: Deseret Book, 2011), 420–21; Mercy Fielding Thompson, "Recollections of the Prophet Joseph Smith," *The Juvenile Instructor* 27, no. 13 (1 July 1892): 398.

22. A literary institution, lecture hall, or teaching place.

23. Mercy Fielding Thompson, "Recollections of the Prophet Joseph Smith," *The Juvenile Instructor* 27, no. 13 (1 July 1892): 398–99.

24. Eliza R. Snow, "Sketch of My Life," 9–11; Eliza R. Snow, "Past and Present," Woman's Exponent 15, no. 5 (1 August 1886): 37.

25. See 1 Thessalonians 5:21.

26. Eliza R. Snow, "Sketch of My Life," 9–11.

CHAPTER 6—PRIESTHOOD

1. Eliza R. Snow, in Edward W. Tullidge, *The Women of Mormondom* (New York: Tullidge and Crandall, 1877), 64.

2. See *Daughters in My Kingdom: The History and Work of Relief Society* (Salt Lake City: The Church of Jesus Christ of Latter-day Saints, 2011), 127.

3. Doctrine and Covenants 132:45.

4. "Death of Mary Ann Pratt," *Woman's Exponent* 20, no. 5 (1 September 1891): 36–37.

5. See Revelation 14:7.

6. See Mark 16:16.

7. Mary Ann M. Pratt, "Questions Answered," *Woman's Exponent* 10, no. 21 (1 April 1882): 162.

8. Eliza R. Snow, "Sketch of My Life," in *The Personal Writings of Eliza R. Snow*, ed. Maureen Ursenbach Beecher (Logan, Utah: Utah State University Press, 2000), 6–9.

9. Snow, in Tullidge, *Women of Mormondom*, 96.

10. Doctrine and Covenants 25:5.

11. Kenneth W. Godfrey, Audrey M. Godfrey, and Jill Mulvay Derr, eds., *Women's Voices: An Untold History of the Latter-Day Saints, 1830–1900* (Salt Lake City: Deseret Book, 1982), 46.

12. Caroline Barnes Crosby, "Reminiscences, undated," ca. 1871–1875, Jonathan Crosby and Caroline B. Crosby papers, 34–35, CHL.

13. "Martha Horne Tingey," *Young Woman's Journal* 16, no. 6 (June 1905): 260; Andrew Jenson, *Latter-day Saint Biographical Encyclopedia* (Salt Lake City: Andrew Jenson Memorial Association, 1936), 4:74–75.

14. Mattie J. Horne, "Young Ladies' Address," *Woman's Exponent* 2, no. 16 (15 January 1874): 123.

15. Doctrine and Covenants 107:18.

16. Cyrena D. Merrill, Autobiography, 1897–1905, typescript, CHL.

17. Ibid.

18. Heber C. Kimball, Biography, josephsmithpapers.org, accessed 30 January 2016.

19. Vilate Kimball, in Tullidge, *Women of Mormondom*, 113.

20. Nancy M. Tracy, "Autobiography: Life and Travels of Nancy M. Tracy," *Woman's Exponent* 38, no. 2 (August 1909): 15–16.

21. Nancy M. Tracy, "Autobiography: Life and Travels of Nancy M. Tracy," *Woman's Exponent* 38, no. 3 (September 1909): 17.

22. Margarette McIntire Burgess, "Recollections of the Prophet Joseph Smith," *The Juvenile Instructor* 27, no. 2 (15 January 1892): 66.

23. Ibid.

24. Doctrine and Covenants 25:7. This section was a revelation given to Emma Smith.

25. Emmeline B. Wells, "A Representative Woman: Mary Isabella Horne," *Woman's Exponent* 10, no. 24 (15 May 1882): 185; Emmeline B. Wells, "A Representative Woman: Mary Isabella Horne," *Woman's Exponent* 11, no. 1 (1 June 1882): 1; Jill Mulvay Derr, Carol Cornwall Madsen, Kate Holbrook, and Matthew J. Grow, eds., *The First Fifty Years of Relief Society: Key Documents in Latter-day Saint Women's History* (Salt Lake City: The Church Historian's Press, 2016), 651; Emmeline B. Wells, "A Representative Woman: Mary Isabella Horne," *Woman's Exponent* 11, no. 9 (1 October 1882): 67.

26. Mary Isabella Horne, "To the Presidents and Members of the Relief Society of Salt Lake Stake of Zion, *Greeting!*," *Woman's Exponent* 6, no. 16 (15 January 1878): 123.

27. Mary Tyndale Ferguson, "Biography of Mary Tyndale Ferguson (Pioneer)," typescript, 1–4, Daughters of Utah Pioneers, Goshen, UT.

28. Mary Baxter, "Address," *Woman's Exponent* 35, no. 8 (March 1907): 58.

29. Andrew Jenson, *Latter-day Saint Biographical Encyclopedia* (Salt Lake City: Andrew Jenson History Company, 1936), 4:186–87.

30. Alice Merrill Horne, in Emmeline B. Wells, "General Relief Society Conference," *Woman's Exponent* 38, no. 9 (April 1910): 69.

31. Jill Mulvay Derr and Carol Cornwall Madsen, "'Something Better' for the Sisters: Joseph Smith and the Female Relief Society of Nauvoo," in *Joseph Smith and the Doctrinal Restoration* (Provo, Utah: BYU Religious Studies Center, 2005), 123–43.

32. Nauvoo Relief Society Minutes, 1842–1844, 31 March 1842, 22, CHL, in Derr et al., *First Fifty Years of Relief Society,* 43.

33. Nauvoo Relief Society Minutes, 1842–1844, 28 April 1842, 36–37, 40, CHL, in Derr et al., *First Fifty Years of Relief Society,* 55–59.

Chapter 7—Sharing the Gospel

1. Lucy Mack Smith to Solomon Mack, 6 January 1831, CHL.

2. "Autobiography of Sarah B. Layton," *Woman's Exponent* 29, nos. 8, 9 (15 September, 1 October 1900): 35; "Autobiography of Sarah B. Layton," *Woman's Exponent* 29, nos. 12, 13 (15 November, 1 December 1900): 55. Ann Sophia Jones Rosser one day distributed fifty tracts and sold seven copies of the Book of Mormon. Elmer B. Edwards, "A Faithful Sister," *The Latter-day Saints' Millennial Star* 78, no. 18 (4 May 1916): 278.

3. Juanita L. Pulsipher [Brooks], ed., *History of Sarah Studevant Leavitt, from her Journal, 1875* (Salt Lake City: Paragon Printing, 1920), 5.

4. Janiece Johnson, *"Give It All Up and Follow Your Lord": Mormon Female Religiosity, 1831–1843* (Provo, Utah: BYU Studies, 2008), 24, 52–53. See also Whittemore Family Papers, Michigan Historical Collections, University of Michigan; Ann Arbor, Michigan.

5. Mercy Fielding Thompson, Autobiographical Sketch, 1880, 1–2, CHL.

6. See Caroline Barnes Crosby, in *No Place to Call Home: The 1807–1857 Life Writings of Caroline Barnes Crosby, Chronicler of Outlying Mormon Communities,* Life Writings of Frontier Women 7, ed. Edward Leo Lyman, Susan Ward Payne, and S. George Ellsworth (Logan, Utah: Utah State University Press, 2005). See Louisa Barnes Pratt, in *The History of Louisa Barnes Pratt: Mormon*

Missionary Widow and Pioneer, Life Writings of Frontier Women 3, ed. S. George Ellsworth (Logan, Utah: Utah State University Press, 1998), xiii–xiv.

7. See Edward W. Tullidge, *The Women of Mormondom* (New York: Tullidge and Crandall, 1877), 413.

8. See 1 Nephi 8:12.

9. Doctrine and Covenants 2:2.

10. Irene Bates, "Lucy Mack Smith—First Mormon Mother," in *Lucy's Book: A Critical Edition of Lucy Mack Smith's Family Memoir*, ed. Lavina Fielding Anderson (Salt Lake City: Signature Books, 2001), 2–10.

11. Lucy Smith to Solomon Mack, 6 January 1831, CHL.

12. Almira Mack Covey to Harriett Whittemore, 19 January 1840, Harriet Mack Whittemore correspondence, CHL; in Johnson, *"Give It All Up and Follow Your Lord,"* 51–53; original in Whittemore Family Papers.

13. Temperance Mack to Harriett Whittemore, 21 October 1845, L. Tom Perry Special Collections, BYU; original in Whittemore Family Papers.

14. Temperance Mack to Harriett Whittemore, 16 September 1841, L. Tom Perry Special Collections, BYU; original in Whittemore Family Papers.

15. Johnson, *"Give Up All and Follow Your Lord,"* 52.

16. Almira Covey to Harriet Whittemore, 9 June 1835, L. Tom Perry Special Collections, BYU; original in Whittemore Family Papers.

17. Johnson, *"Give Up All and Follow Your Lord,"* 25–26.

18. Phebe Crosby Peck to Anna Pratt, 10 August 1832, CHL.

19. The letter also included a message to Patty Crosby, Phebe's sister. Phebe Crosby Peck to Anna Pratt, 10 August 1832, CHL.

20. Reed Smoot, Conference Address, Conference Report, October 1923, 76–77.

21. Kirstine Mauritz-datter, letter, 1 September 1854, in Smoot, Conference Address, 77.

22. Doctrine and Covenants 4:3.

23. Steven L. Staker, "'I Had Made God My Friend': Elizabeth Anderson Howard (1823–1893)," in *Women of Faith in the Latter Days: Volume Two, 1821–1845*, ed. Richard E. Turley Jr. and Brittany A. Chapman (Salt Lake City: Deseret Book, 2012), 113–14.

24. Elizabeth Anderson Howard, Autobiography, typescript in "William and Elizabeth Anderson Howard," comp. Sydney Howard Minette, L. Tom Perry Special Collections, BYU.

25. Janiece Johnson, "'My Happy Soul Is Witness': Laura Farnsworth Owen (1806–1881)," in *Women of Faith in the Latter Days: Volume One, 1775–1820*, ed. Richard E. Turley Jr. and Brittany A. Chapman (Salt Lake City: Deseret Book, 2011), 193–98.

26. Laura Owen, "Defence Against the Various Charges That Have Gone Abroad," *Times and Seasons* 2, no. 7 (1 February 1841): 301.

27. Doctrine and Covenants 88:81.

28. Hannah Tapfield King, in Tullidge, *Women of Mormondom*, 456–57.

29. Hannah Tapfield King, Autobiography, vol. 3, ca. 1864, CHL; see 1 Thessalonians 5:21.

30. Kenneth W. Godfrey, Audrey M. Godfrey, and Jill Mulvay Derr, eds., *Women's Voices: An Untold History of the Latter-Day Saints, 1830–1900* (Salt Lake City: Deseret Book, 1982), 26.

31. Juanita Leavitt Pulsipher [Brooks], "History of Sarah Studevant Leavitt," typescript, 1919, 5–7, CHL.

32. See Elizabeth Lewis Jones, Edward Tullidge, *Women of Mormondom*, 460–61; "Death of Sister Jones," *Deseret Evening News*, 6 May 1893.

33. Elizabeth Lewis, to "Dear Brother in the Gospel," 1851; published in *Udgorn Seion* [*Zion's*

Trumpet, or Star of the Saints], no. 17 (23 August, 1851); reprinted in *Zion's Trumpet: 1851 Welsh Mormon Periodical,* trans. and ed. Ronald D. Dennis (Provo, Utah: BYU Religious Studies Center; and Salt Lake City: Deseret Book, 2012), 272–74.

34. Doctrine and Covenants 4:4.
35. Louisa Barnes Pratt, in *The History of Louisa Barnes Pratt,* xv.
36. Louisa Barnes Pratt, in Tullidge, *Women of Mormondom,* 449–50.

CHAPTER 8—CONSECRATION

1. Elizabeth Ann Whitney, "A Leaf from an Autobiography," *Woman's Exponent* 7, no. 7 (1 September 1878): 51.
2. Doctrine and Covenants 38:27.
3. Doctrine and Covenants 82:19.
4. See Steven C. Harper, "All Things Are the Lord's," in *The Doctrine and Covenants: Revelations in Context,* ed. Andrew H. Hedges, J. Spencer Fluhman, and Alonzo L. Gaskill (Provo, Utah: BYU Religious Studies Center; Salt Lake City: Deseret Book, 2008), 212–27.
5. Doctrine and Covenants 42:30.
6. Doctrine and Covenants 51:3.
7. Gordon B. Hinckley, *Teachings of Gordon B. Hinckley* (Salt Lake City: Deseret Book, 1997), 639.
8. See Harper, "All Things are the Lord's," 212–27.
9. "Great Events Transpiring," *Woman's Exponent* 35, no. 7 (February 1907): 52.
10. Doctrine and Covanants 42:2.
11. Emily M. Austin, *Mormonism; or, Life Among the Mormons* (Madison, WI: M.J. Cantwell, 1882), 1–86.
12. Ibid., 66–67.
13. Karen Lynn Davidson and Jill Mulvay Derr, *Eliza: The Life and Faith of Eliza R. Snow* (Salt Lake City: Deseret Book, 2013), 22.
14. Eliza R. Snow, in Box Elder Relief Society Minutes, 1875–1884, 10 September 1878, CHL.
15. Helen Mar Whitney, "Scenes and Incidents at Winter Quarters," *Woman's Exponent* 14, no. 13 (1 December 1885): 98.
16. Ibid.
17. H. L., "Woman's Voice," *Woman's Exponent* 5, no. 1 (15 June 1876): 14.
18. Doctrine and Covenants 42:30.
19. Nauvoo Relief Society Minutes, 1842–1844, 17 March 1842, 22–23, CHL; Jill Mulvay Derr, Carol Cornwall Madsen, Kate Holbrook, and Matthew J. Grow, eds., *The First Fifty Years of Relief Society: Key Documents in Latter-day Saint Women's History* (Salt Lake City: The Church Historian's Press, 2016), 43.
20. Eliza R. Snow, "The Female Relief Society: What is It?" *Times and Seasons* 3, no. 17 (1 July 1842), 846.
21. Jane Manning James, Biography, 1902, 21, CHL; Linda King Newell and Valeen Tippetts Avery, "Jane Manning James: Black Saint, 1847 Pioneer," *Ensign,* August 1979.
22. Eliza P. Lyman, Journal, 1846–1885, 45–47, CHL.
23. Edward Tullidge, *The Women of Mormondom* (New York: Tullidge and Crandall, 1877), 460–61.
24. "Wife of the Famous Dan Jones," in Tullidge, *Women of Mormondom,* 460–61.
25. Doctrine and Covenants 82:18.
26. Derr et al., *First Fifty Years of Relief Society,* 655.
27. Sarah M. Kimball, "Autobiography," *Woman's Exponent* 12, no. 7 (1 September 1883): 51.

28. Doctrine and Covenants 82:18.

29. M. A. F. J., "Personal Development: 'There, is no excellence without Labor,'" *Woman's Exponent* 1, no. 1 (1 June 1872): 2.

30. "Mrs. [Alvira] Cox Dies," *Salt Lake Herald*, 22 May 1913.

31. A. L. Cox, "Dear Exponent," *Woman's Exponent* 3, no. 2 (15 June 1874):10.

32. "History of Joseph Hyrum Hanks and Almira Sophronia Jackman Hanks," https://family search.org/photos/stories/5769287, accessed 20 April 2016.

33. Almira Jackman, "R.S. Reports," *Woman's Exponent* 4, no. 21 (1 April 1876): 162.

34. "In Memoriam. Mary Ellen and Ruth Reese Kimball," *Woman's Exponent* 31, nos . 15, 16 (February 1903): 60–61.

35. M. E. Kimball, "An Address to the Juvenile Relief Society of the 17th Ward," *Woman's Exponent* 3, no. 17 (1 February 1875): 132. See Alma 34:28–29.

36. Emmeline Wells, "Woman's Council: National and International," *Woman's Exponent* 32, no. 5 (October 1903): 36.

37. Blanche Beechwood [Emmeline Wells], "Why, Ah! Why," *Woman's Exponent* 3, no. 9 (30 September 1874): 67.

38. Doctrine and Covenants 59:5.

39. Derr et al., *First Fifty Years of Relief Society*, 684; "N. K. Whitney & Co.," http://josephsmith papers.org/topic/n-k-whitney-co?p=1&highlight=ashery, accessed 20 April 2016.

40. Elizabeth Ann Whitney, "A Leaf from an Autobiography," *Woman's Exponent* 7, no. 7 (1 September 1878): 51.

41. Elizabeth Ann Whitney, "A Leaf from an Autobiography," *Woman's Exponent* 7, no. 9 (1 October 1878): 71.

42. Carol Cornwall Madsen and Cherry B. Silver, "'I Believe in Women, Especially Thinking Women': Emmeline Blanche Woodward Wells (1828–1921)," in *Women of Faith in the Latter Days: Volume Two, 1821–1845*, ed. Richard E. Turley Jr. and Brittany A. Chapman (Salt Lake City: Deseret Book, 2012), 384–97.

43. Emmeline Wells, "Editorial Thoughts," *Woman's Exponent* 16, no. 13 (1 December 1887): 100; see James 1:5.

44. Josephine Meyer Morris, Obituary, *Salt Lake Telegram*, 15 December 1923.

45. Josephine Meyer, "Humility," *Woman's Exponent* 5, no. 15 (1 January 1877): 119.

46. Lisa Olsen Tait, "'Thank God That I Have Been Counted Worthy,' Susa Amelia Young Dunford Gates (1856–1933)," in *Women of Faith in the Latter-days: Volume Three, 1846–1870*, ed. Richard E. Turley Jr. and Brittany A. Chapman (Salt Lake City: Deseret Book, 2014), 57–68.

47. Susa Young Gates, "Consecration," *Young Woman's Journal* 21:9 (September 1910): 502.

CHAPTER 9—GIFTS OF THE SPIRIT

1. Elizabeth Ann Whitney, "A Leaf from an Autobiography," *Woman's Exponent* 7, no. 11 (1 November 1878): 83.

2. Mark 16:17–18.

3. Richard L. Bushman, *Joseph Smith: Rough Stone Rolling* (New York: Alfred A. Knopf, 2005) 147–52.

4. Articles of Faith 1:7.

5. Doctrine and Covenants 109:36–37; see also Acts 2:1–4.

6. Acts 2:4.

7. Kenneth W. Godfrey, Audrey M. Godfrey, and Jill Mulvay Derr, eds., *Women's Voices: An Untold History of the Latter-day Saints, 1830–1900* (Salt Lake City: Deseret Book, 1982), 58.

8. Mary Fielding Smith to Mercy Fielding Thompson, 8 July 1837, 1–2, CHL.

9. Gary L. Boatright Jr., "'My Feet Never Slipped': Presendia Lathrop Huntington Kimball (1810–1891)," in *Women of Faith in the Latter Days: Volume One, 1775–1820*, ed. Richard E. Turley Jr. and Brittany A. Chapman (Salt Lake City: Deseret Book, 2011), 81–82.

10. Zina Diantha Huntington Jacobs Young.

11. See Doctrine and Covenants 109:37; Acts 2:2; see also Presendia Kimball, in Emmeline B. Wells, "A Venerable Woman: Presendia Lathrop Kimball," *Woman's Exponent* 11, no. 18 (15 February 1883): 139.

12. Doctrine and Covenants 46:24–25.

13. Zina Huntington Young, *Young Woman's Journal* 4, no. 7 (April 1893): 317–19.

14. Ibid.

15. Elizabeth Ann Whitney, "A Leaf from an Autobiography," *Woman's Exponent* 7, no. 6 (15 August 1878): 41; Emmeline B. Wells, "Elizabeth Ann Whitney," *Woman's Exponent* 10, no. 20 (15 March 1882): 153–54.

16. Elizabeth Ann Whitney, "A Leaf from an Autobiography," *Woman's Exponent* 7, no. 11 (1 November 1878): 83.

17. Emmeline B. Wells, "Elizabeth Ann Whitney," *Woman's Exponent* 10, no. 20 (15 March 1882): 153.

18. William G. Hartley, "Newel and Lydia Bailey Knight's Kirtland Love Story and Historic Wedding," *BYU Studies* 39, no. 4 (2000): 8–13; Homespun [Susa Young Gates], *Lydia Knight's History* (Salt Lake City: Juvenile Instructor, 1883), 21–22.

19. Homespun [Susa Young Gates], *Lydia Knight's History* (Salt Lake City: Juvenile Instructor, 1883), 21–22.

20. Doctrine and Covenants 46:19–20.

21. Edward W. Tullidge, *The Women of Mormondom* (New York: Tullidge and Crandall, 1877), 419–20.

22. Rhoda Richards, in Tullidge, *Women of Mormondom*, 420–21.

23. Hannah Cornaby, *Autobiography and Poems* (Salt Lake City: J. C. Graham, 1881), 49–50, 52–53.

24. Ibid., 52–53, 58.

25. Doctrine and Covenants 46:22.

26. Heber J. Grant, "Discourse of Heber J. Grant," Conference Report, October 1919, 31–32.

27. Heber J. Grant, "A Gospel Gift," *Young Woman's Journal* 16, no. 3 (March 1905), 128–29.

28. Heber J. Grant, "Discourse of Heber J. Grant," 31–32.

29. Hannah Cornaby, *Autobiography and Poems*, 44–47.

30. Ibid., 46–47.

CHAPTER 10—COMMANDMENTS

1. Drusilla Hendricks, "Historical Sketch of James Hendricks and Drusilla Dorris Hendricks (His Wife)," Typescript, L. Tom Perry Special Collections, BYU.

2. Doctrine and Covenants 82:8–9.

3. Matthew 22:37.

4. Excelette, "Woman's Voice," *Woman's Exponent* 4, no. 11 (1 November 1875): 83.

5. C. R., "Providence and Duty," *Woman's Exponent* 3, no. 18 (15 February 1875): 140.

6. Doctrine and Covenants 89:3.

7. "A Venerable Woman: Presendia Lathrop Kimball," *Woman's Exponent* 11, no. 17 (1 February 1883): 131.

8. Ibid.

9. Donna Toland Smart, ed., *Mormon Midwife: The 1846–1888 Diaries of Patty Bartlett Sessions* (Logan, Utah: Utah State University Press, 1997), 1–2.

10. Patty Sessions, in Edward W. Tullidge, *The Women of Mormondom* (New York: Tullidge and Crandall, 1877), 428.

11. Malachi 3:10.

12. Joseph F. Smith, *70th Annual Conference, April 6th, 7th, & 8th*, 1900, 48.

13. Ibid.

14. Annie Noble, "Some Sacred Experiences in the Life of Annie Emma Dexter Noble, 1931–1940," 76–78, CHL.

15. Ibid., 15.

16. Doctrine and Covenants 68:29.

17. Ronald W. Walker, "Rachel R. Grant: The Continuing Legacy of the Feminine Ideal," in *Supporting Saints: Life Stories of Nineteenth-Century Mormons* (Provo, Utah: BYU Religious Studies Center, 1985), 17–22; Rachel Ridgeway Grant, "How I Became a 'Mormon,'" 1, CHL.

18. Rachel Ridgeway Grant, "How I Became a 'Mormon,'" 1, CHL.

19. Doctrine and Covenants 59:14.

20. "'All Things Move in Order in the City': The Nauvoo Diary of Zina Diantha Jacobs," ed. Maureen Ursenbach Beecher, in *BYU Studies* 19, no. 3 (Spring 1979): 285–320.

21. Zina Diantha Huntington Jacobs Young, Diaries 1844–1845, CHL. Though Zina called this July, it was actually August.

22. Doctrine and Covenants 68:25.

23. See Doctrine and Covenants 68:25–31.

24. Janiece Johnson, *"Give It All Up and Follow Your Lord": Mormon Female Religiosity, 1831–1843* (Provo, Utah: BYU Studies, 2008), 25–27.

25. Phebe Crosby Peck to Anna Pratt, 10 August 1832, photocopy, CHL.

26. Carol Cornwall Madsen and Cherry B. Silver, "'I Believe in Women, Especially Thinking Women': Emmeline Blanche Woodward Wells (1828–1921)," in *Women of Faith in the Latter Days: Volume Two, 1821–1845*, ed. Richard E. Turley Jr. and Brittany A. Chapman (Salt Lake City: Deseret Book, 2012), 384–98.

27. Emmeline B. Wells, "Home Work," *Woman's Exponent* 2, no. 13 (1 December 1873): 98.

28. Doctrine and Covenants 30:8.

29. Ardeth Greene Kapp, "'I Shall Know They Are True': Susan Kent Greene, 1816–1860," in *Heroines of the Restoration* (Salt Lake City: Bookcraft, 1997), 79–92.

30. Susan Kent Greene, "Dear Exponent," *Woman's Exponent* 2: no. 23 (1 May 1874): 183.

31. Jane Manning James, Autobiography, 1893 [ca. 1902], dictated to J. D. Roundy, holograph, CHL.

32. Ibid.

Chapter 11—Temples

1. Doctrine and Covenants 88:119.

2. Doctrine and Covenants 42:36.

3. Doctrine and Covenants 88:119.

4. Women often donated eggs that their chickens laid on Sundays as a type of tithing. See Truman O. Angell, Autobiography, holograph, 7–8, CHL; see also Helen Mar Whitney, "Scenes in

Nauvoo, and Incidents from H.C. Kimball's Journal," *Woman's Exponent* 12, no. 9 (1 October 1883): 71; "R.S. Reports," *Woman's Exponent* 3, no. 23 (1 May 1875): 178; "R.S. Reports," *Woman's Exponent* 3, no. 15 (1 January 1875): 114.

5. George A. Smith, "Gathering and Sanctification of the People of God," 18 March 1855, in *Journal of Discourses*, ed. Brigham Young (Liverpool, England: F. D. Richards, 1855–1886), 2:215.

6. Mercy Fielding Thompson, "Recollections of the Prophet Joseph Smith," *Juvenile Instructor* 27, no. 13 (1 July 1892): 400.

7. Mary Ann Rankin, "Little Letters," *Woman's Exponent* 3, no. 23 (1 May 1875): 181.

8. Virginia H. Pearce, "'In Blessing Others We Are Blessed': Sarah Melissa Granger Kimball," in *Women of Faith in the Latter Days: Volume One, 1775–1820*, ed. Richard E. Turley Jr. and Brittany A. Chapman (Salt Lake City: Deseret Book, 2011), 116.

9. "R.S. Reports," *Woman's Exponent* 5, no. 7 (1 September 1876): 50.

10. Eliza R. Snow, "Sketch of My Life," in *The Personal Writings of Eliza R. Snow*, ed. Maureen Ursenbach Beecher (Logan, Utah: Utah State University Press, 2000), 6–8, 11.

11. Ibid., 11. The money that Eliza R. Snow contributed for the temple was most likely part of her inheritance from her father, claimed at the time she left Mantua, Portage County, Ohio. See Beecher, 260, fn. 19.

12. Jill Mulvay Derr, Carol Cornwall Madsen, Kate Holbrook, and Matthew J. Grow, eds., *The First Fifty Years of Relief Society: Key Documents in Latter-day Saint Women's History* (Salt Lake City: The Church Historian's Press, 2016), 655.

13. "Historical Sketch of the Church from the Time of the Martyrdom of the Prophets Joseph Smith and Hyrum Smith," *Young Woman's Journal* 3, no. 11 (August 1892): 514.

14. Angell, Autobiography, 7–8.

15. In Edward W. Tullidge, *The Women of Mormondom* (New York: Tullidge and Crandall, 1877), 76.

16. "The Life of Jeremiah and Elmeda Stringham," transcript, FamilySearch, https://family search.org/tree/#view=ancestor&person=KWJH-BLD&section=memories, accessed 18 March 2016.

17. Elmeda Harmon, in *Tennant Family History*, ed. Inez Tennant Swenson and Richard M. Swensen, 1997, 47.

18. "Sketch of Sister Mercy R. Thompson: Worker in the Nauvoo Temple," *Young Woman's Journal* 4, no. 7 (April 1893): 291.

19. Mercy Fielding Thompson, Autobiographical Sketch, 1880, holograph, 7–9, CHL.

20. "R.S. Reports," *Woman's Exponent* 5, no. 7 (1 September 1876): 50.

21. M. G. H., "Building Temples," *Woman's Exponent* 3, no. 14 (15 December 1874): 108–9; see Malachi 3:1.

22. Alice Anderson Harris, "Caroline Frances Angell [Davis] Holbrook," biography, original in family possession, http://boap.org/LDS/Early-Saints/CAngell.html, accessed 20 April 2016.

23. Caroline Frances Angell Davis Holbrook, "A Sketch of the Life and Experiences of Caroline Frances Angell Davis Holbrook," typescript, CHL.

24. Eliza R. Snow, in Tullidge, *Women of Mormondom*, 65.

25. Ibid.

26. Ibid., 95.

27. Augusta Joyce Crocheron, *Representative Women of Deseret, a Book of Biographical Sketches to Accompany the Picture Bearing the Same Title* (Salt Lake City: J. C. Graham, 1884), 76–77.

28. Elvira Stevens Barney, "Ruins of the Nauvoo Temple," comments on postcard pictures of the temple sketched by her sister, CHL.

29. Nancy N. Tracy, "Life History of Nancy Naomi Alexander Tracy, Written by Herself," typescript, L. Tom Perry Special Collections, BYU, 7–8, 26; Eleanor C. Jensen and Rachel G. Christensen, "Our Lamps Trimmed and Burning: Nancy Naomi Alexander Tracy," in *Women of Faith in the Latter Days: Volume One, 1775–1820*, ed. Richard E. Turley Jr. and Brittany A. Chapman (Salt Lake City: Deseret Book, 2011), 437–38.

30. Nancy N. Tracy, "Life History of Nancy Naomi Alexander Tracy," 9–10.

31. Sylvia Cutler Webb, "The Autobiography of Sylvia C. Webb," *Saints' Herald* 62, no. 12 (24 March 1915): 289–90.

32. Ibid.

33. Hannah Tapfield King, "To a Young Lady Friend," *Woman's Exponent* 2, no. 23 (1 May 1874): 182.

34. Ibid.

35. Hannah Sorenson, "Letter to the Young Women of Zion," *Young Woman's Journal* 2, no. 11 (August 1891): 514–16.

36. Esther, "Celestial Marriage, Opening a New Era," *Woman's Exponent* 6, no. 11 (1 November 1877): 83.

Chapter 12—Education

1. Doctrine and Covenants 93:36.

2. Doctrine and Covenants 88:118.

3. Doctrine and Covenants 93:36, 40.

4. Fifteenth Ward, Riverside Stake, Relief Society Minutes and Records, vol. 5, 1874–1894, 11 April 1894, and vol. 8, 1893–1899, 25 November 1896, 140, CHL; "President Sarah M. Kimball," *Woman's Exponent* 27, no. 14 (15 December 1898): 77.

5. Eliza R. Snow, "Sketch of My Life," in *The Personal Writings of Eliza R. Snow*, ed. Maureen Ursenbach Beecher (Logan, Utah: Utah State University Press, 2000), 10–11, 18.

6. Maria Morris, "Woman Intellectually," *Young Woman's Journal* 4, no. 5 (February 1893): 237.

7. Milton Backman, *The Heavens Resound* (Salt Lake City: Deseret Book, 1983), 262–75.

8. Elizabeth Haven Barlow to Elizabeth H. Bullard, 24 February 1839, Barlow Family Collection, CHL.

9. S. E. R., "Night Thoughts," *Young Woman's Journal* 1, no. 6 (March 1890): 177.

10. Hope [Sarah E. Russell, "Life is Worth the Living," and "Sarah E. Russell," *Woman's Exponent* 41, no. 13 (January 1914): 89, 92.

11. S. E. R., "Night Thoughts," 177.

12. Jill Mulvay Derr, Carol Cornwall Madsen, Kate Holbrook, and Matthew J. Grow, ed., *The First Fifty Years of Relief Society: Key Documents in Latter-day Saint Women's History* (Salt Lake City: The Church Historian's Press, 2016),655; Helen Mar Whitney, "Scenes and Incidents in Nauvoo," Woman's Exponent 10, no. 21 (1 April 1882): 162.

13. Helen Mar Whitney, "Scenes and Incidents in Nauvoo," *Woman's Exponent* 10, no. 21 (1 April 1882): 162.

14. Homespun [Susa Young Gates, *Lydia Knight's History* (Salt Lake City: Juvenile Instructor Office, 1883), 22–23, 27; Nicholas J. Frederick, "'God Rules!' Lydia Goldthwaite Knight," in *Women of Faith in the Latter Days: Volume One, 1775–1820*, ed. Richard E. Turley Jr. and Brittany A. Chapman (Salt Lake City: Deseret Book, 2011), 143–50.

15. Lydia Knight to Brigham and Mary Ann Young, 24 May 1849, Brigham Young Incoming Correspondence, 1839–1877, CHL.

16. Augusta Joyce Crocheron, *Representative Women of Deseret, a Book of Biographical Sketches to Accompany the Picture Bearing the Same Title* (Salt Lake City: J. C. Graham, 1884), 64.

17. Ibid., 64–67.

18. Eliza R. Snow, "Practical Education," *Woman's Exponent* 11, no. 8 (15 September 1882): 61.

19. "In Memoriam," *Woman's Exponent* 29, nos. 6, 7 (15 August, 1 September 1900): 29.

20. Lizzie Smith, "Equality of the Sexes," *Young Woman's Journal* 1, no. 6 (March 1890): 176.

21. Jill Mulvay Derr, "'Cheerfully Respond to Every Call': Eliza Roxcy Snow (1804–1887)," in *Women of Faith in the Latter Days: Volume One, 1775–1820*, ed. Richard E. Turley Jr. and Brittany A. Chapman (Salt Lake City: Deseret Book, 2011), 389–406.

22. Eliza R. Snow, "Practical Education," 61.

23. Crocheron, *Representative Women*, 76.

24. Ibid., 76–81.

25. Ibid., 77–81.

26. Ibid., 72–73.

27. 1 Nephi 19:14; see also 3 Nephi 16:9.

28. Romania B. Pratt, Memoir, 19 March 1881, 11–16, CHL.

29. M. J. C., "Time is Precious," *Woman's Exponent* 4, no. 6 (15 August 1875): 41.

30. Mary Jane Johnson Crosby, Mormon Pioneer Overland Travel Database, history.lds.org /overlandtravels, accessed 19 March 2016.

31. Mary Jane Crosby, *Woman's Exponent* 17, no. 18 (15 February 1889): 144.

32. M. J. C, "Time is Precious," 41.

33. "Anna May Sirrine," familysearch.org, accessed 10 May 2016; Thurza A. Hall, "Conjoint Session," *Young Woman's Journal* 5, no. 12 (September 1894): 596.

34. Anna Covington, "Why Should We Read?" *Young Woman's Journal* 4, no. 5 (February 1893): 237–40.

35. "Rachel Amanda Reynolds," familysearch.org, accessed May 10, 2016; "Another Pioneer Laid to Rest—Funeral of Warren F. Reynolds," *Deseret Evening News*, 16 July 1900.

36. Rachel Reynolds, "Education," *Young Woman's Journal* 3, no. 9 (June 1892): 431–32.

37. Lisa Olsen Tait, "'Thank God That I Have Been Counted Worthy,' Susa Amelia Young Dunford Gates (1856–1933)," in *Women of Faith in the Latter-days: Volume Three, 1846–1870*, ed. Richard E. Turley Jr. and Brittany A. Chapman (Salt Lake City: Deseret Book, 2014), 57–68.

38. See Articles of Faith 1:8.

39. Susa Young Gates, "Education," History of Women Files, Early Chapters, Susa Young Gates Papers, 24–25, CHL.

Chapter 13—Personal Apostasy

1. Doctrine and Covenants 49:23.

2. Ann Marsh Abbott to Nathan Marsh, 20 June 1843, in private possession.

3. Temperance Mack to Harriett Whittemore, 30 December 1838, in Janiece Johnson, *"Give It All Up and Follow Your Lord": Mormon Female Religiosity, 1831–1843* (Provo, Utah: BYU Studies, 2008), 53; original in Whittemore Family Papers, Michigan Historical Collections, University of Michigan; Ann Arbor, Michigan.

4. Milton Backman, *The Heavens Resound* (Salt Lake City: Deseret Book, 1983), 310–11, 323–29.

5. Doctrine and Covenants 49:23. See Doctrine and Covenants 45; 46; 50; 52.

6. Caroline Barnes Crosby, in *No Place to Call Home: The 1807–1857 Life Writings of Caroline Barnes Crosby, Chronicler of Outlying Mormon Communities*, Life Writings of Frontier Women 7, ed. Edward Leo Lyman, Susan Ward Payne, and S. George Ellsworth (Logan, Utah: Utah State University Press, 2005), 48.

7. *Women's Voices: An Untold History of the Latter-day Saints, 1830–1900*, ed. Kenneth W. Godfrey, Audrey M. Godfrey, and Jill Mulvay Derr (Salt Lake City:Deseret Book Company, 1982), 46; Crosby, in *No Place to Call Home*, 43.

8. Crosby, in *No Place to Call Home*, 47–48.

9. Sally Parker to Mr. Francis Tufts, 24 July [ca. 1837], Kirtland Mills, Ohio, Doris Whittier Pierce File, Delaware County Historical Society, Delaware, Ohio, as transcribed in Janiece Johnson, "The Scriptures Is a Fulfilling: Sally Parker's Weave," *BYU Studies* 44, no. 2 (2005): 120fn4.

10. Johnson, "The Scriptures Is a Fulfilling," 110–14.

11. See Proverbs 26:11.

12. Sally Parker to Brother and Sister, 26 August1838, Sunbury, Delaware County, Ohio, Doris Whittier Pierce File, Delaware County Historical Society, Delaware, Ohio, as transcribed in Johnson, "The Scriptures Is a Fulfilling," 116–17.

13. Johnson, *"Give It All Up and Follow Your Lord,"* 41–42, 47; Mary Fielding to Mercy Thompson, August–September 1837, Mary Fielding Smith Collection, CHL.

14. Mary Fielding to Mercy Thompson, August–September 1837, Mary Fielding Smith Collection, CHL.

15. Kenneth W. and Audrey W. Godfrey, and Jill Mulvay Derr, eds. *Women's Voices: An Untold History of The Latter-day Saints* (Salt Lake City: Deseret Book, 1982), 69.

16. On January 12, 1838, Joseph received a revelation not included in the Doctrine and Covenants to "Get out of this place." Clearly Hepzibah was aware of the revelation. Joseph Smith, Revelation, 12 January 1838–C, Page 1, Joseph Smith Papers, josephsmithpapers.org, accessed 28 April 2016.

17. Hepzibah Richards to William Richards, 22 January 1838, Richards Family Papers, CHL.

18. Hepzibah Richards to Friends, 23 March 1838, Richards Family Papers, CHL.

19. Johnson, *"Give It All Up and Follow Your Lord,"* 89; see also Doctrine and Covenants 112.

20. Ann Marsh Abbott to Nathan Marsh, 20 June 1843.

21. Desdemona Wadsworth Fullmer, Reminiscence, 1868, Desdemona Wadsworth Fullmer Papers, CHL.

22. Ibid.

23. Ibid.

24. Willard Richards, in Edward W. Tullidge, *The Women of Mormondom* (New York: Tullidge and Crandall, 1877), 245.

25. Johnson, *"Give It All Up and Follow Your Lord,"* 48–50.

26. Jennetta Richards to Willard Richards, 11 August 1838, photocopy, CHL.

27. Jennetta Richards to Willard Richards, 8 September 1838, photocopy, CHL.

28. Janiece Johnson, "'My Happy Soul Is Witness': Laura Farnsworth Owen (1806–1881)," in *Women of Faith in the Latter Days: Volume One, 1775–1820*, ed. Richard E. Turley Jr. and Brittany A. Chapman (Salt Lake City: Deseret Book, 2011), 193–95.

29. Laura Farnsworth Owen, Autobiography, 1868, CHL.

30. Melissa Morgan Dodge to William T. Morgan, 23 June 1839, William T. Morgan Correspondence, CHL.

31. Johnson, *"Give It All Up and Follow Your Lord,"* 63, 68; see also Luke 8:15.

32. See Luke 8:4–15.

33. Melissa Morgan Dodge to William T. Morgan, 23 June 1839, CHL.

34. Johnson, *"Give It All Up and Follow Your Lord,"* 51–53.

35. See Matthew 13; see also Doctrine and Covenants 86.

36. See 3 Nephi 11:11; see also Doctrine and Covenants 19:18.

37. Temperance Mack to Harriett Whittemore, 30 December 1838, in Johnson, *"Give It All Up and Follow Your Lord,"* 53; original in Whittemore Family Papers.

38. Linda King Newell and Valeen Tippets Avery, *Mormon Enigma: Emma Hale Smith, 2nd ed.* (Urbana: University of Illinois Press, 1994), 190–91.

39. Emma Smith, blessing, 1844, typescript, CHL.

40. Ibid.

41. Johnson, *"Give It All Up and Follow Your Lord,"* 27–28.

42. See Matthew 25:1–13.

43. Almira Scobey Covey to Harriet Whittemore, 9 June 1835, microfilm, L. Tom Perry Special Collections, BYU; original in Whittemore Family Papers.

Chapter 14—Gathering and Building Zion

1. Obadiah 1:17.

2. Psalm 128:5; see also Isaiah 2:2–3; Psalm 48:11; 87:2; 125:1; Obadiah 1:21.

3. Moses 7:18.

4. See 3 Nephi 21:20–24; Ether 13:1–11.

5. Doctrine and Covenants 57:3.

6. Doctrine and Covenants 100:16.

7. Elizabeth Haven Barlow to Elizabeth Howe Bullard, 24 February 1839, Barlow Family Collection, CHL, in *The Israel Barlow Story and Mormon Mores* (Salt Lake City: Ora H. Barlow, 1968), 143. See also Psalm 137:1.

8. Helen Mar Whitney, "Scenes and Incidents in Nauvoo," *Woman's Exponent* 10, no. 20 (15 March 1882): 159.

9. Bathsheba W. Smith, in Edward W. Tullidge, *The Women of Mormondom* (New York: Tullidge and Crandall, 1877), 151.

10. Kenneth W. and Audrey M. Godfrey, Jill Mulvay Derr, ed., *Women's Voices: An Untold History of the Latter-day Saints, 1830–1900* (Salt Lake City: Deseret Book Company, 1982), 46; Caroline Barnes Crosby, in *No Place to Call Home: The 1807–1857 Life Writings of Caroline Barnes Crosby, Chronicler of Outlying Mormon Communities*, Life Writings of Frontier Women 7, ed. Edward Leo Lyman, Susan Ward Payne, and S. George Ellsworth (Logan, Utah: Utah State University Press, 2005), 35–36.

11. Crosby, in *No Place to Call Home*, ed. Lyman, Payne, and Ellsworth, 35–37.

12. Emily M. Austin, *Mormonism; or, Life Among the Mormons* (Madison, WI: M.J. Cantwell, 1882), 57–58, 63, 86, 112–13.

13. See Hebrews 11:13–16.

14. Austin, *Mormonism*, 58–60, 63, 68.

15. Bathsheba W. Smith, Autobiography, ca. 1875–1906, typescript, 2–5, CHL.

16. Ibid., 2–3; emphasis in original.

17. August Dorius Stevens, Autobiography, 1922, 1, CHL.

18. Ibid., 1–2.

19. Barlow to Bullard, 147.

20. Sarah DeArmon Pea Rich, Autobiography, 1885–1893, 36, 41–42, CHL; Godfrey, Godfrey, and Derr, *Women's Voices*, 97–98.

21. Sarah DeArmon Pea Rich, Autobiography, 41–42, CHL.

22. *The Israel Barlow Story*, 138–42.

23. Barlow to Bullard, 142–52.

24. Augusta Joyce Crocheron, *Representative Women of Deseret, a Book of Biographical Sketches to Accompany the Picture Bearing the Same Title* (Salt Lake City: J. C. Graham, 1884), 29–30; "A Venerable Woman: Presendia Lathrop Kimball," *Woman's Exponent* 11, no. 21 (1 April 1883): 163; "A Venerable Woman: Presendia Lathrop Kimball," *Woman's Exponent* 11, no. 23 (1 May 1883): 183.

25. Presendia Kimball, in Crocheron, *Representative Women*, 31.

26. Eliza R. Snow, "Sketch of My Life," in *The Personal Writings of Eliza R. Snow*, ed. Maureen Ursenbach Beecher (Logan, Utah: Utah State University Press, 2000), 12–14.

27. Eliza R. Snow, "A Word to the Saints Who Are Gathering," in *Poems, Religious, Historical, and Political*, vol. 1 (Liverpool, England: F. D. Richards, 1856), 234–35; in *Eliza R. Snow: The Complete Poetry*, ed. Jill Mulvay Derr and Karen Lynn Davidson (Provo: BYU Press; Salt Lake City: University of Utah Press, 2009), 518–20.

28. Mary Fielding Smith to Joseph Fielding, June 1839, in Tullidge, *Women of Mormondom*, 257.

29. Sarah DeArmon Pea Rich, Autobiography, CHL.

30. Ibid., 66.

31. Jay A. Parry, "'Called to Drink Deep of the Bitter Cup': Mary Fielding Smith (1801–1852)," in *Women of Faith in the Latter Days: Volume One, 1775–1820*, ed. Richard E. Turley Jr. and Brittany A. Chapman (Salt Lake City: Deseret Book, 2011), 376–77, 380–81.

32. Mary Fielding Smith to Joseph Fielding, June 1839, in Tullidge, *Women of Mormondom*, 256–57.

33. Moses 7:18.

34. Nauvoo Relief Society Minute Book, 24 March 1842, 17, in Jill Mulvay Derr, Carol Cornwall Madsen, Kate Holbrook, and Matthew J. Grow, ed., *The First Fifty Years of Relief Society: Key Documents in Latter-day Saint Women's History* (Salt Lake City: The Church Historian's Press, 2016), 38.

35. Nauvoo Relief Society Minute Book, 19 April 1842, 31, in Derr et al., *First Fifty Years of Relief Society*, 50.

36. Nauvoo Relief Society Minute Book, 24 March 1842, 18–19, in Derr et al., *First Fifty Years of Relief Society*, 40.

37. Derr et al., *First Fifty Years of Relief Society*, 157, 640.

38. Ellen Douglas, letter, 14 April 1844, CHL, in Derr et al., *First Fifty Years of Relief Society*, 158–59.

39. Derr et al., *First Fifty Years of Relief Society*, 214.

40. Lucy Meserve Smith, "Historical Sketches of My Great Grandfathers," 12 June 1889, manuscript, Special Collections, Marriott Library, University of Utah, 53–54, in Derr et al., *First Fifty Years of Relief Society*, 217–18.

Chapter 15—Affliction

1. Laura Clark Phelps to John Cooper, 1839, Zula Rich Cole Collection, CHL; see Psalm 12:6.

2. See 2 Nephi 2:11.

3. Lilburn W. Boggs to John B. Clark, Executive Order No. 44, 27 October 1838, Mormon War Papers, 1837–1841, Missouri State Archives.

4. Melissa Morgan Dodge to William T. Morgan, 23 June 1839, William T. Morgan Correspondence, CHL; Ann Marsh Abbott to Nathan Marsh, 20 June 1843, in private possession.

5. Mercy Fielding Thompson, in Edward W. Tullidge, *The Women of Mormondom* (New York: Tullidge and Crandall, 1877), 255.

6. Jennifer Reeder, "'The Blessing of the Lord has Attended Me': Mercy Fielding Thompson," in *Women of Faith in the Latter Days: Volume One, 1775–1820*, ed. Richard E. Turley Jr. and Brittany A. Chapman (Salt Lake City: Deseret Book, 2011), 420–22.

7. Thompson, in Tullidge, *Women of Mormondom*, 254–55.

8. Janiece Johnson, "Give It All Up and Follow Your Lord": Mormon Female Religiosity, 1831–1843 (Provo, Utah: BYU Studies, 2008), 41–42, 57, 62.

9. Mary Fielding Smith to Hyrum Smith, 11 April 1839, Mary Fielding Smith Collection, CHL; Mary Fielding Smith to Joseph Fielding, June 1839, in Tullidge, *Women of Mormondom*, 255–56.

10. The epistles that Mary references are likely the two parts of Joseph Smith's March 1839 letter to "the Church and Edward Partridge," now found in Doctrine and Covenants 121–123. See Joseph Smith, Hyrum Smith, Lyman Wight, Caleb Baldwin, and Alexander McRae to the Church and Edward Partridge, 20 March 1839, parts A and B, Revelations Collection, CHL; also on josephsmithpapers.org, accessed 11 May 2016.

11. Mary Fielding Smith to Hyrum Smith, 11 April 1839, CHL.

12. Johnson, *"Give It All Up and Follow Your Lord,"* 73, 78.

13. Joseph Smith and the others imprisoned in Liberty Jail were allowed to escape in early April 1839. See Richard Lyman Bushman, *Joseph Smith: Rough Stone Rolling* (New York: Alfred A. Knopf, 2005), 382.

14. Laura's mother, Polly Keeler Clark, had passed away earlier in 1839, on February 27.

15. See Revelation 7:14.

16. Laura Clark Phelps to John Cooper, 1839, Zula Rich Cole Collection, CHL; see Psalm 12:6.

17. Temperance Mack to Harriett Whittemore, 30 December 1838, in Johnson, *"Give It All Up and Follow Your Lord,"* 53; original in Whittemore Family Papers, Michigan Historical Collections, University of Michigan; Ann Arbor, Michigan.

18. Johnson, *"Give It All Up and Follow Your Lord,"* 51–53.

19. Temperance Mack to Harriett Whittemore, 30 December 1838, in Johnson, *"Give It All Up and Follow Your Lord,"* 53; original in Whittemore Family Papers, Michigan Historical Collections, University of Michigan; Ann Arbor, Michigan.

20. Alexander L. Baugh, "'I'll Never Forsake': Amanda Barnes Smith," in *Women of Faith in the Latter Days: Volume One, 1775–1820*, ed. Richard E. Turley Jr. and Brittany A. Chapman (Salt Lake City: Deseret Book, 2011), 327–42.

21. "How Firm a Foundation," *Hymns of The Church of Jesus Christ of Latter-day Saints* (Salt Lake City: The Church of Jesus Christ of Latter-day Saints, 1985), no. 85. This hymn was included in the first LDS hymnbook. Emma Smith, A Collection of Sacred Hymns for the Church of Jesus Christ of Latter-day Saints (Kirtland, Ohio: F.G. Williams Printer, 1835), 111–13.

22. Amanda Barnes Smith, in Tullidge, *Women of Mormondom*, 129–31.

23. Johnson, *"Give It All Up and Follow Your Lord,"* 63, 68.

24. See Hebrews 10:34.

25. Melissa Morgan Dodge to William T. Morgan, 23 June 1839, CHL.

26. Johnson, *"Give It All Up and Follow Your Lord,"* 89.

27. Ann Marsh Abbott to Nathan Marsh, 20 June 1843.

CHAPTER 16—ORDINANCES AND COVENANTS

1. Lydia Knight to Brigham Young and Mary Ann Young, 28 May 1849, Brigham Young Office Files, Incoming Correspondence, 1839–1877, CHL.
2. Doctrine and Covenants 25:13.
3. See Doctrine and Covenants 132:46.
4. David E. Sorensen, "Small Temples—Large Blessings," Conference Report, October 1998.
5. Doctrine and Covenants 84:20.
6. Elder Boyd K. Packer defined order, ordain, and ordinance: "Order—to put in ranks or rows, in proper sequence or relationship. Ordain—the process of putting things in rows of proper relationship. Ordinance—the ceremony by which things are put in proper order." Boyd K. Packer, *The Holy Temple* (Salt Lake City: Bookcraft, 1980), 145.
7. Temperance Bond Mack to Harriet Mack Whittemore, 16 September 1841, L. Tom Perry Special Collections, BYU. Original in Whittemore Family Papers, Michigan Historical Collection, University of Michigan, Ann Arbor, Michigan.
8. Eliza R. Snow to Phebe Snow, 6 April 1868, Lorenzo Snow papers, CHL.
9. Zina D. H. Young, Nauvoo diary, 24 May 1845, CHL.
10. Mary Fielding Smith to Joseph Fielding, June 1839, in Edward W. Tullidge, *The Women of Mormondom* (New York: Tullidge and Crandall, 1877), 258.
11. Elizabeth Haven, in *The Israel Barlow Story and Mormon Mores* (Salt Lake City: Ora H. Barlow, 1968), 141.
12. Lucy Mack Smith, History, 1844–1845, vol. 9, manuscript, 12, CHL.
13. Ibid.
14. Elizabeth B. Pratt, "Autobiography," *Woman's Exponent* 19, no. 12 (1 December 1890): 94–95.
15. Ibid.
16. Elizabeth Haven, in *The Israel Barlow Story and Mormon Mores* (Salt Lake City: Ora H. Barlow, 1968), 139–41.
17. Ibid.
18. Priscilla Mogridge Staines, in Tullidge, *Women of Mormondom*, 285–86.
19. Ibid., 286–88.
20. Eliza Dana Gibbs, Autobiography, typescript, Utah State Historical Society; http://boap.org /LDS/Early-Saints/EGibbs.html, accessed 20 April 2016.
21. Ibid.
22. Mary Brown Pulsipher, History, typescript, 1–2, 4–5, L. Tom Perry Special Collections, BYU.
23. Ibid.
24. Vilate Kimball to Heber C. Kimball, 11 October 1840, Vilate M. Kimball letters, CHL.
25. Louisa Barnes Pratt, "Obituaries," *Woman's Exponent* 9, no. 1 (1 June 1880): 4–5; Jane Neyman statements, 29 November 1854, Joseph Smith History Documents, 1839–1860, CHL.
26. Carol Cornwall Madsen, "Mormon Women and the Temple: Toward a New Understanding," in *Sisters in Spirit: Mormon Women in Historical and Cultural Perspective*, ed. Maureen Ursenbach Beecher and Lavina Fielding Anderson (Urbana, IL: University of Illinois Press, 1987), 81. In the months following the initial teaching of baptism for the dead, Joseph Smith added additional guidelines of witnesses and recorders (see Doctrine and Covenants 124; 127; 128). In 1845, Brigham Young suggested the practice of women being baptized for women and men for men. Brigham Young, "Speech," *Times and Seasons* 6, no. 12 (1 July 1845): 953–57.
27. Jane Neyman statement, Joseph Smith History Documents, 13 September 1840, CHL.
28. Jill Mulvay Derr, Carol Cornwall Madsen, Kate Holbrook, and Matthew J. Grow, eds., *The First

Fifty Years of Relief Society: Key Documents in Latter-day Saint Women's History (Salt Lake City: The Church Historian's Press, 2016), 654–55.

29. Vilate Kimball to Heber C. Kimball, 11 October 1840, CHL.
30. Elizabeth Anderson Howard, Autobiography, typescript, L. Tom Perry Special Collections, BYU.
31. Ibid.
32. Sally Carlisle Randall, letters, 1843–1852, typescripts, 6 October 1843 and 12 November 1843, CHL.
33. Sally Carlisle Randall, 21 April 1844, CHL.
34. Mercy Fielding Thompson, "Recollections of the Prophet Joseph Smith," *Juvenile Instructor* 27, no. 13 (July 1, 1892): 400.
35. Derr et al., *First Fifty Years of Relief Society*, 674; Clara L. Clawson, "R.S. Reports: Pioneer Stake," *Woman's Exponent* 34, no. 2–3 (July and August 1905): 14.
36. Bathsheba W. Smith, "Affidavit," 19 November 1903, in Affidavits about Celestial Marriage, 1869–1915, CHL.
37. Mary Ellen Harris Abel Kimball, "Sketch of Pioneer History," 1895, manuscript, 12, 21, CHL.
38. Ibid.
39. Hannah Cornaby, *Autobiography and Poems* (Salt Lake City: J. C. Graham, 1881), 23–25, 35.
40. Ibid., 39.
41. Bathsheba W. Smith, Autobiography, 9, CHL.
42. Lydia Knight and Susa Young Gates, *Lydia Knight's History*, Noble Women's Lives Series 1 (Salt Lake City: Juvenile Instructor Office, 1883), 10–11, 25–30.
43. Knight and Gates, *Lydia Knight's History*, 30–31.
44. Orson F. Whitney, *Life of Heber C. Kimball: An Apostle, the Father and Founder of the British Mission* (Salt Lake City: Juvenile Instructor Office, 1888), 333–35.
45. Vilate Kimball to Heber C. Kimball, 8 June 1843, in Orson F. Whitney, journal, 1840–1845, CHL.
46. Eliza R. Snow, "Sacramental Hymn," *Millennial Star* 23, no. 24 (13 June 1871): 384, in *Eliza R. Snow: The Complete Poetry*, ed. Jill Mulvay Derr and Karen Lynn Davidson (Provo: BYU Press; Salt Lake City: University of Utah Press, 2009), 837–38; "Again We Meet Around the Board," *Hymns of The Church of Jesus Christ of Latter-day Saints* (Salt Lake City: The Church of Jesus Christ of Latter-day Saints, 1985), no. 186.
47. Nancy A. Tracy, "Diary of Nancy Naomi Alexander Tracy," typescript, 7–8, Nancy A. Tracy Reminiscences and Diary, CHL.
48. Ibid., 10.
49. Josephine Savage Jones, *Henry Savage and His Family* (privately published, 1968), 67, 71, 84.
50. Ibid., 71.
51. *The Complete Poetry*, ed. Derr and Davidson, 837–43.
52. Gunnison Ward, Sevier and Sanpete Stakes, Relief Society Minutes, vol. 1 (1872–1879), 28 June 1878, 151, CHL.
53. Eliza R. Snow, "Hymn 334," in *Sacred Hymns and Spiritual Songs for The Church of Jesus Christ of Latter-day Saints*, 14th ed. (Salt Lake City: Deseret News Office, 1871), 401–402, in *The Complete Poetry*, ed. Derr and Davidson, 841–842; "How Great the Wisdom and the Love," *Hymns*, no. 195.

CHAPTER 17—ABRAHAMIC SACRIFICES

1. Philippians 3:10.
2. Doctrine and Covenants 98:12; see also Abraham 3:25; Doctrine and Covenants 101:3–5.

3. Philippians 3:8, 10.
4. Neal A. Maxwell, "I Will Arise and Go to My Father," *Ensign*, September 1993, 67; see also Bruce C. Hafen, *A Disciple's Life* (Salt Lake City, Utah: Deseret Book, 2002), 20.
5. See Doctrine and Covenants 122:7.
6. See Doctrine and Covenants 101:4; 132:50–51.
7. See Doctrine and Covenants 101:3.
8. Doctrine and Covenants 132:51; see also Doctrine and Covenants 132:36, 50.
9. Eliza R. Snow Smith, *Biography and Family Record of Lorenzo Snow* (Salt Lake City: Deseret News Company Printers, 1884), 69–70.
10. B. H. Roberts, *The Life of John Taylor, Third President of the Church of Jesus Christ of Latter-day Saints* (Salt Lake City: Deseret Book Company, 1892), 100.
11. Augusta Joyce Crocheron, *Representative Women of Deseret, a Book of Biographical Sketches to Accompany the Picture Bearing the Same Title* (Salt Lake City: J. C. Graham, 1884), 58.
12. "Great Indignation Meeting of the Ladies of Salt Lake City, to Protest against the Passage of Cullom's Bill," *Deseret Evening News*, 14 January 1870.
13. Mary Fielding Smith to Joseph Fielding, June 1839, in Edward W. Tullidge, *The Women of Mormondom* (New York, 1877), 255–56.
14. Smithfield Branch, "Relief Society Minutes and Records, 1868–1906," 7 August 1871, 98–99, CHL.
15. Ibid.
16. Drusilla D. Hendricks, in Historical Sketch of James Hendricks and Drusilla Dorris Hendricks, typescript, 17–19, CHL.
17. Phoebe K. Woodbury to George and Maria Plumb, 9 December [year unknown], Phoebe K. Woodbury Letters, L. Tom Perry Special Collections, BYU.
18. *Deseret Evening News*, 6 May 1868, 3.
19. Phoebe K. Woodbury, notebook, holograph, Phoebe K. Woodbury Letters, L. Tom Perry Special Collections, BYU.
20. Woodbury to Plumb and Plumb, 9 December [year unknown].
21. Eliza P. Lyman, Journal, 1846–1885, 35, CHL.
22. Ibid., 31–35.
23. Ibid., 33–35.
24. Annie Wells Cannon, "Jane Snyder Richards, In Memoriam," *Woman's Exponent* 41, no. 3 (November 1912): 17; see also "Mrs. Richards is Dead; Weber Loses by Demise—Prominent Woman in Ninetieth Year Taken By Death," *Salt Lake Herald-Republican*, 18 November 1912.
25. Jane Snyder Richards, Reminiscence, 1880, holograph, 20–21, CHL.
26. Helen Mar Whitney, "Scenes in Nauvoo After the Martyrdom of the Prophet and Patriarch," *Woman's Exponent* 11, no. 19 (1 March 1883): 146.
27. Helen Mar Whitney, "Scenes and Incidents in Nauvoo," *Woman's Exponent* 10, no. 10 (15 October 1881): 74.
28. See James 1:5.
29. See Matthew 7:7.
30. Helen Mar Whitney, "Scenes and Incidents in Nauvoo," 74.
31. Helen Mar Whitney, "Scenes in Nauvoo After the Martyrdom," 146.
32. Helen Mar Whitney, Autobiography, 30 March 1881, CHL.
33. Helen Mar Whitney, "Scenes in Nauvoo After the Martyrdom," 146.
34. Helen Mar Whitney, Autobiography, 30 March 1881, CHL.
35. See Doctrine and Covenants 68:25; 20:71.

36. Cordelia Morley Cox, "Sketch of Cordelia Morley Cox," *Woman's Exponent* 41, no. 5 (Midwinter 1913), 1–2.

37. Cordelia Calista Morley Cox, Collection of Biographies, holograph, L. Tom Perry Special Collections, BYU.

38. Carol Cornwall Madsen, *An Advocate for Women: The Public Life of Emmeline B. Wells, 1870–1920* (Provo, Utah: Brigham Young University Press; Salt Lake City: Deseret Book, 2006), 18–19.

39. Emmeline Harris [Wells] to Newel K. Whitney, holograph, Newel K. Whitney Collection, L. Tom Perry Collection, Harold B. Lee Library, Brigham Young University, Provo, Utah.

40. Grace Ingels Frost, "Beyond the Darkness," *Young Woman's Journal* 21, no. 9 (September 1910): 490.

41. Eliza R. Snow, "For the Times and Seasons," *Times and Seasons* 2, no. 6 (15 January 1841): 286–87; *Sacred Hymns and Spiritual Songs: For the Church of Jesus Christ of Latter-day Saints*, 11th ed. (Liverpool, England: F. D. Richards, 1856), 374–75; see also *Eliza R. Snow: The Complete Poetry*, ed. Jill Mulvay Derr and Karen Lynn Davidson (Provo, Utah: BYU Press; Salt Lake City: University of Utah Press, 2009), 130–32, 1080.

42. Eliza R. Snow, "For the Times and Seasons," 286–87.

Chapter 18—The Death of Joseph and Hyrum Smith

1. Mary Isabella Horne, in Edward W. Tullidge, *The Women of Mormondom* (New York: Tullidge and Crandall, 1877), 323.

2. Nauvoo Relief Society Minutes, 28 April 1842, 37, CHL, in Jill Mulvay Derr, Carol Cornwall Madsen, Kate Holbrook, and Matthew J. Grow, ed., *The First Fifty Years of Relief Society: Key Documents in Latter-day Saint Women's History* (Salt Lake City: The Church Historian's Press, 2016), 56.

3. Jane Manning James, Autobiography, 1903, 20, CHL.

4. Mary Ellen Kimball, *The Juvenile Instructor* 27, no. 16 (15 August 1892): 491.

5. Mary Ellen Harris Abel Kimball, "Sketch of Pioneer History," 1895, manuscript, 12, 21–23, CHL.

6. Mary Ellen Kimball, *The Juvenile Instructor* 27, 490–91.

7. Eunice B. Snow, "A Sketch of the Life of Eunice Billings Snow," Woman's Exponent 39, no. 3 (September 1910): 22.

8. Ibid.

9. Elizabeth B. Pratt, "Autobiography of Elizabeth B. Pratt," *Woman's Exponent* 19, no. 12 (1 December 1890): 94–95.

10. Elizabeth B. Pratt, "Autobiography of Elizabeth B. Pratt," *Woman's Exponent* 19, no. 13 (15 December 1890): 102.

11. Zina D. H. Young, diaries, 1844–1845, 29 June 1844, CHL.

12. Eliza Clayton Margetts, "Reminiscence of Nauvoo," 1870, 1, CHL.

13. Ibid., 1–2.

14. Derr et al., *First Fifty Years of Relief Society,* 689; Zina D. H. Young, diaries, 1844–1845, CHL.

15. Zina D. H. Young, diaries, 1844–1845, CHL.

16. Lucy Mack Smith, in Sarah M. Kimball to "Mrs. Sarepta Haywood," ca. 1844, Joseph L. Heywood letters, CHL.

17. Lucy Mack Smith, in Tullidge, *Women of Mormondom*, 299–300.

18. Martha Ann Harris, "Statement of Martha Ann Smith Harris, Provo City, March 22, 1881,"

Martha A. Smith Harris Autobiography, CHL. See also Richard P. Harris, "Martha Ann Smith Harris," *Relief Society Magazine* 11, no. 1 (January 1924): 12.

19. Martha Ann Harris, "Statement of Martha Ann Smith Harris."

20. Caroline Barnes Crosby, in *No Place to Call Home: The 1807–1857 Life Writings of Caroline Barnes Crosby, Chronicler of Outlying Mormon Communities*, Life Writings of Frontier Women 7, ed. Edward Leo Lyman, Susan Ward Payne, and S. George Ellsworth (Logan, Utah: Utah State University Press, 2005), 63.

21. Ibid., 4, 62.

22. Ibid., 62–63.

23. Augusta Joyce Crocheron, *Representative Women of Deseret, a Book of Biographical Sketches to Accompany the Picture Bearing the Same Title* (Salt Lake City: J. C. Graham, 1884), 18–19.

24. Mary Isabella Horne, in Tullidge, *Women of Mormondom*, 323–24.

25. Derr et al., *First Fifty Years of Relief Society*, 654–55.

26. Vilate M. Kimball to Heber C. Kimball, 30 June 1844, photocopy, CHL.

27. Eliza R. Snow, "The Assassination of Gen's Joseph Smith and Hyrum Smith First Presidents of the Church of Latter-day Saints; Who Were Massacred by a Mob, in Carthage, Hancock County, Ill., on the 27th of June, 1844," *Times and Seasons* 5, no. 12 (1 July 1844): 575; also in *Eliza R. Snow: The Complete Poetry*, ed. Jill Mulvay Derr and Karen Lynn Davidson (Provo, Utah: BYU Press; Salt Lake City: University of Utah Press, 2009), 295–99.

28. Louisa Barnes Pratt, in *The History of Louisa Barnes Pratt: Mormon Missionary Widow and Pioneer*, ed. S. George Ellsworth, (Logan, Utah: Utah State University Press, 1998), 69–72.

29. Mary Alice Cannon Lambert, in "Joseph Smith, the Prophet," *Young Woman's Journal* 16, no. 12 (December 1905): 554.

30. Louisa Barnes Pratt, in *The History of Louisa Barnes Pratt*, 65–71.

31. Ibid., 70–72.

32. Sally Carlisle Randall, letter, 1 July 1844, Sally Randall Letters, 1843–1852, copy, CHL.

33. Jane Manning James, Autobiography, 1903, CHL.

34. "The teachers" could have been either visiting teachers or men in the priesthood office of teachers.

35. Jane Manning James, in "Joseph Smith, the Prophet," *Young Woman's Journal* 16, no. 12 (December 1905): 553.

36. Sally Carlisle Randall, letters, 1843–1852, copy, CHL; see Jordan Watkins and Steven C. Harper, "'It Seems That All Nature Mourns': Sally Randall's Response to the Murder of Joseph and Hyrum Smith," *BYU Studies* 46, no. 1 (2007): 95–100.

37. Randall, letter, 1 July 1844; see Watkins and Harper, "'It Seems That All Nature Mourns,'" 95–100.

Chapter 19—Postscript

1. Doctrine and Covenants 25:16.

2. Doctrine and Covenants 25:3, 7, 16.

IMAGE CREDITS

INDEX

About the Authors

JANIECE JOHNSON is a transplanted Bay Area, California, native who loves history, design, art, good food, and traveling. She has master's degrees in American religious history and theology from Brigham Young University and Vanderbilt's Divinity School, respectively. After working as a historian in the LDS Chuch History Department for several years, she returned to school to complete doctoral work at the University of Leicester in England. Janiece has published work in women's and religious history—specializing in Mormon history and the Mountain Meadows Massacre. She is the general editor of the Mountain Meadows Massacre Legal Papers (University of Oklahoma Press, 2017). She is currently a visiting professor in religious education at Brigham Young University–Idaho.

JENNIFER REEDER is a nineteenth-century women's history specialist in the LDS Church History Department. She has a PhD in American history from George Mason University and an MA in history, documentary editing, and archival management from New York University, with a BA in humanities and English teaching from BYU. She is originally from Provo, Utah, and served a mission to Catania, Italy. Check out another book coedited by Reeder with Kate Holbrook: *At the Pulpit: 185 Years of Discourses by Latter-day Saint Women* (Church Historian's Press, 2017).